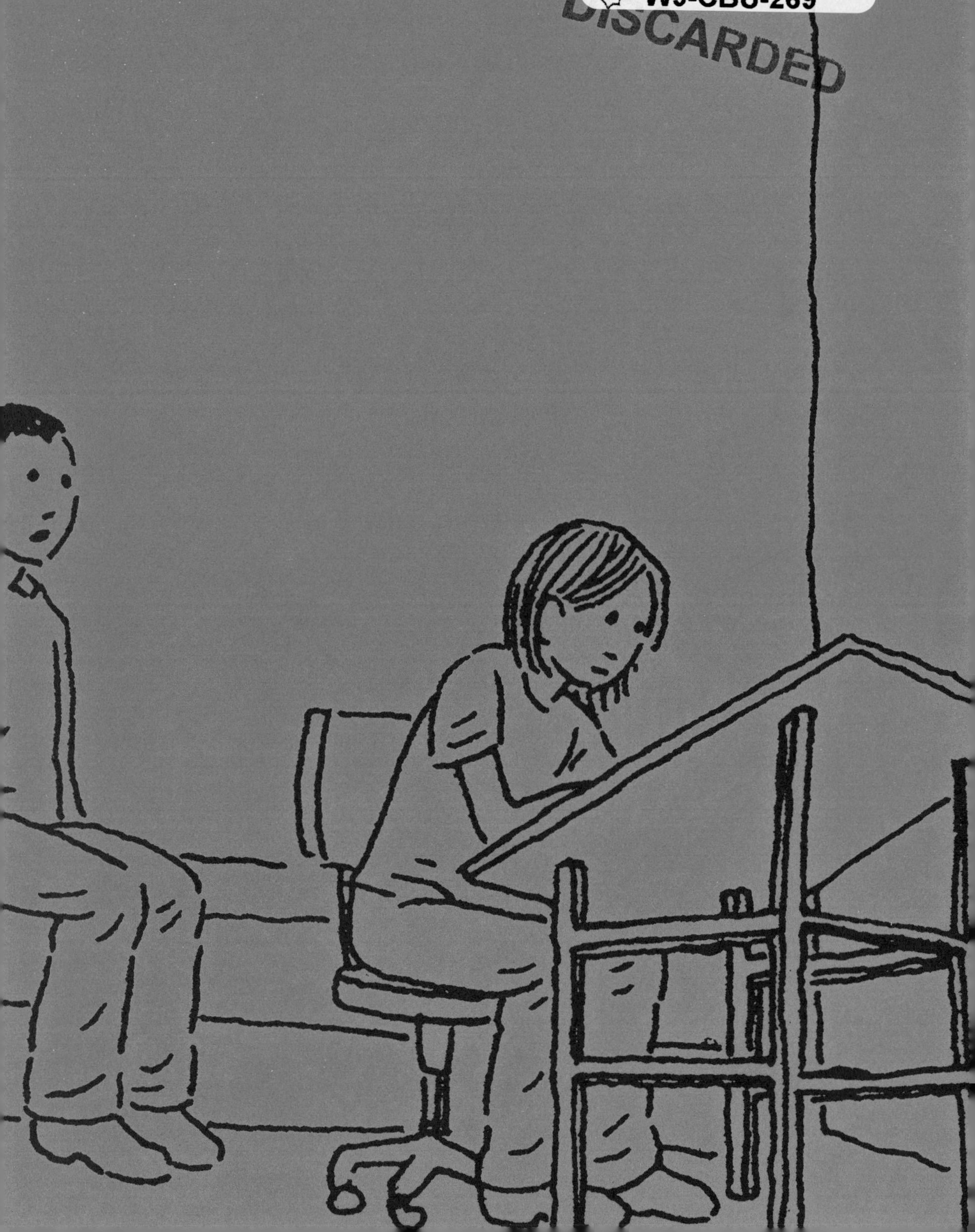

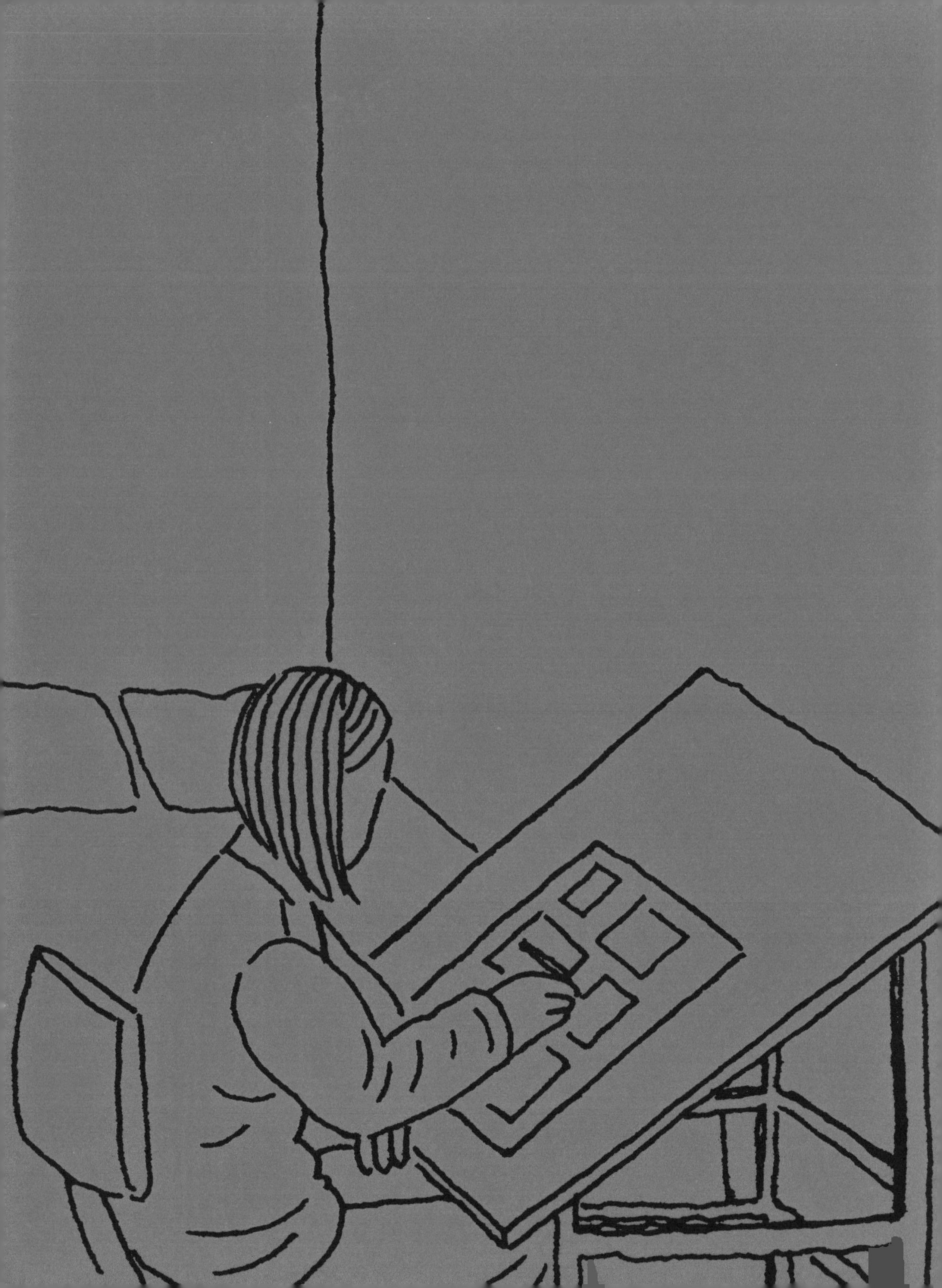

# An Introduction

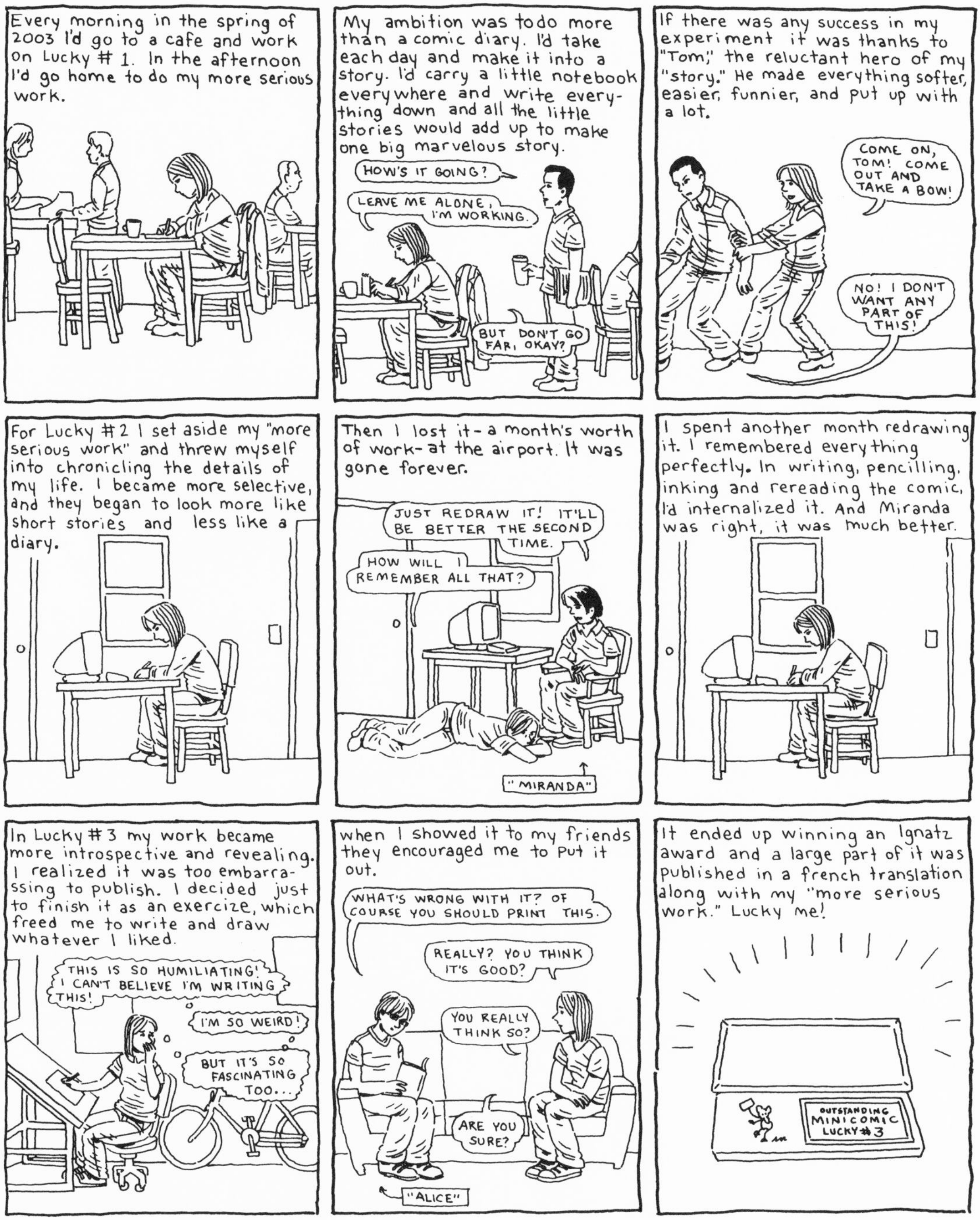
Every morning in the spring of 2003 I'd go to a cafe and work on Lucky # 1. In the afternoon I'd go home to do my more serious work.
My ambition was to do more than a comic diary. I'd take each day and make it into a story. I'd carry a little notebook everywhere and write everything down and all the little stories would add up to make one big marvelous story.
HOW'S IT GOING?
LEAVE ME ALONE, I'M WORKING.
BUT DON'T GO FAR, OKAY?
If there was any success in my experiment it was thanks to "Tom," the reluctant hero of my "story." He made everything softer, easier, funnier, and put up with a lot.
COME ON, TOM! COME OUT AND TAKE A BOW!
NO! I DON'T WANT ANY PART OF THIS!
For Lucky #2 I set aside my "more serious work" and threw myself into chronicling the details of my life. I became more selective, and they began to look more like short stories and less like a diary.
Then I lost it - a month's worth of work - at the airport. It was gone forever.
JUST REDRAW IT! IT'LL BE BETTER THE SECOND TIME.
HOW WILL I REMEMBER ALL THAT?
"MIRANDA"
I spent another month redrawing it. I remembered everything perfectly. In writing, pencilling, inking and rereading the comic, I'd internalized it. And Miranda was right, it was much better.
In Lucky #3 my work became more introspective and revealing. I realized it was too embarrassing to publish. I decided just to finish it as an exercize, which freed me to write and draw whatever I liked.
THIS IS SO HUMILIATING! I CAN'T BELIEVE I'M WRITING THIS!
I'M SO WEIRD!
BUT IT'S SO FASCINATING TOO...
when I showed it to my friends they encouraged me to put it out.
WHAT'S WRONG WITH IT? OF COURSE YOU SHOULD PRINT THIS.
REALLY? YOU THINK IT'S GOOD?
YOU REALLY THINK SO?
ARE YOU SURE?
"ALICE"
It ended up winning an Ignatz award and a large part of it was published in a french translation along with my "more serious work." Lucky me!
OUTSTANDING MINICOMIC LUCKY #3

# LUCKY

## GABRIELLE BELL

DRAWN & QUARTERLY
MONTREAL

Lucky by Gabrielle Bell


DRAWN & QUARTERLY
Post Office Box 48056
Montreal, Quebec
Canada H2V 4S8
www.drawnandquarterly.com

First hardcover edition: September 2006
Printed in Singapore
10 9 8 7 6 5 4 3 2 1

Library and Archives Canada Cataloguing in Publication
Bell, Gabrielle
Lucky / Gabrielle Bell
ISBN 1-897299-01-X
I. Title. PN6727.B3775L82 2006
741.5973 C2006-902880-X

Distributed in the USA by:
FARRAR, STRAUS AND GIROUX
19 Union Square West
New York, NY 10003
Orders: 888.330.8477

Distributed in Canada by:
RAINCOAST BOOKS
9050 Shaughnessy Street
Vancouver, BC V6P 6E5
Orders: 800.663.5714

Lucky #1 (May 2003)

Tuesday, April 22nd

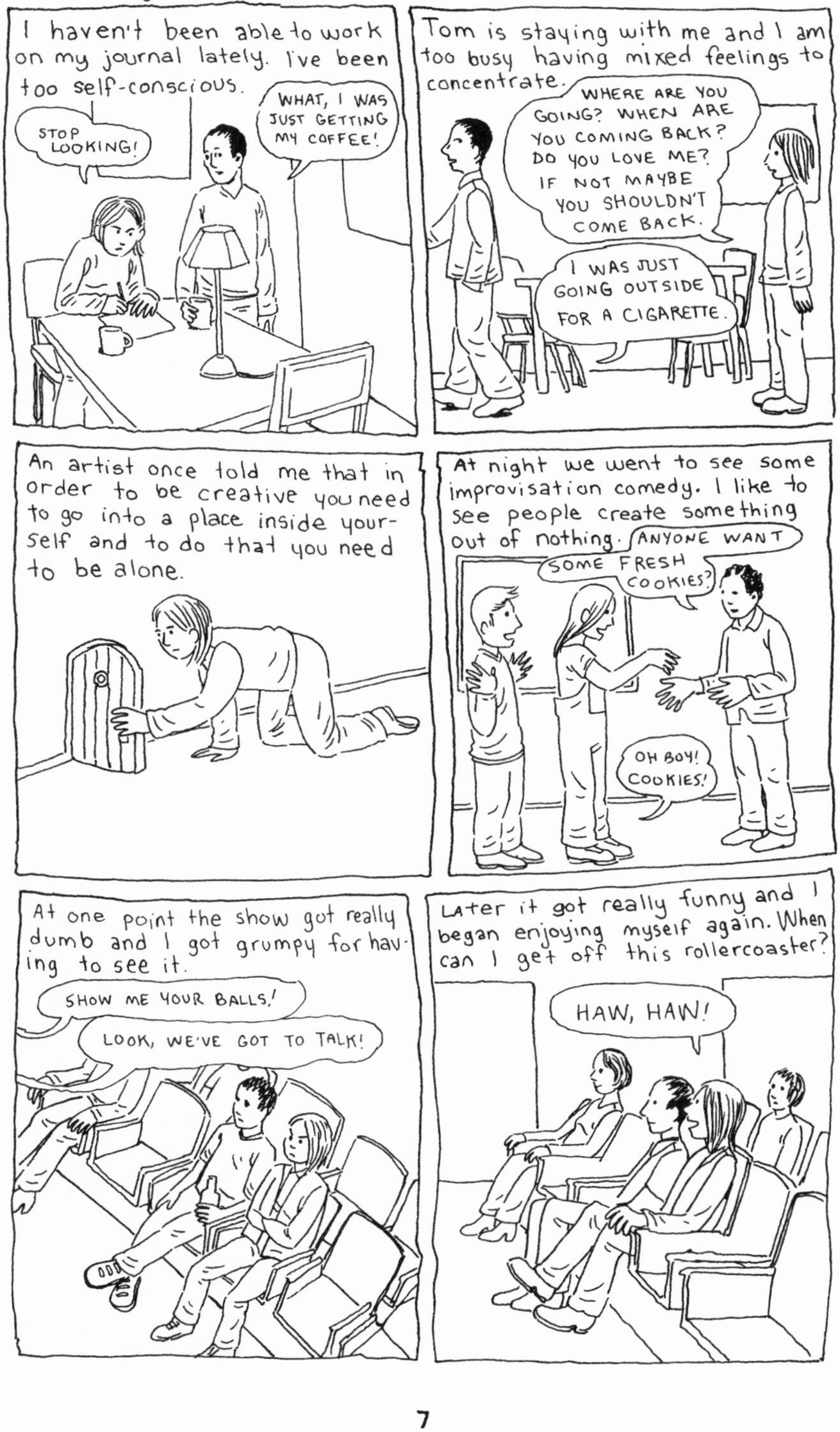
I haven't been able to work on my journal lately. I've been too self-conscious.
STOP LOOKING!
WHAT, I WAS JUST GETTING MY COFFEE!
Tom is staying with me and I am too busy having mixed feelings to concentrate.
WHERE ARE YOU GOING? WHEN ARE YOU COMING BACK? DO YOU LOVE ME? IF NOT MAYBE YOU SHOULDN'T COME BACK.
I WAS JUST GOING OUTSIDE FOR A CIGARETTE.
An artist once told me that in order to be creative you need to go into a place inside yourself and to do that you need to be alone.
At night we went to see some improvisation comedy. I like to see people create something out of nothing.
ANYONE WANT SOME FRESH COOKIES?
OH BOY! COOKIES!
At one point the show got really dumb and I got grumpy for having to see it.
SHOW ME YOUR BALLS!
LOOK, WE'VE GOT TO TALK!
Later it got really funny and I began enjoying myself again. When can I get off this rollercoaster?
HAW, HAW!

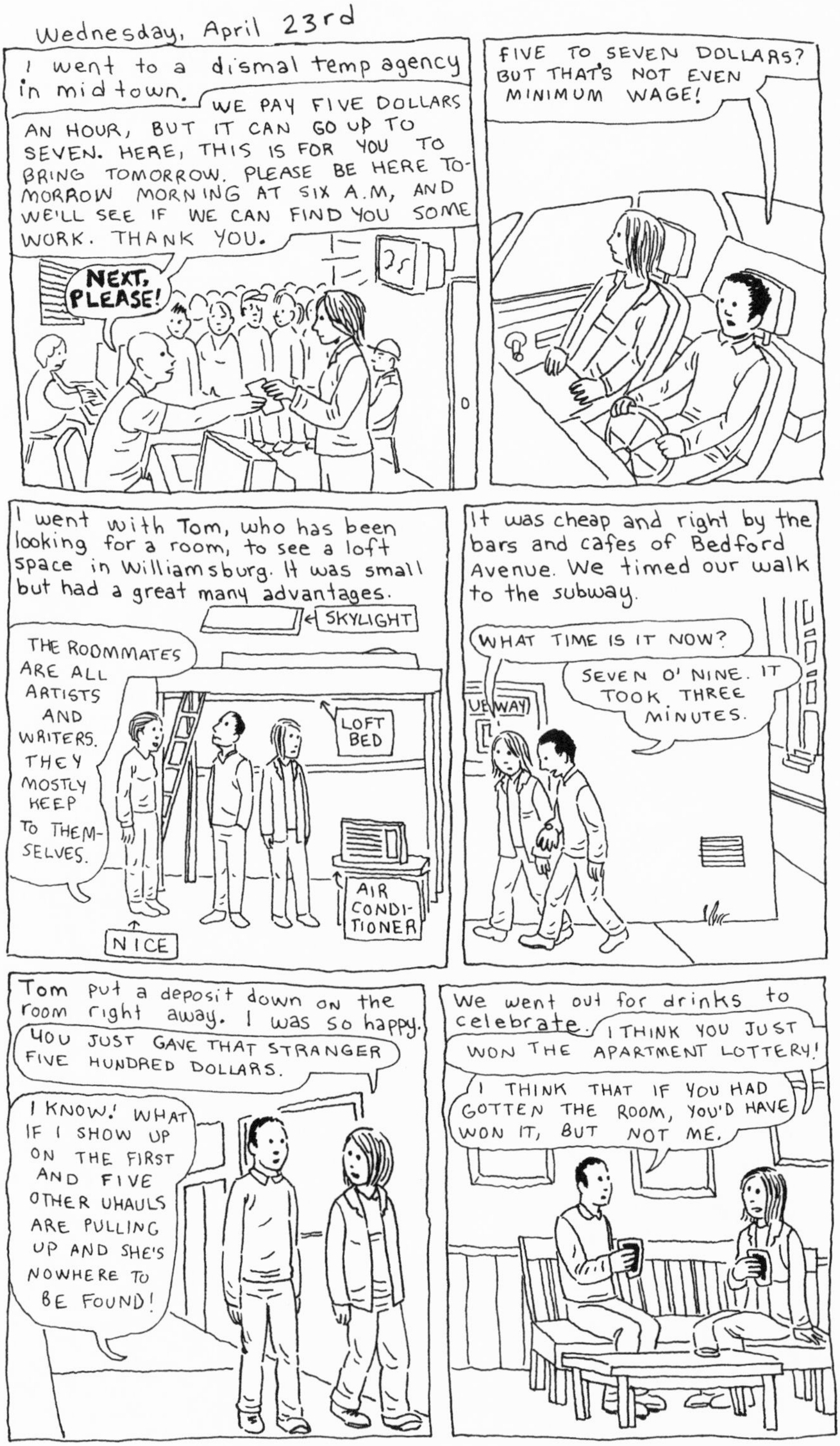
Wednesday, April 23rd
I went to a dismal temp agency in midtown.
WE PAY FIVE DOLLARS AN HOUR, BUT IT CAN GO UP TO SEVEN. HERE, THIS IS FOR YOU TO BRING TOMORROW. PLEASE BE HERE TOMORROW MORNING AT SIX A.M, AND WE'LL SEE IF WE CAN FIND YOU SOME WORK. THANK YOU.
NEXT, PLEASE!
FIVE TO SEVEN DOLLARS? BUT THAT'S NOT EVEN MINIMUM WAGE!
I went with Tom, who has been looking for a room, to see a loft space in Williamsburg. It was small but had a great many advantages.
SKYLIGHT
THE ROOMMATES ARE ALL ARTISTS AND WRITERS. THEY MOSTLY KEEP TO THEMSELVES.
LOFT BED
AIR CONDITIONER
NICE
It was cheap and right by the bars and cafes of Bedford Avenue. We timed our walk to the subway.
WHAT TIME IS IT NOW?
SEVEN O' NINE. IT TOOK THREE MINUTES.
Tom put a deposit down on the room right away. I was so happy.
YOU JUST GAVE THAT STRANGER FIVE HUNDRED DOLLARS.
I KNOW! WHAT IF I SHOW UP ON THE FIRST AND FIVE OTHER UHAULS ARE PULLING UP AND SHE'S NOWHERE TO BE FOUND!
We went out for drinks to celebrate.
I THINK YOU JUST WON THE APARTMENT LOTTERY!
I THINK THAT IF YOU HAD GOTTEN THE ROOM, YOU'D HAVE WON IT, BUT NOT ME.

Thursday, April 24th

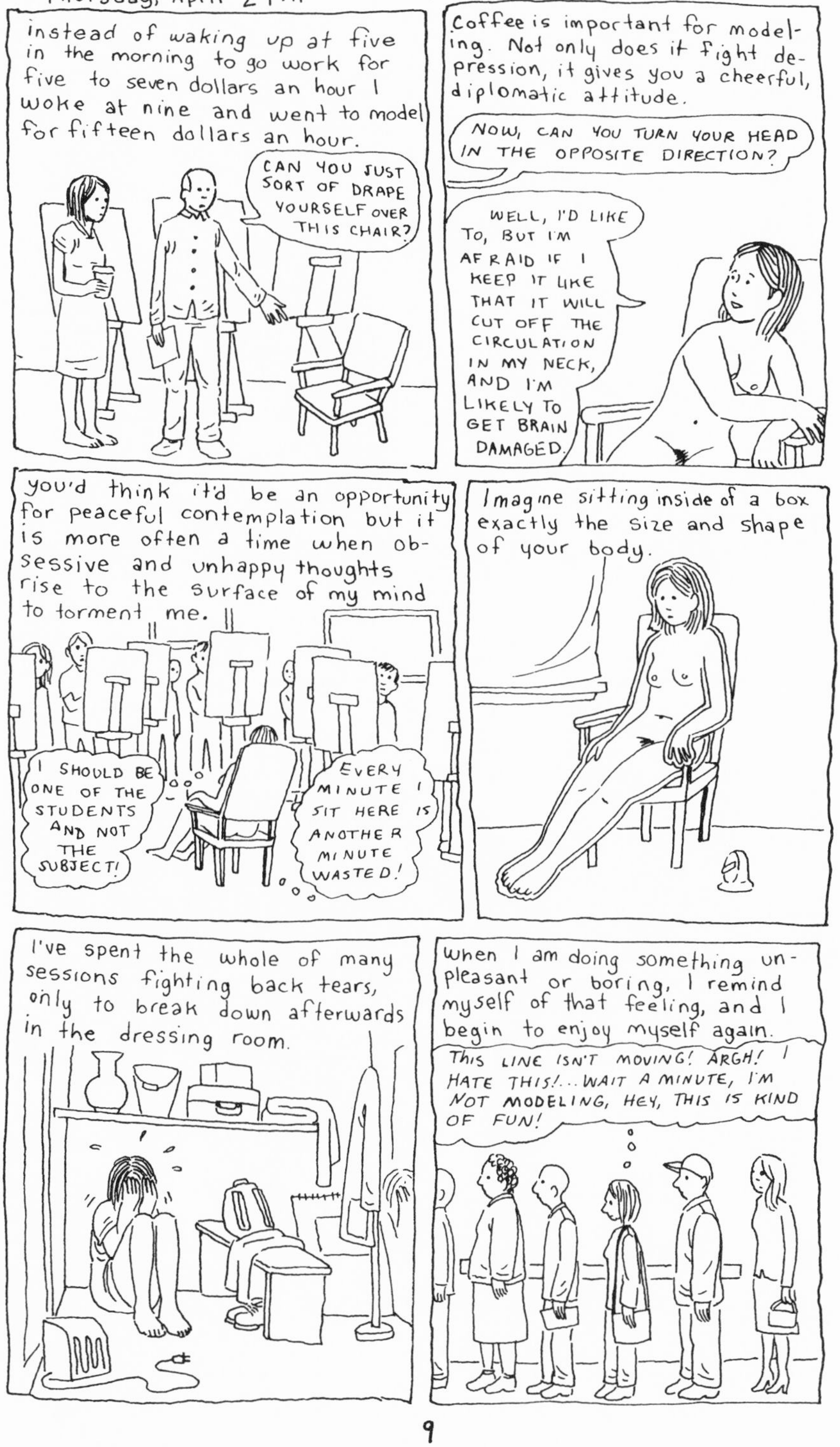
instead of waking up at five in the morning to go work for five to seven dollars an hour I woke at nine and went to model for fifteen dollars an hour.
CAN YOU JUST SORT OF DRAPE YOURSELF OVER THIS CHAIR?
Coffee is important for modeling. Not only does it fight depression, it gives you a cheerful, diplomatic attitude.
NOW, CAN YOU TURN YOUR HEAD IN THE OPPOSITE DIRECTION?
WELL, I'D LIKE TO, BUT I'M AFRAID IF I KEEP IT LIKE THAT IT WILL CUT OFF THE CIRCULATION IN MY NECK, AND I'M LIKELY TO GET BRAIN DAMAGED.
you'd think it'd be an opportunity for peaceful contemplation but it is more often a time when obsessive and unhappy thoughts rise to the surface of my mind to torment me.
I SHOULD BE ONE OF THE STUDENTS AND NOT THE SUBJECT!
EVERY MINUTE I SIT HERE IS ANOTHER MINUTE WASTED!
Imagine sitting inside of a box exactly the size and shape of your body.
I've spent the whole of many sessions fighting back tears, only to break down afterwards in the dressing room.
when I am doing something unpleasant or boring, I remind myself of that feeling, and I begin to enjoy myself again.
THIS LINE ISN'T MOVING! ARGH! I HATE THIS!... WAIT A MINUTE, I'M NOT MODELING, HEY, THIS IS KIND OF FUN!

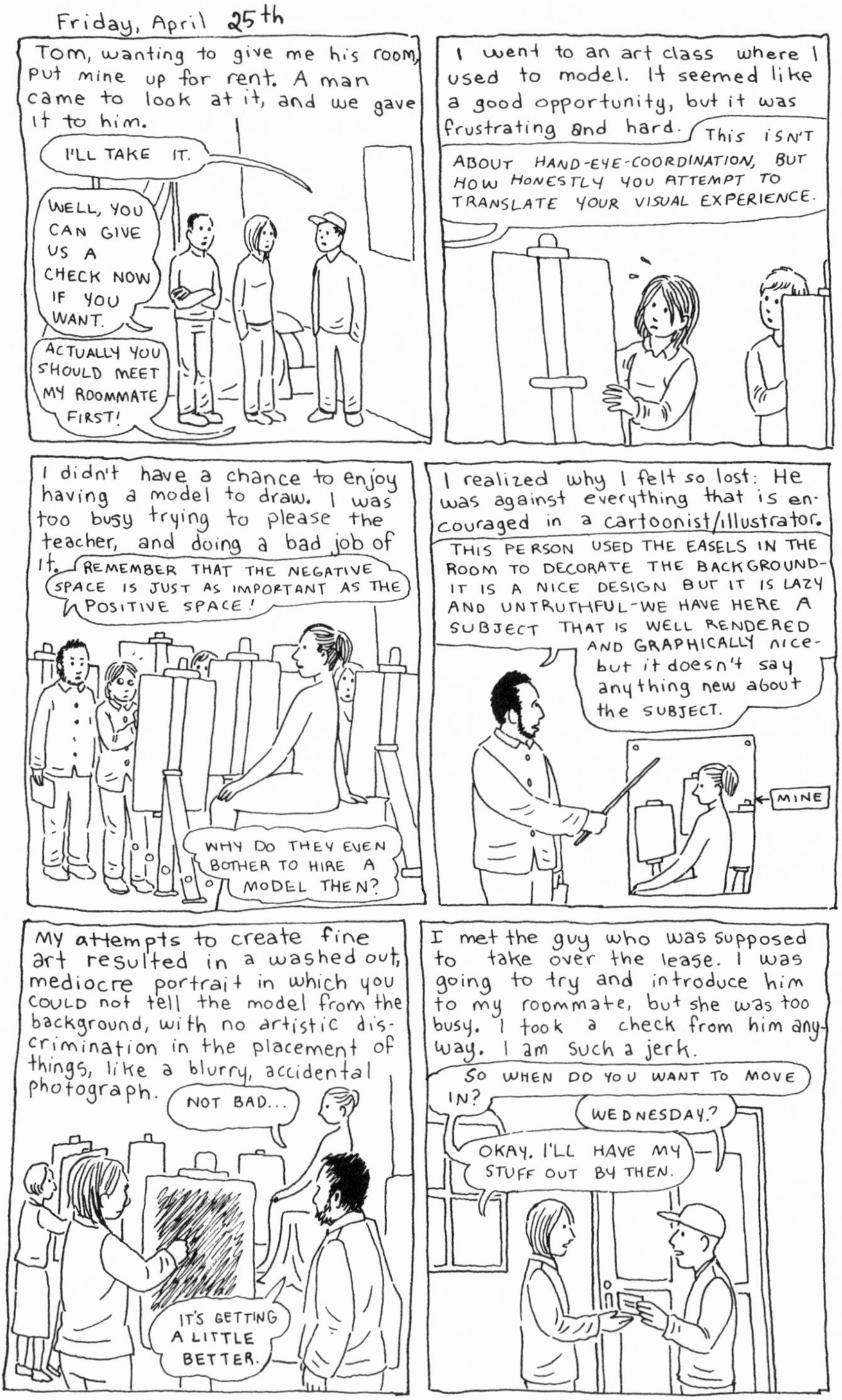
Friday, April 25th
Tom, wanting to give me his room, put mine up for rent. A man came to look at it, and we gave it to him.
I'LL TAKE IT.
WELL, YOU CAN GIVE US A CHECK NOW IF YOU WANT.
ACTUALLY YOU SHOULD MEET MY ROOMMATE FIRST!
I went to an art class where I used to model. It seemed like a good opportunity, but it was frustrating and hard.
This ISN'T ABOUT HAND-EYE-COORDINATION, BUT HOW HONESTLY YOU ATTEMPT TO TRANSLATE YOUR VISUAL EXPERIENCE.
I didn't have a chance to enjoy having a model to draw. I was too busy trying to please the teacher, and doing a bad job of it.
REMEMBER THAT THE NEGATIVE SPACE IS JUST AS IMPORTANT AS THE POSITIVE SPACE!
WHY DO THEY EVEN BOTHER TO HIRE A MODEL THEN?
I realized why I felt so lost: He was against everything that is encouraged in a cartoonist/illustrator.
THIS PERSON USED THE EASELS IN THE ROOM TO DECORATE THE BACKGROUND-IT IS A NICE DESIGN BUT IT IS LAZY AND UNTRUTHFUL-WE HAVE HERE A SUBJECT THAT IS WELL RENDERED AND GRAPHICALLY NICE-but it doesn't say anything new about the SUBJECT.
MINE
My attempts to create fine art resulted in a washed out, mediocre portrait in which you COULD not tell the model from the background, with no artistic discrimination in the placement of things, like a blurry, accidental photograph.
NOT BAD...
IT'S GETTING A LITTLE BETTER.
I met the guy who was supposed to take over the lease. I was going to try and introduce him to my roommate, but she was too busy. I took a check from him anyway. I am such a jerk.
SO WHEN DO YOU WANT TO MOVE IN?
WEDNESDAY?
OKAY. I'LL HAVE MY STUFF OUT BY THEN.

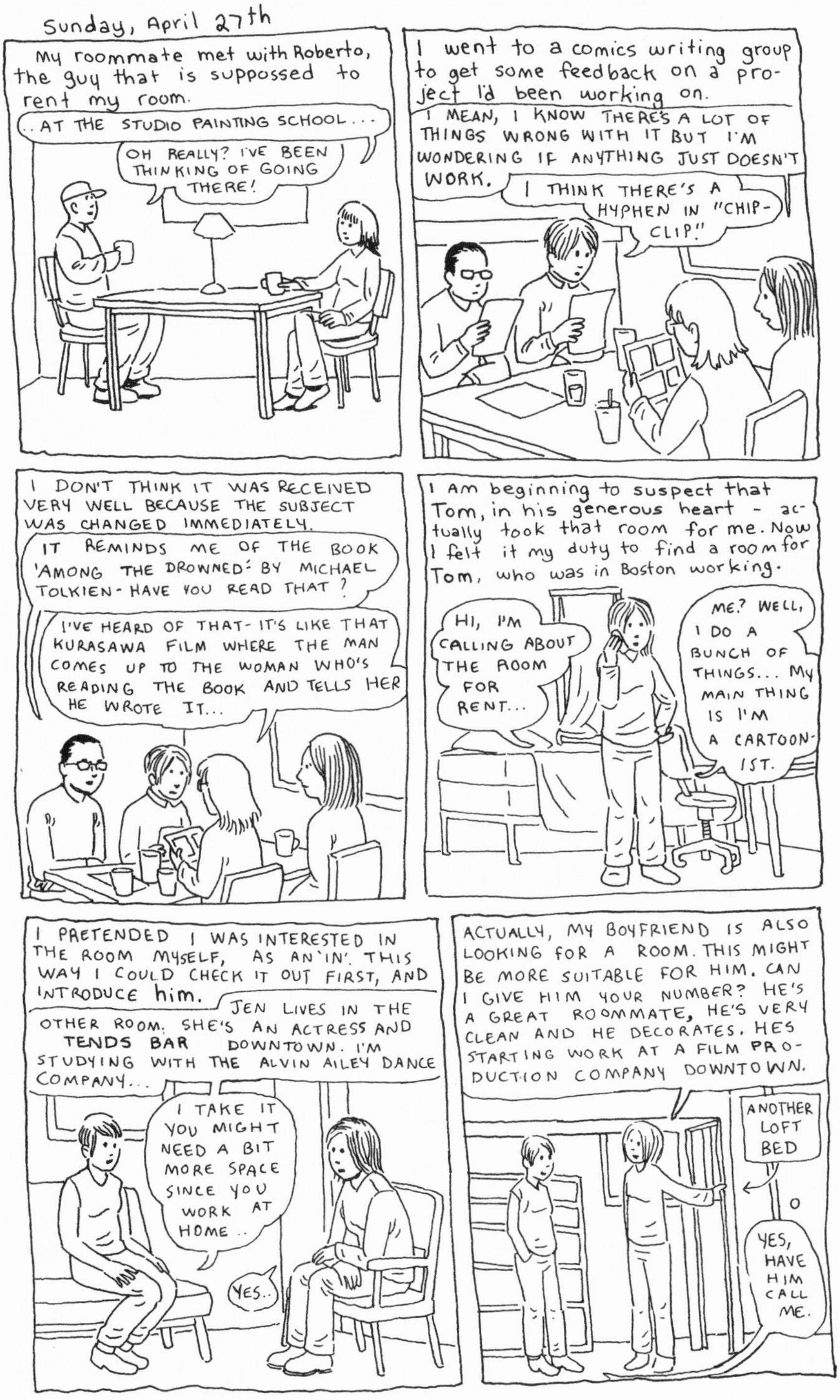
Sunday, April 27th
My roommate met with Roberto, the guy that is suppossed to rent my room.
..AT THE STUDIO PAINTING SCHOOL...
OH REALLY? I'VE BEEN THINKING OF GOING THERE!
I went to a comics writing group to get some feedback on a project I'd been working on.
I MEAN, I KNOW THERE'S A LOT OF THINGS WRONG WITH IT BUT I'M WONDERING IF ANYTHING JUST DOESN'T WORK.
I THINK THERE'S A HYPHEN IN "CHIP-CLIP."
I DON'T THINK IT WAS RECEIVED VERY WELL BECAUSE THE SUBJECT WAS CHANGED IMMEDIATELY.
IT REMINDS ME OF THE BOOK 'AMONG THE DROWNED' BY MICHAEL TOLKIEN - HAVE YOU READ THAT?
I'VE HEARD OF THAT - IT'S LIKE THAT KURASAWA FILM WHERE THE MAN COMES UP TO THE WOMAN WHO'S READING THE BOOK AND TELLS HER HE WROTE IT...
I am beginning to suspect that Tom, in his generous heart - actually took that room for me. Now I felt it my duty to find a room for Tom, who was in Boston working.
HI, I'M CALLING ABOUT THE ROOM FOR RENT...
ME? WELL, I DO A BUNCH OF THINGS... MY MAIN THING IS I'M A CARTOONIST.
I PRETENDED I WAS INTERESTED IN THE ROOM MYSELF, AS AN 'IN'. THIS WAY I COULD CHECK IT OUT FIRST, AND INTRODUCE him.
JEN LIVES IN THE OTHER ROOM. SHE'S AN ACTRESS AND TENDS BAR DOWNTOWN. I'M STUDYING WITH THE ALVIN AILEY DANCE COMPANY...
I TAKE IT YOU MIGHT NEED A BIT MORE SPACE SINCE YOU WORK AT HOME..
YES..
ACTUALLY, MY BOYFRIEND IS ALSO LOOKING FOR A ROOM. THIS MIGHT BE MORE SUITABLE FOR HIM. CAN I GIVE HIM YOUR NUMBER? HE'S A GREAT ROOMMATE, HE'S VERY CLEAN AND HE DECORATES. HES STARTING WORK AT A FILM PRODUCTION COMPANY DOWNTOWN.
ANOTHER LOFT BED
YES, HAVE HIM CALL ME.

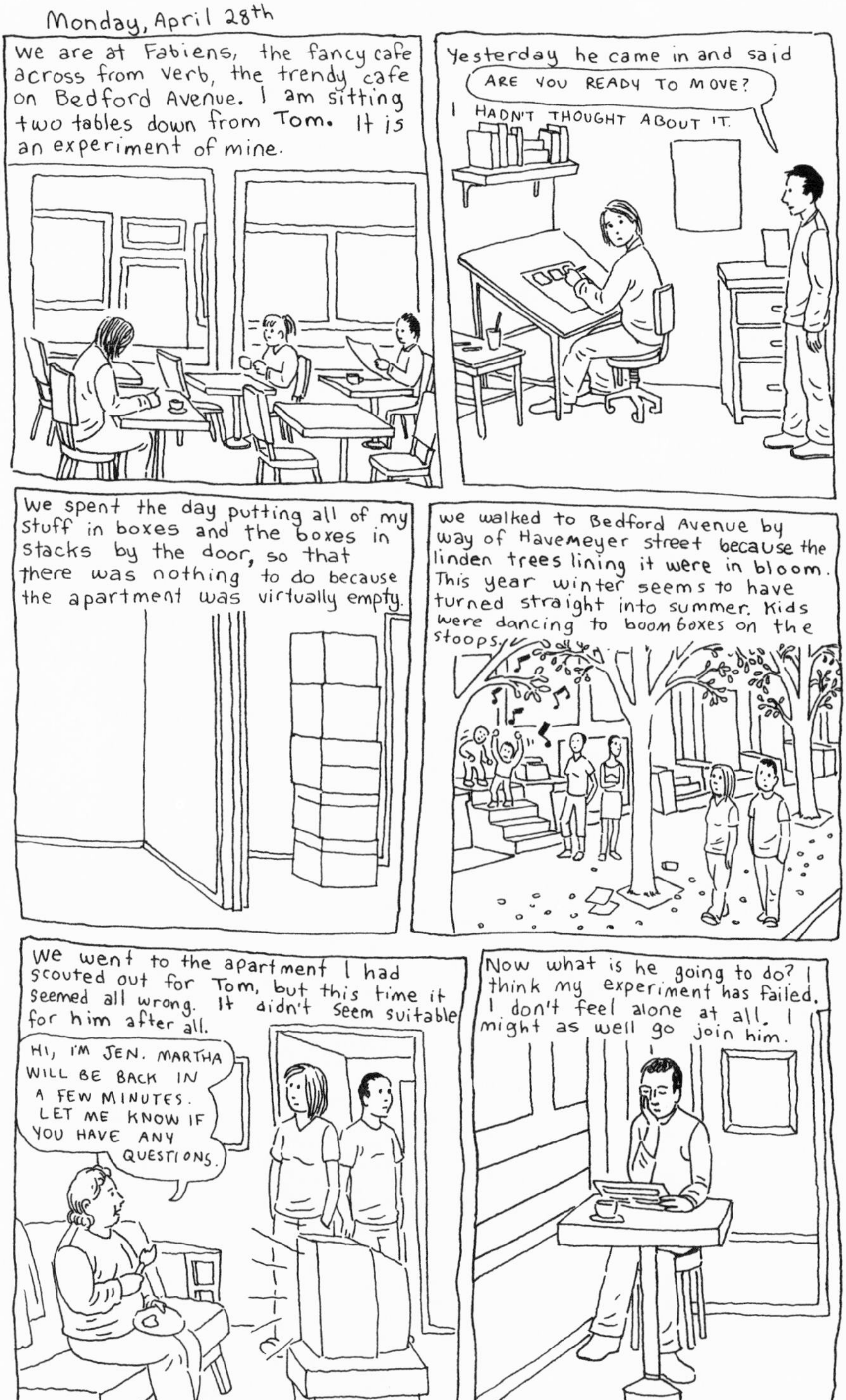
Monday, April 28th
We are at Fabiens, the fancy cafe across from Verb, the trendy cafe on Bedford Avenue. I am sitting two tables down from Tom. It is an experiment of mine.
Yesterday he came in and said
ARE YOU READY TO MOVE?
I HADN'T THOUGHT ABOUT IT.
We spent the day putting all of my stuff in boxes and the boxes in stacks by the door, so that there was nothing to do because the apartment was virtually empty.
We walked to Bedford Avenue by way of Havemeyer street because the linden trees lining it were in bloom. This year winter seems to have turned straight into summer. Kids were dancing to boom boxes on the stoops.
We went to the apartment I had scouted out for Tom, but this time it seemed all wrong. It didn't seem suitable for him after all.
HI, I'M JEN. MARTHA WILL BE BACK IN A FEW MINUTES. LET ME KNOW IF YOU HAVE ANY QUESTIONS.
Now what is he going to do? I think my experiment has failed. I don't feel alone at all. I might as well go join him.

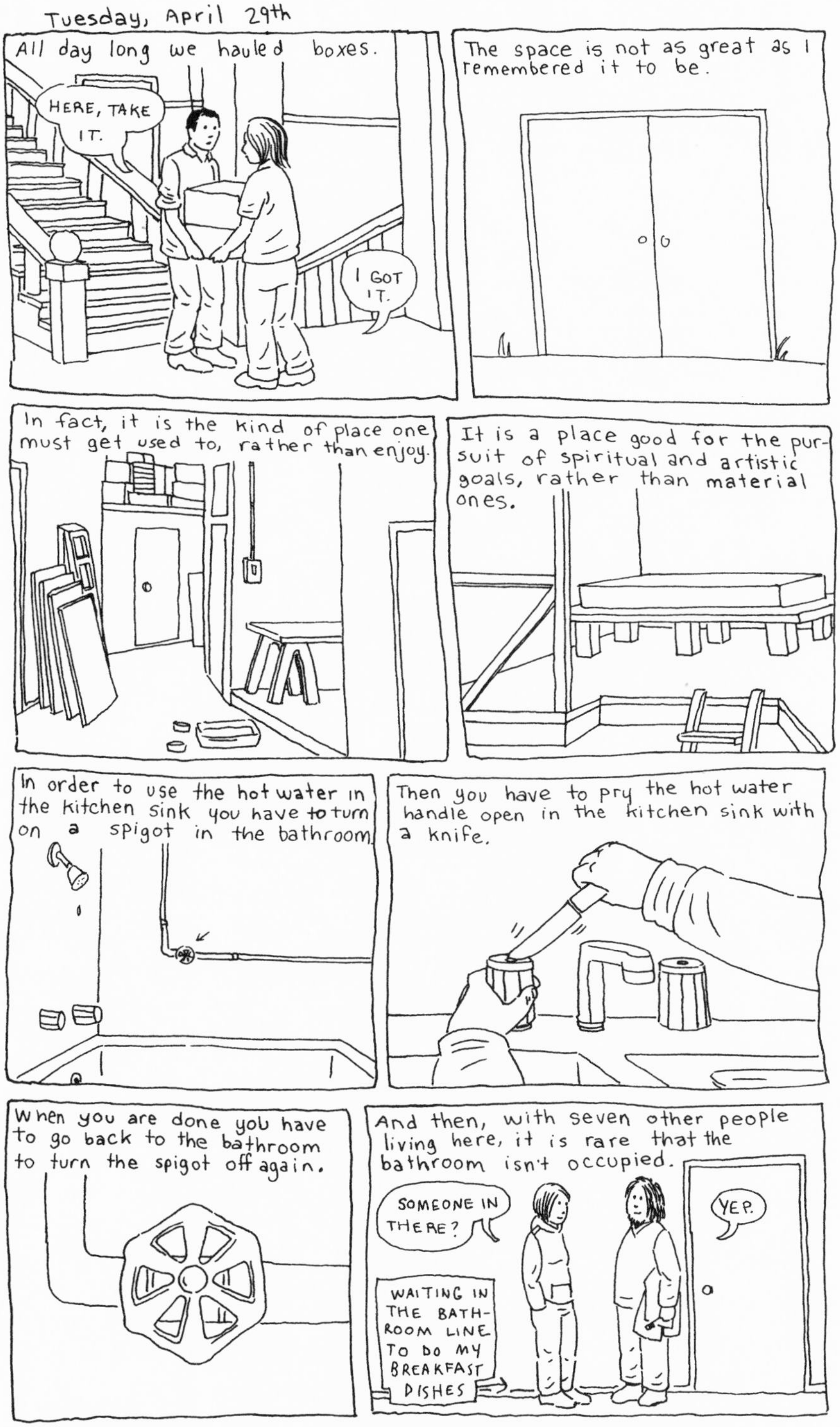
Tuesday, April 29th
All day long we hauled boxes.
HERE, TAKE IT.
I GOT IT.
The space is not as great as I remembered it to be.
In fact, it is the kind of place one must get used to, rather than enjoy.
It is a place good for the pursuit of spiritual and artistic goals, rather than material ones.
In order to use the hot water in the kitchen sink you have to turn on a spigot in the bathroom.
Then you have to pry the hot water handle open in the kitchen sink with a knife.
When you are done you have to go back to the bathroom to turn the spigot off again.
And then, with seven other people living here, it is rare that the bathroom isn't occupied.
SOMEONE IN THERE?
YEP.
WAITING IN THE BATHROOM LINE TO DO MY BREAKFAST DISHES

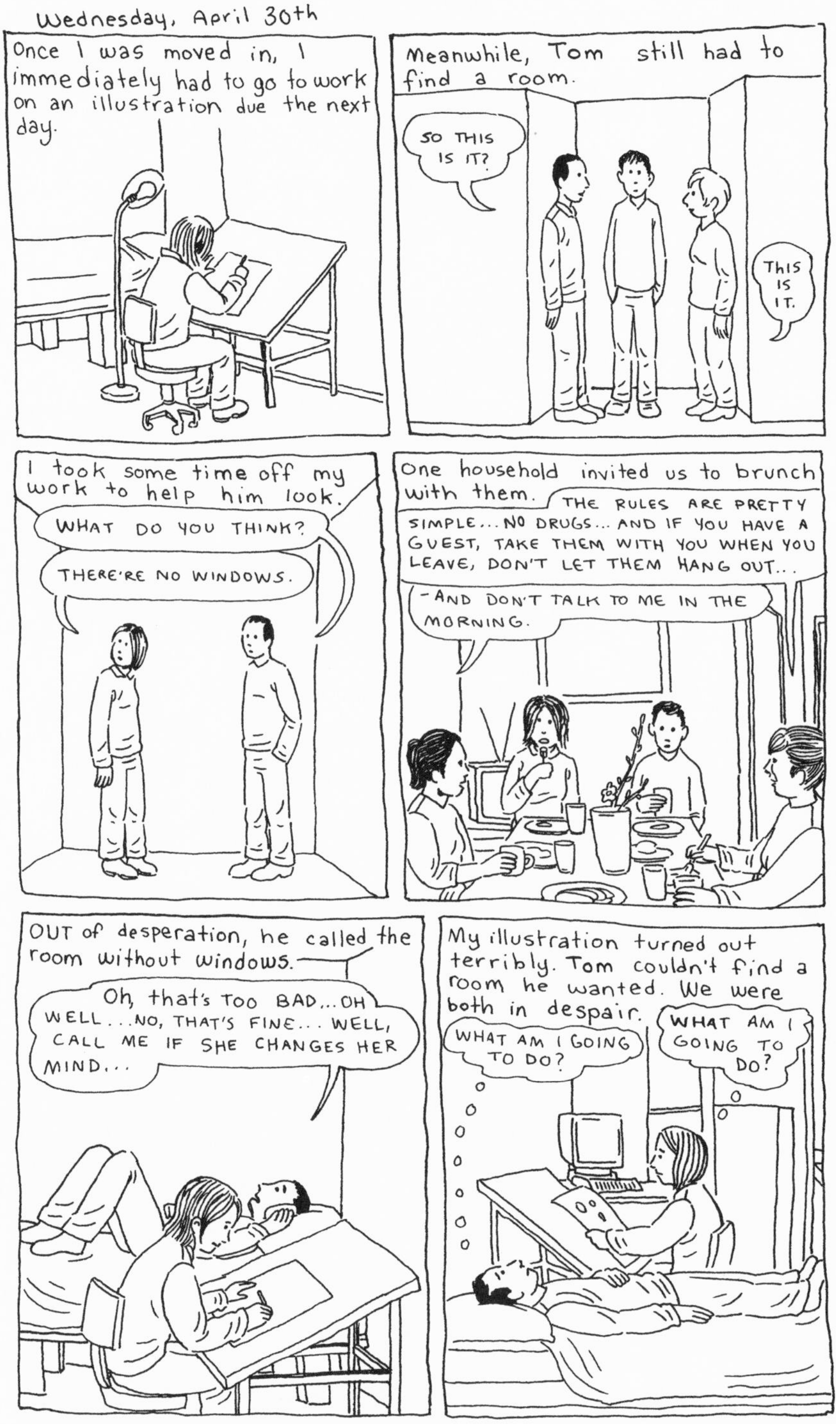
Wednesday, April 30th
Once I was moved in, I immediately had to go to work on an illustration due the next day.
Meanwhile, Tom still had to find a room.
SO THIS IS IT?
THIS IS IT.
I took some time off my work to help him look.
WHAT DO YOU THINK?
THERE'RE NO WINDOWS.
One household invited us to brunch with them.
THE RULES ARE PRETTY SIMPLE... NO DRUGS... AND IF YOU HAVE A GUEST, TAKE THEM WITH YOU WHEN YOU LEAVE, DON'T LET THEM HANG OUT...
-AND DON'T TALK TO ME IN THE MORNING.
OUT of desperation, he called the room without windows.
Oh, that's TOO BAD,...OH WELL...NO, THAT'S FINE... WELL, CALL ME IF SHE CHANGES HER MIND...
My illustration turned out terribly. Tom couldn't find a room he wanted. We were both in despair.
WHAT AM I GOING TO DO?
WHAT AM I GOING TO DO?

Thursday, May 1st

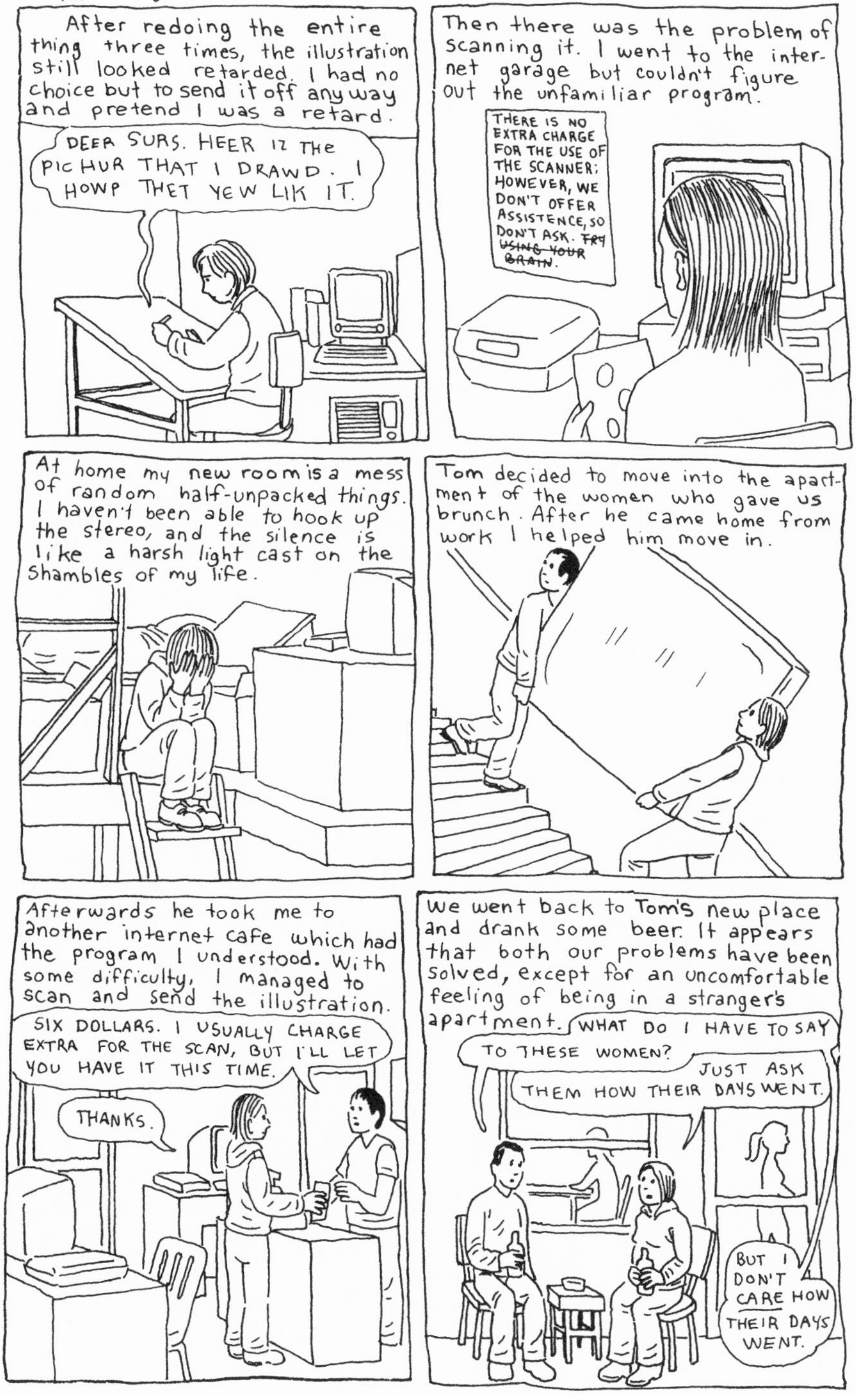
After redoing the entire thing three times, the illustration still looked retarded. I had no choice but to send it off anyway and pretend I was a retard.
DEER SURS. HEER IZ THE PICHUR THAT I DRAWD. I HOWP THET YEW LIK IT.
Then there was the problem of scanning it. I went to the internet garage but couldn't figure out the unfamiliar program.
THERE IS NO EXTRA CHARGE FOR THE USE OF THE SCANNER; HOWEVER, WE DON'T OFFER ASSISTENCE, SO DON'T ASK. ~~TRY USING YOUR BRAIN~~.
At home my new room is a mess of random half-unpacked things. I haven't been able to hook up the stereo, and the silence is like a harsh light cast on the shambles of my life.
Tom decided to move into the apartment of the women who gave us brunch. After he came home from work I helped him move in.
Afterwards he took me to another internet cafe which had the program I understood. With some difficulty, I managed to scan and send the illustration.
SIX DOLLARS. I USUALLY CHARGE EXTRA FOR THE SCAN, BUT I'LL LET YOU HAVE IT THIS TIME.
THANKS.
We went back to Tom's new place and drank some beer. It appears that both our problems have been solved, except for an uncomfortable feeling of being in a stranger's apartment.
WHAT DO I HAVE TO SAY TO THESE WOMEN?
JUST ASK THEM HOW THEIR DAYS WENT.
BUT I DON'T CARE HOW THEIR DAYS WENT.

Friday, May 2nd

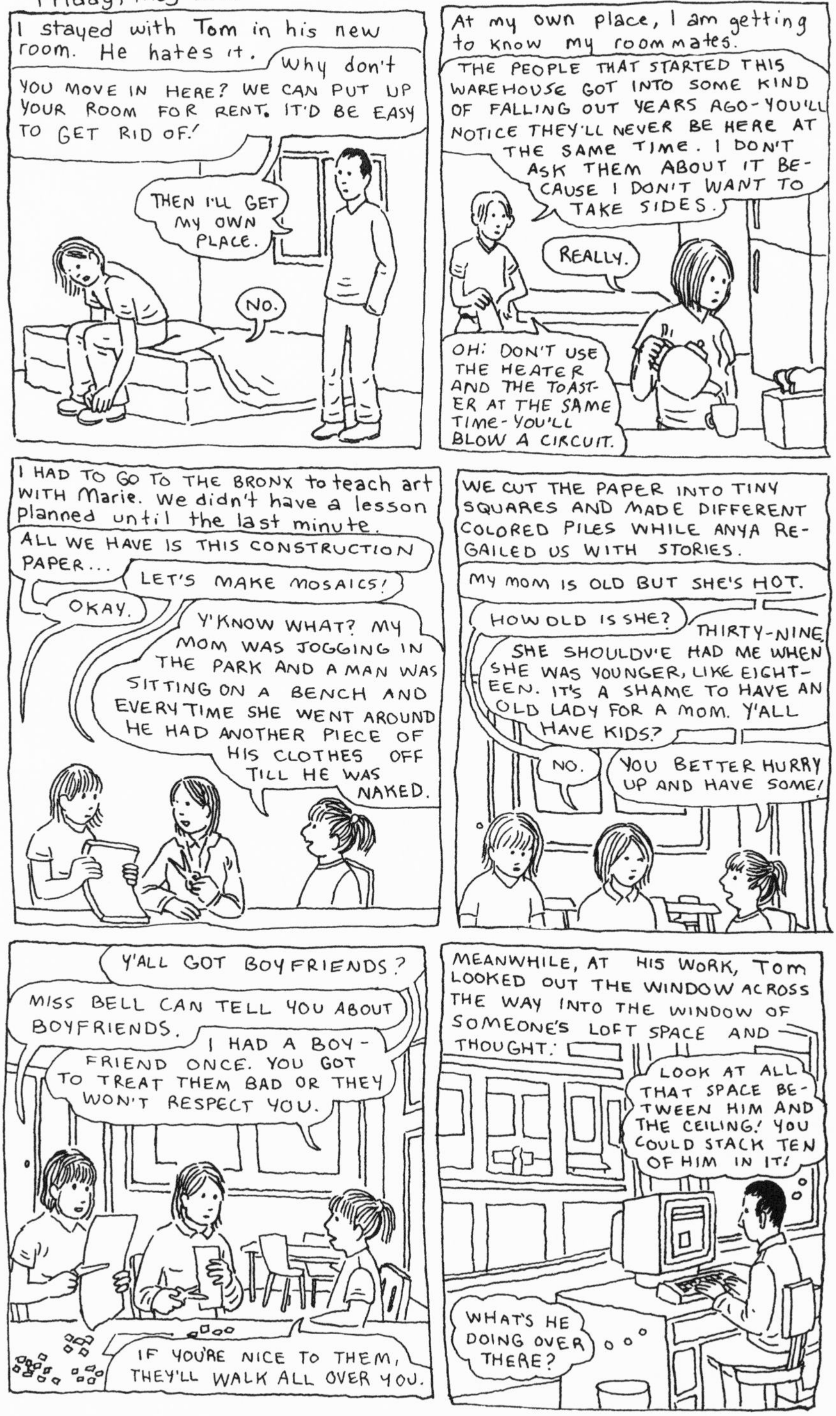
I stayed with Tom in his new room. He hates it.
Why don't YOU MOVE IN HERE? WE CAN PUT UP YOUR ROOM FOR RENT. IT'D BE EASY TO GET RID OF!
THEN I'LL GET MY OWN PLACE.
NO.
At my own place, I am getting to know my roommates.
THE PEOPLE THAT STARTED THIS WAREHOUSE GOT INTO SOME KIND OF FALLING OUT YEARS AGO- YOU'LL NOTICE THEY'LL NEVER BE HERE AT THE SAME TIME. I DON'T ASK THEM ABOUT IT BECAUSE I DON'T WANT TO TAKE SIDES.
REALLY.
OH: DON'T USE THE HEATER AND THE TOASTER AT THE SAME TIME- YOU'LL BLOW A CIRCUIT.
I HAD TO GO TO THE BRONX to teach art WITH Marie. We didn't have a lesson planned until the last minute.
ALL WE HAVE IS THIS CONSTRUCTION PAPER...
LET'S MAKE MOSAICS!
OKAY.
Y'KNOW WHAT? MY MOM WAS JOGGING IN THE PARK AND A MAN WAS SITTING ON A BENCH AND EVERY TIME SHE WENT AROUND HE HAD ANOTHER PIECE OF HIS CLOTHES OFF TILL HE WAS NAKED.
WE CUT THE PAPER INTO TINY SQUARES AND MADE DIFFERENT COLORED PILES WHILE ANYA REGAILED US WITH STORIES.
MY MOM IS OLD BUT SHE'S HOT.
HOW OLD IS SHE?
THIRTY-NINE. SHE SHOULDV'E HAD ME WHEN SHE WAS YOUNGER, LIKE EIGHTEEN. IT'S A SHAME TO HAVE AN OLD LADY FOR A MOM. Y'ALL HAVE KIDS?
NO.
YOU BETTER HURRY UP AND HAVE SOME!
Y'ALL GOT BOYFRIENDS?
MISS BELL CAN TELL YOU ABOUT BOYFRIENDS.
I HAD A BOYFRIEND ONCE. YOU GOT TO TREAT THEM BAD OR THEY WON'T RESPECT YOU.
IF YOU'RE NICE TO THEM, THEY'LL WALK ALL OVER YOU.
MEANWHILE, AT HIS WORK, Tom LOOKED OUT THE WINDOW ACROSS THE WAY INTO THE WINDOW OF SOMEONE'S LOFT SPACE AND THOUGHT:
LOOK AT ALL THAT SPACE BETWEEN HIM AND THE CEILING! YOU COULD STACK TEN OF HIM IN IT!
WHAT'S HE DOING OVER THERE?

Saturday, May 3rd

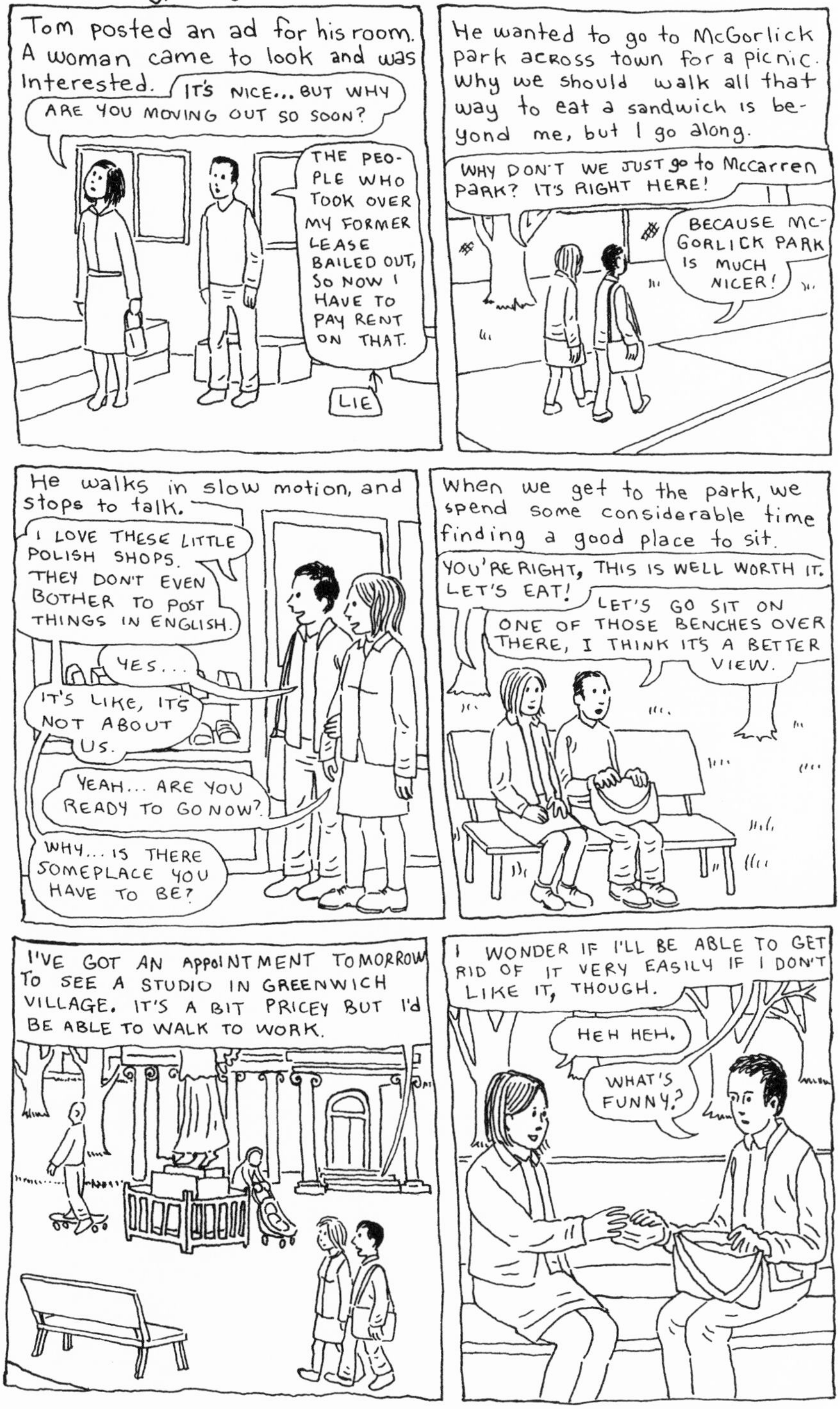
Tom posted an ad for his room. A woman came to look and was interested.
IT'S NICE... BUT WHY ARE YOU MOVING OUT SO SOON?
THE PEOPLE WHO TOOK OVER MY FORMER LEASE BAILED OUT, SO NOW I HAVE TO PAY RENT ON THAT.
LIE
He wanted to go to McGorlick park across town for a picnic. Why we should walk all that way to eat a sandwich is beyond me, but I go along.
WHY DON'T WE JUST go to McCarren PARK? IT'S RIGHT HERE!
BECAUSE McGORLICK PARK IS MUCH NICER!
He walks in slow motion, and stops to talk.
I LOVE THESE LITTLE POLISH SHOPS. THEY DON'T EVEN BOTHER TO POST THINGS IN ENGLISH.
YES...
IT'S LIKE, IT'S NOT ABOUT US.
YEAH... ARE YOU READY TO GO NOW?
WHY... IS THERE SOMEPLACE YOU HAVE TO BE?
When we get to the park, we spend some considerable time finding a good place to sit.
YOU'RE RIGHT, THIS IS WELL WORTH IT. LET'S EAT!
LET'S GO SIT ON ONE OF THOSE BENCHES OVER THERE, I THINK IT'S A BETTER VIEW.
I'VE GOT AN APPOINTMENT TOMORROW TO SEE A STUDIO IN GREENWICH VILLAGE. IT'S A BIT PRICEY BUT I'd BE ABLE TO WALK TO WORK.
I WONDER IF I'LL BE ABLE TO GET RID OF IT VERY EASILY IF I DON'T LIKE IT, THOUGH.
HEH HEH.
WHAT'S FUNNY?

Sunday, May 4th

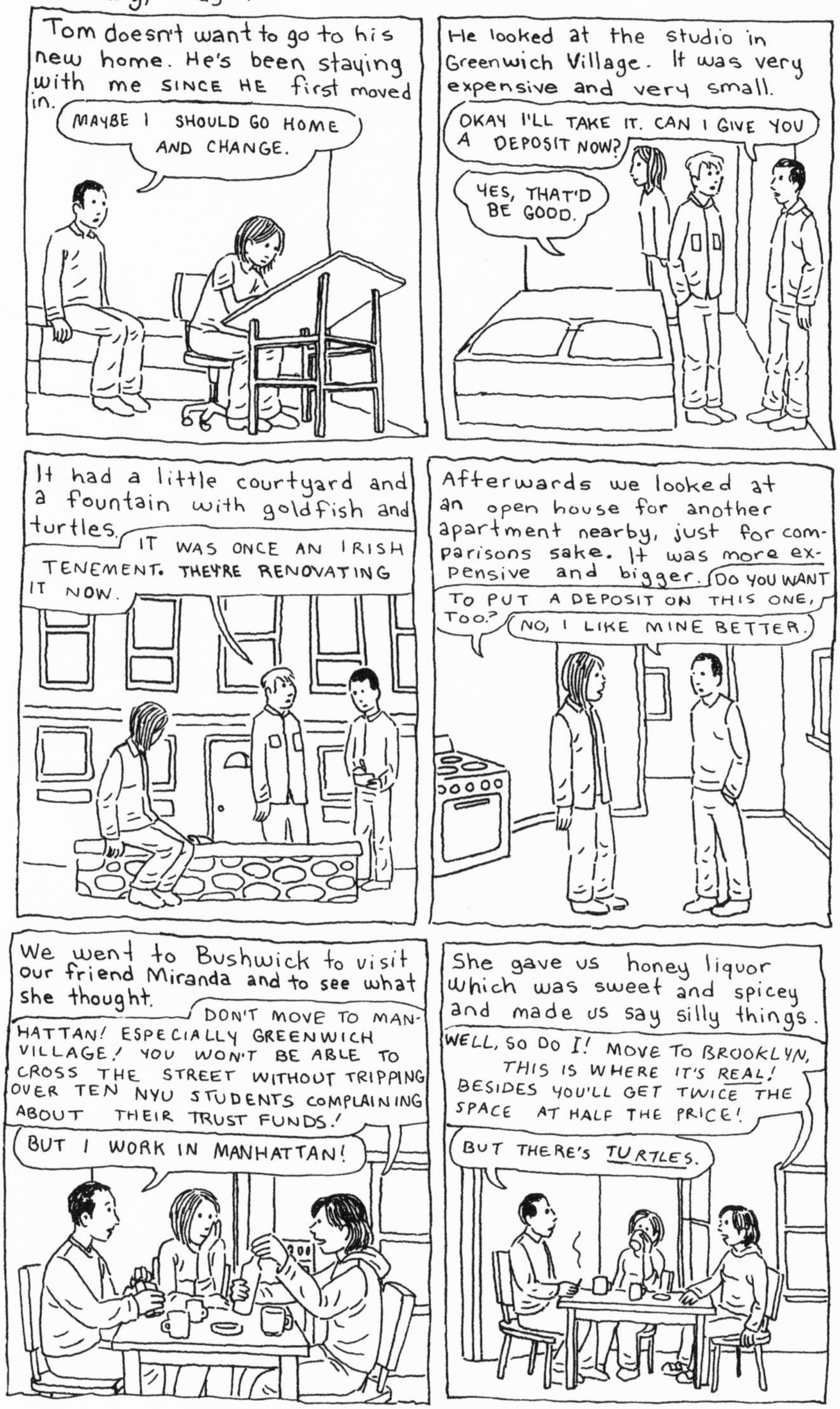
Tom doesn't want to go to his new home. He's been staying with me SINCE HE first moved in.
MAYBE I SHOULD GO HOME AND CHANGE.
He looked at the studio in Greenwich Village. It was very expensive and very small.
OKAY I'LL TAKE IT. CAN I GIVE YOU A DEPOSIT NOW?
YES, THAT'D BE GOOD.
It had a little courtyard and a fountain with goldfish and turtles.
IT WAS ONCE AN IRISH TENEMENT. THEY'RE RENOVATING IT NOW.
Afterwards we looked at an open house for another apartment nearby, just for comparisons sake. It was more expensive and bigger.
DO YOU WANT TO PUT A DEPOSIT ON THIS ONE, TOO?
NO, I LIKE MINE BETTER.
We went to Bushwick to visit our friend Miranda and to see what she thought.
DON'T MOVE TO MANHATTAN! ESPECIALLY GREENWICH VILLAGE! YOU WON'T BE ABLE TO CROSS THE STREET WITHOUT TRIPPING OVER TEN NYU STUDENTS COMPLAINING ABOUT THEIR TRUST FUNDS!
BUT I WORK IN MANHATTAN!
She gave us honey liquor which was sweet and spicey and made us say silly things.
WELL, SO DO I! MOVE TO BROOKLYN, THIS IS WHERE IT'S REAL! BESIDES YOU'LL GET TWICE THE SPACE AT HALF THE PRICE!
BUT THERE'S TURTLES.

Monday, May 5th

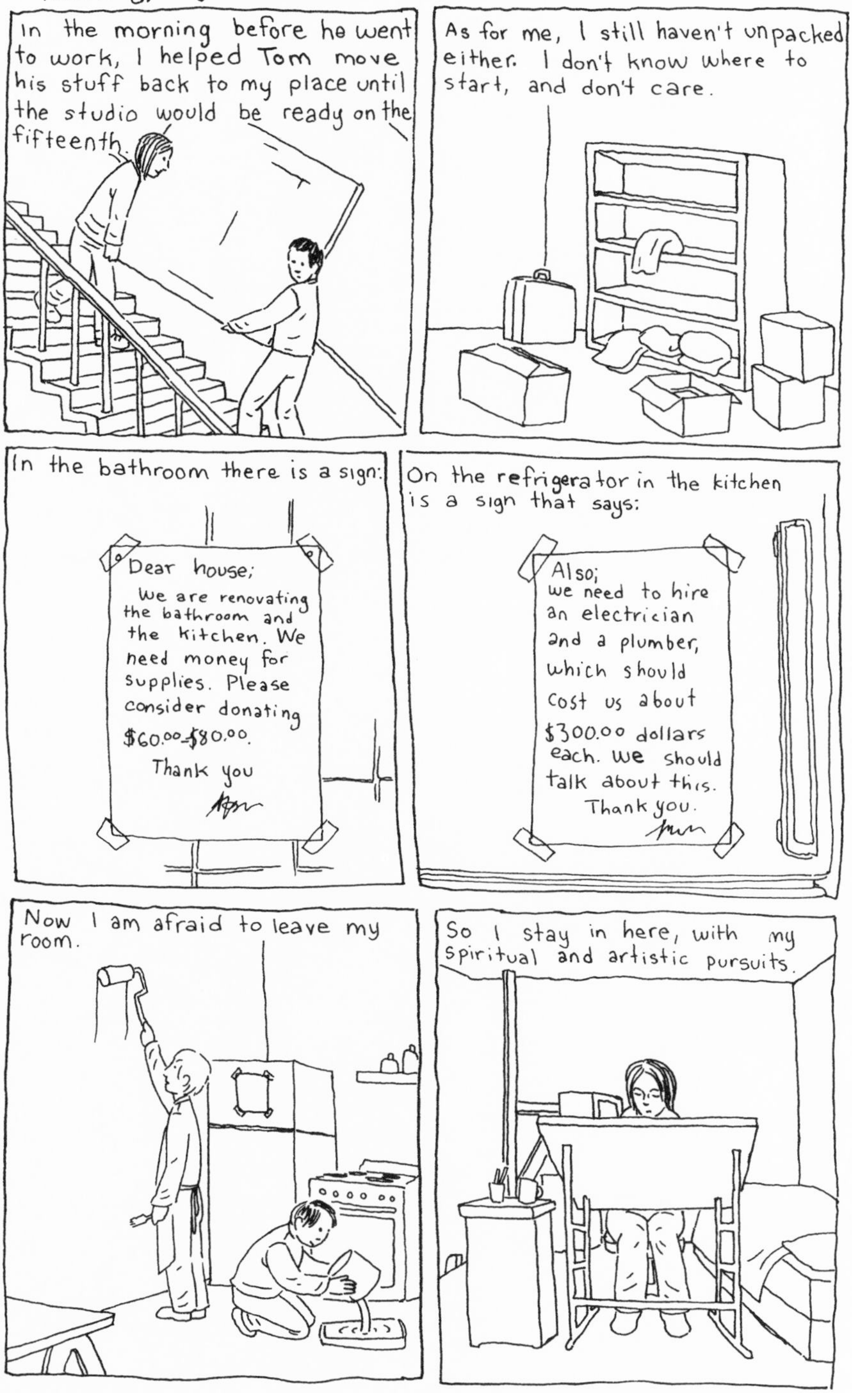
In the morning before he went to work, I helped Tom move his stuff back to my place until the studio would be ready on the fifteenth.
As for me, I still haven't unpacked either. I don't know where to start, and don't care.
In the bathroom there is a sign:
Dear house;
We are renovating the bathroom and the kitchen. We need money for supplies. Please consider donating $60.00-$80.00.
Thank you
On the refrigerator in the kitchen is a sign that says:
Also;
we need to hire an electrician and a plumber, which should cost us about $300.00 dollars each. We should talk about this.
Thank you.
Now I am afraid to leave my room.
So I stay in here, with my spiritual and artistic pursuits.

Wednesday, May 7th

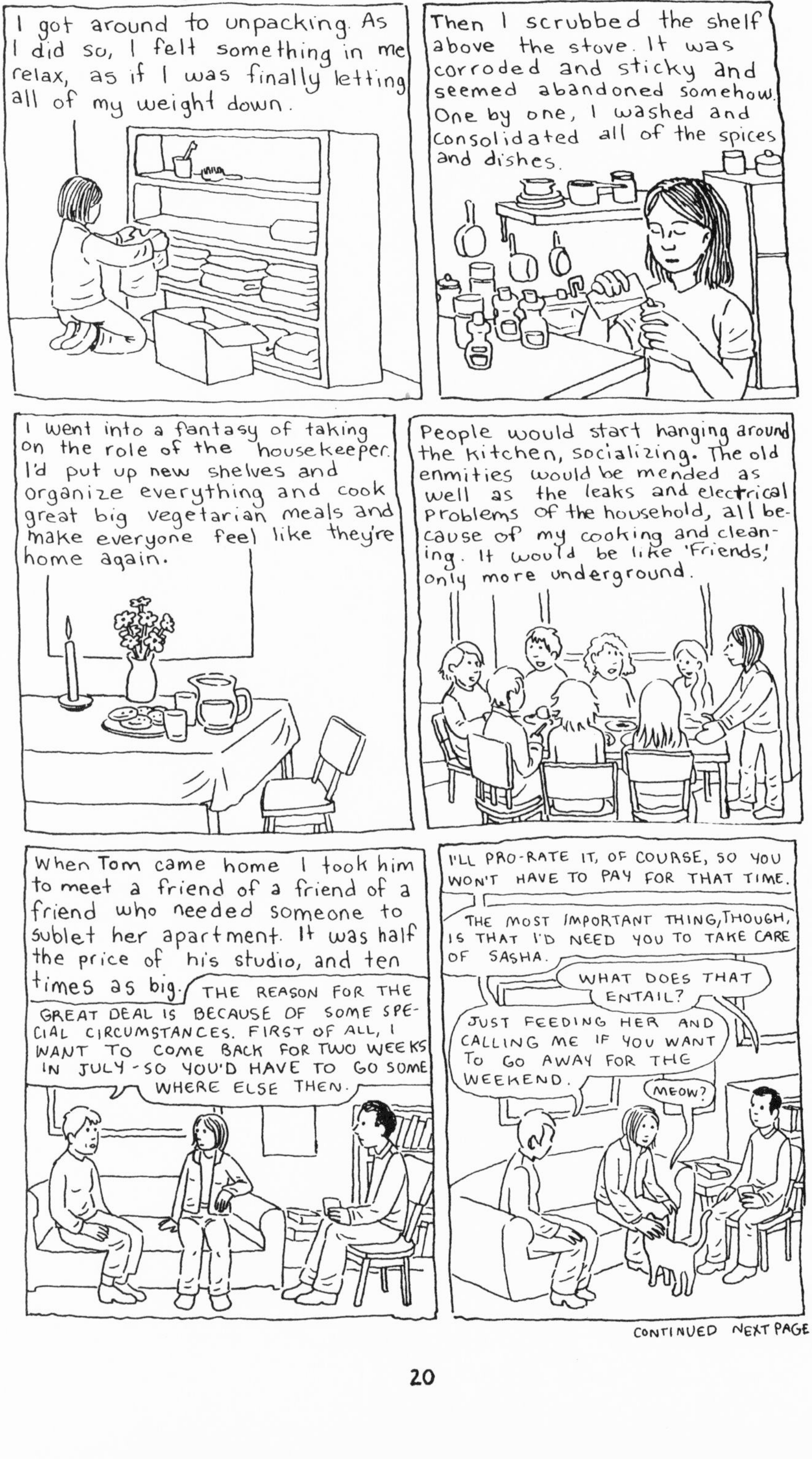
I got around to unpacking. As I did so, I felt something in me relax, as if I was finally letting all of my weight down.
Then I scrubbed the shelf above the stove. It was corroded and sticky and seemed abandoned somehow. One by one, I washed and consolidated all of the spices and dishes.
I went into a fantasy of taking on the role of the housekeeper. I'd put up new shelves and organize everything and cook great big vegetarian meals and make everyone feel like they're home again.
People would start hanging around the kitchen, socializing. The old enmities would be mended as well as the leaks and electrical problems of the household, all because of my cooking and cleaning. It would be like 'Friends,' only more underground.
When Tom came home I took him to meet a friend of a friend of a friend who needed someone to sublet her apartment. It was half the price of his studio, and ten times as big.
THE REASON FOR THE GREAT DEAL IS BECAUSE OF SOME SPECIAL CIRCUMSTANCES. FIRST OF ALL, I WANT TO COME BACK FOR TWO WEEKS IN JULY - SO YOU'D HAVE TO GO SOME WHERE ELSE THEN.
I'LL PRO-RATE IT, OF COURSE, SO YOU WON'T HAVE TO PAY FOR THAT TIME.
THE MOST IMPORTANT THING, THOUGH, IS THAT I'D NEED YOU TO TAKE CARE OF SASHA.
WHAT DOES THAT ENTAIL?
JUST FEEDING HER AND CALLING ME IF YOU WANT TO GO AWAY FOR THE WEEKEND.
MEOW?

CONTINUED NEXT PAGE

(continued)

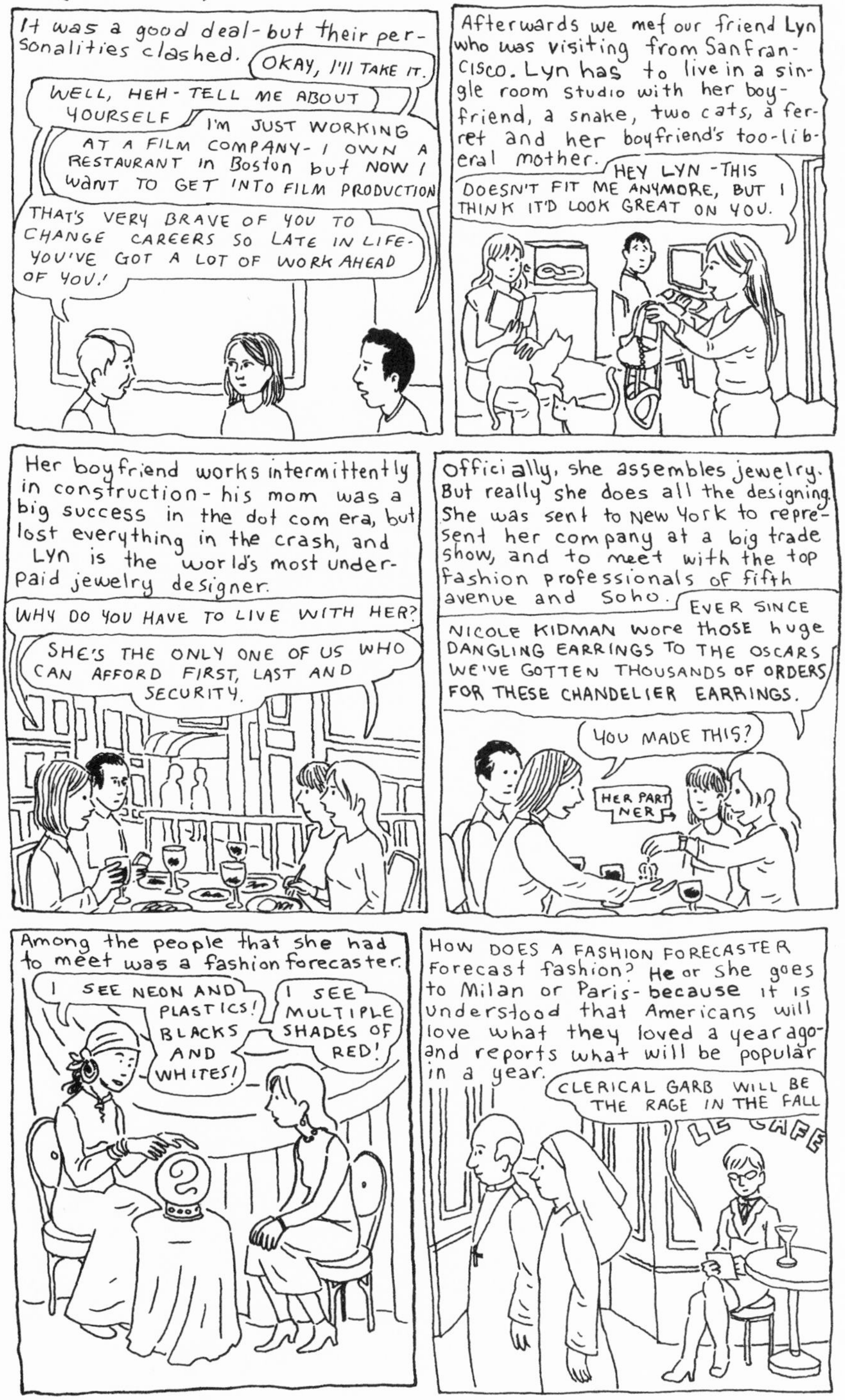
It was a good deal-but their personalities clashed.
OKAY, I'LL TAKE IT.
WELL, HEH-TELL ME ABOUT YOURSELF
I'M JUST WORKING AT A FILM COMPANY- I OWN A RESTAURANT in Boston but NOW I WANT TO GET INTO FILM PRODUCTION
THAT'S VERY BRAVE OF YOU TO CHANGE CAREERS SO LATE IN LIFE-YOU'VE GOT A LOT OF WORK AHEAD OF YOU!
Afterwards we met our friend Lyn who was visiting from San Francisco. Lyn has to live in a single room studio with her boyfriend, a snake, two cats, a ferret and her boyfriend's too-liberal mother.
HEY LYN -THIS DOESN'T FIT ME ANYMORE, BUT I THINK IT'D LOOK GREAT ON YOU.
Her boyfriend works intermittently in construction- his mom was a big success in the dot com era, but lost everything in the crash, and Lyn is the world's most underpaid jewelry designer.
WHY DO YOU HAVE TO LIVE WITH HER?
SHE'S THE ONLY ONE OF US WHO CAN AFFORD FIRST, LAST AND SECURITY.
Officially, she assembles jewelry. But really she does all the designing. She was sent to New York to represent her company at a big trade show, and to meet with the top fashion professionals of fifth avenue and Soho.
EVER SINCE NICOLE KIDMAN wore those huge DANGLING EARRINGS TO THE OSCARS WE'VE GOTTEN THOUSANDS OF ORDERS FOR THESE CHANDELIER EARRINGS.
YOU MADE THIS?
HER PARTNER
Among the people that she had to meet was a fashion forecaster.
I SEE NEON AND PLASTICS! BLACKS AND WHITES!
I SEE MULTIPLE SHADES OF RED!
HOW DOES A FASHION FORECASTER Forecast fashion? He or she goes to Milan or Paris- because it is understood that Americans will love what they loved a year ago- and reports what will be popular in a year.
CLERICAL GARB WILL BE THE RAGE IN THE FALL
LE CAFE

Thursday, May 8th

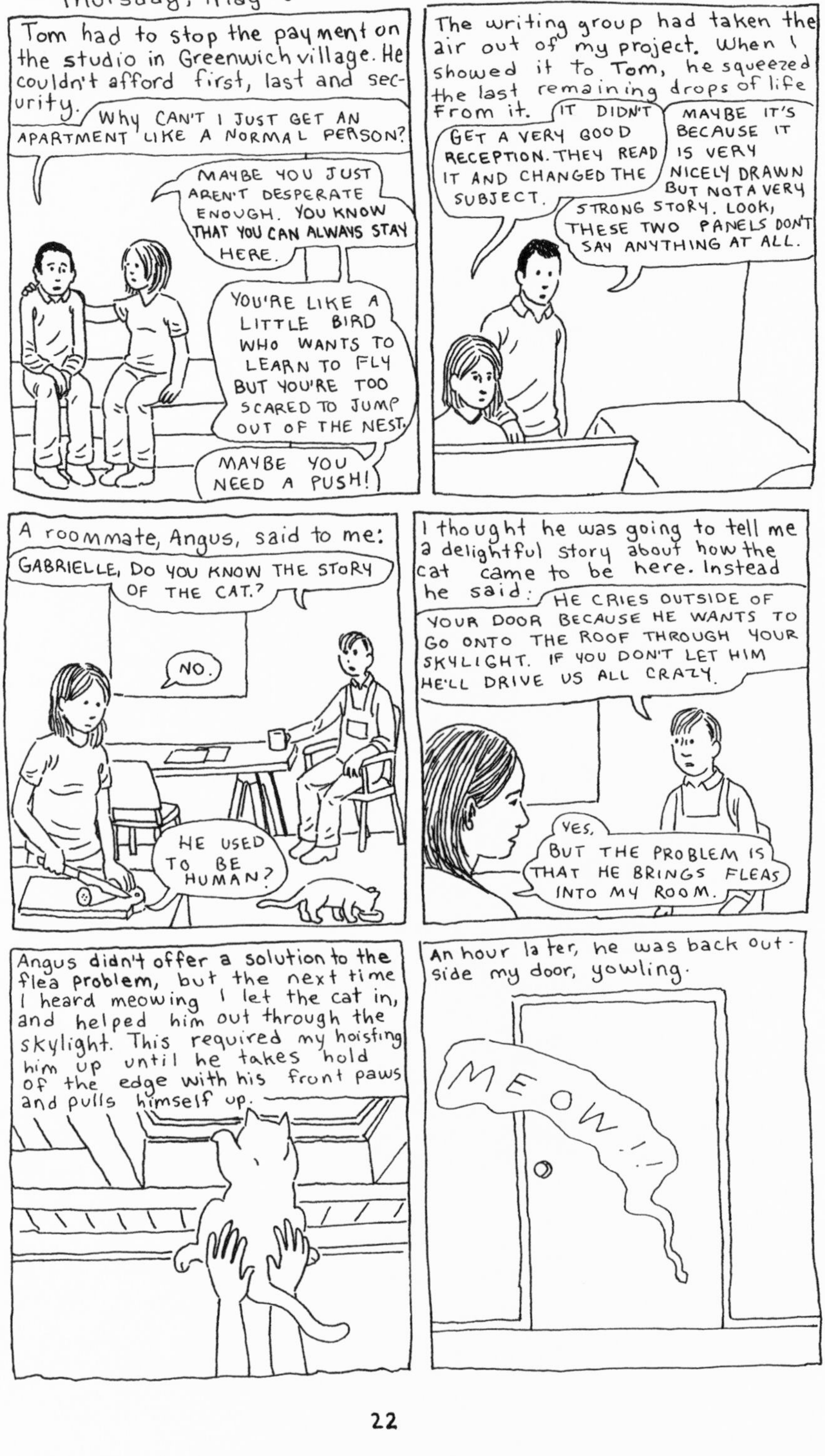
Tom had to stop the payment on the studio in Greenwich village. He couldn't afford first, last and security.
WHY CAN'T I JUST GET AN APARTMENT LIKE A NORMAL PERSON?
MAYBE YOU JUST AREN'T DESPERATE ENOUGH. YOU KNOW THAT YOU CAN ALWAYS STAY HERE.
YOU'RE LIKE A LITTLE BIRD WHO WANTS TO LEARN TO FLY BUT YOU'RE TOO SCARED TO JUMP OUT OF THE NEST.
MAYBE YOU NEED A PUSH!
The writing group had taken the air out of my project. When I showed it to Tom, he squeezed the last remaining drops of life from it.
IT DIDN'T GET A VERY GOOD RECEPTION. THEY READ IT AND CHANGED THE SUBJECT.
MAYBE IT'S BECAUSE IT IS VERY NICELY DRAWN BUT NOT A VERY STRONG STORY. LOOK, THESE TWO PANELS DON'T SAY ANYTHING AT ALL.
A roommate, Angus, said to me:
GABRIELLE, DO YOU KNOW THE STORY OF THE CAT?
NO.
HE USED TO BE HUMAN?
I thought he was going to tell me a delightful story about how the cat came to be here. Instead he said:
HE CRIES OUTSIDE OF YOUR DOOR BECAUSE HE WANTS TO GO ONTO THE ROOF THROUGH YOUR SKYLIGHT. IF YOU DON'T LET HIM HE'LL DRIVE US ALL CRAZY.
YES.
BUT THE PROBLEM IS THAT HE BRINGS FLEAS INTO MY ROOM.
Angus didn't offer a solution to the flea problem, but the next time I heard meowing I let the cat in, and helped him out through the skylight. This required my hoisting him up until he takes hold of the edge with his front paws and pulls himself up.
An hour later, he was back outside my door, yowling.
MEOW!!

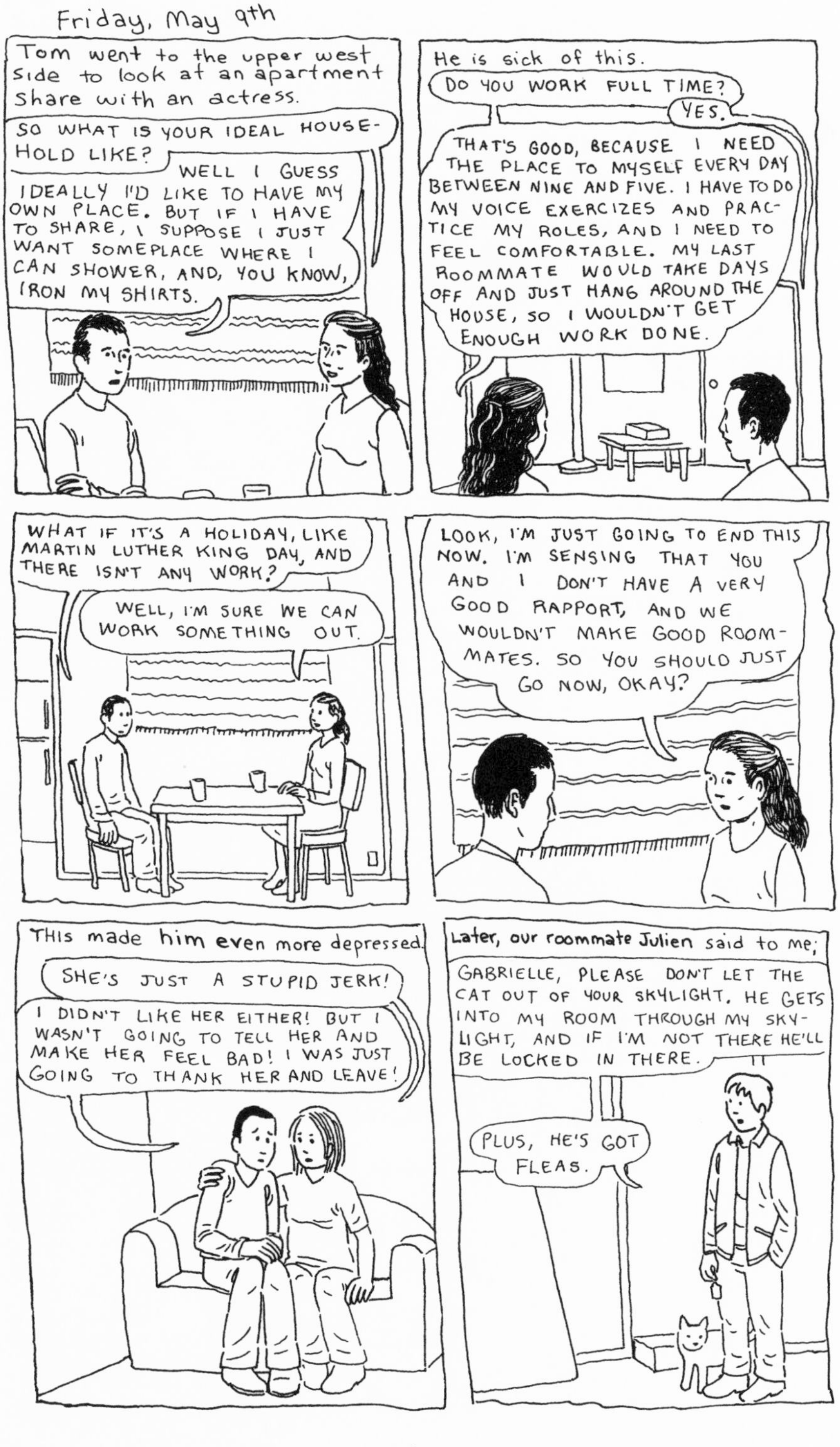
Friday, May 9th
Tom went to the upper west side to look at an apartment share with an actress.
SO WHAT IS YOUR IDEAL HOUSE-HOLD LIKE?
WELL I GUESS IDEALLY I'D LIKE TO HAVE MY OWN PLACE. BUT IF I HAVE TO SHARE, I SUPPOSE I JUST WANT SOMEPLACE WHERE I CAN SHOWER, AND, YOU KNOW, IRON MY SHIRTS.
He is sick of this.
DO YOU WORK FULL TIME?
YES.
THAT'S GOOD, BECAUSE I NEED THE PLACE TO MYSELF EVERY DAY BETWEEN NINE AND FIVE. I HAVE TO DO MY VOICE EXERCIZES AND PRAC-TICE MY ROLES, AND I NEED TO FEEL COMFORTABLE. MY LAST ROOMMATE WOULD TAKE DAYS OFF AND JUST HANG AROUND THE HOUSE, SO I WOULDN'T GET ENOUGH WORK DONE.
WHAT IF IT'S A HOLIDAY, LIKE MARTIN LUTHER KING DAY, AND THERE ISN'T ANY WORK?
WELL, I'M SURE WE CAN WORK SOMETHING OUT.
LOOK, I'M JUST GOING TO END THIS NOW. I'M SENSING THAT YOU AND I DON'T HAVE A VERY GOOD RAPPORT, AND WE WOULDN'T MAKE GOOD ROOM-MATES. SO YOU SHOULD JUST GO NOW, OKAY?
This made him even more depressed.
SHE'S JUST A STUPID JERK!
I DIDN'T LIKE HER EITHER! BUT I WASN'T GOING TO TELL HER AND MAKE HER FEEL BAD! I WAS JUST GOING TO THANK HER AND LEAVE!
Later, our roommate Julien said to me;
GABRIELLE, PLEASE DON'T LET THE CAT OUT OF YOUR SKYLIGHT. HE GETS INTO MY ROOM THROUGH MY SKY-LIGHT, AND IF I'M NOT THERE HE'LL BE LOCKED IN THERE.
PLUS, HE'S GOT FLEAS.

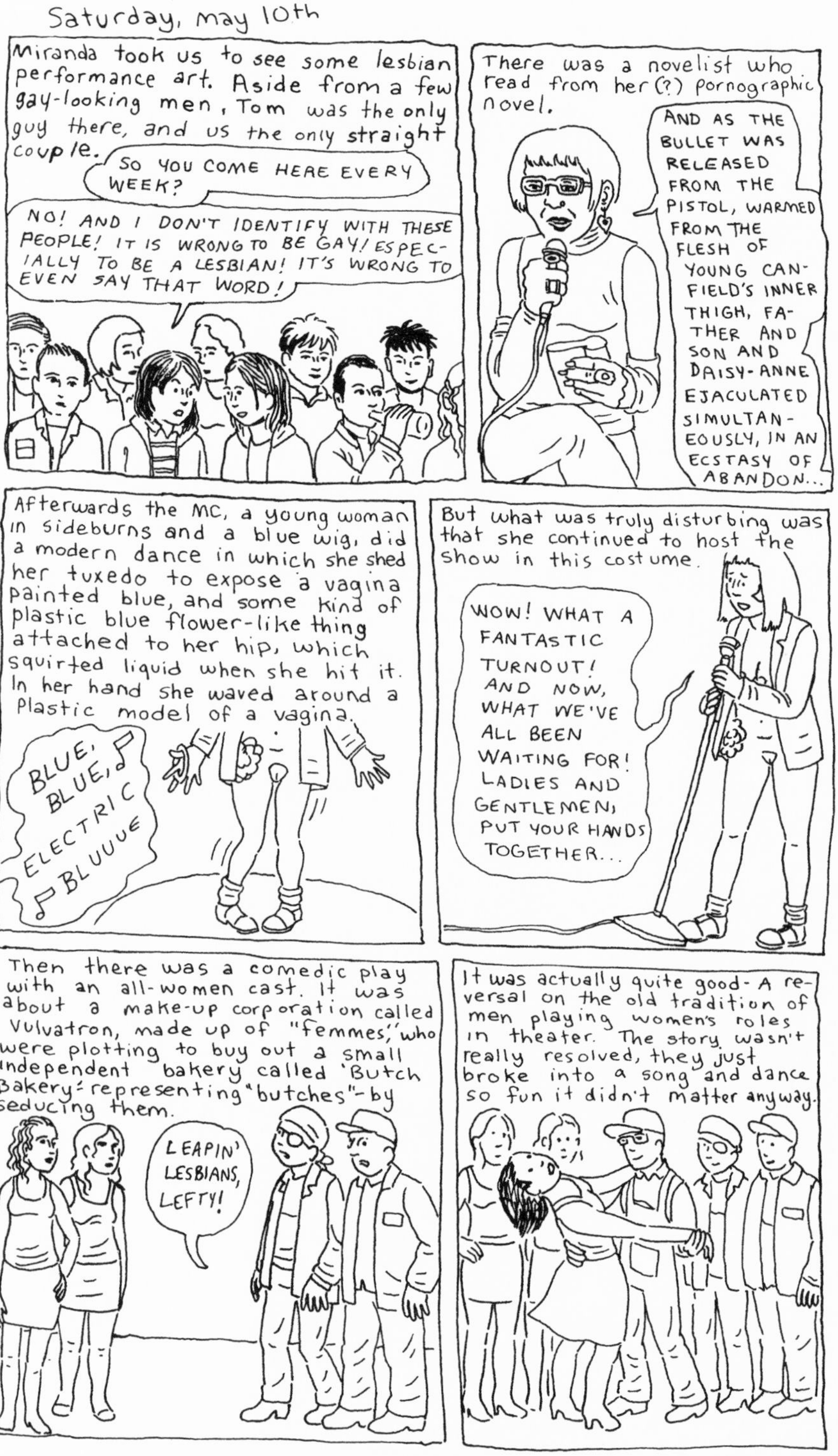
Saturday, May 10th
Miranda took us to see some lesbian performance art. Aside from a few gay-looking men, Tom was the only guy there, and us the only straight couple.
SO YOU COME HERE EVERY WEEK?
NO! AND I DON'T IDENTIFY WITH THESE PEOPLE! IT IS WRONG TO BE GAY! ESPECIALLY TO BE A LESBIAN! IT'S WRONG TO EVEN SAY THAT WORD!
There was a novelist who read from her(?) pornographic novel.
AND AS THE BULLET WAS RELEASED FROM THE PISTOL, WARMED FROM THE FLESH OF YOUNG CANFIELD'S INNER THIGH, FATHER AND SON AND DAISY-ANNE EJACULATED SIMULTANEOUSLY, IN AN ECSTASY OF ABANDON...
Afterwards the MC, a young woman in sideburns and a blue wig, did a modern dance in which she shed her tuxedo to expose a vagina painted blue, and some kind of plastic blue flower-like thing attached to her hip, which squirted liquid when she hit it. In her hand she waved around a plastic model of a vagina.
BLUE, BLUE, ELECTRIC BLUUUE
But what was truly disturbing was that she continued to host the show in this costume.
WOW! WHAT A FANTASTIC TURNOUT! AND NOW, WHAT WE'VE ALL BEEN WAITING FOR! LADIES AND GENTLEMEN, PUT YOUR HANDS TOGETHER...
Then there was a comedic play with an all-women cast. It was about a make-up corporation called Vulvatron, made up of "femmes," who were plotting to buy out a small independent bakery called 'Butch Bakery'- representing "butches"- by seducing them.
LEAPIN' LESBIANS, LEFTY!
It was actually quite good- A reversal on the old tradition of men playing women's roles in theater. The story wasn't really resolved, they just broke into a song and dance so fun it didn't matter anyway.

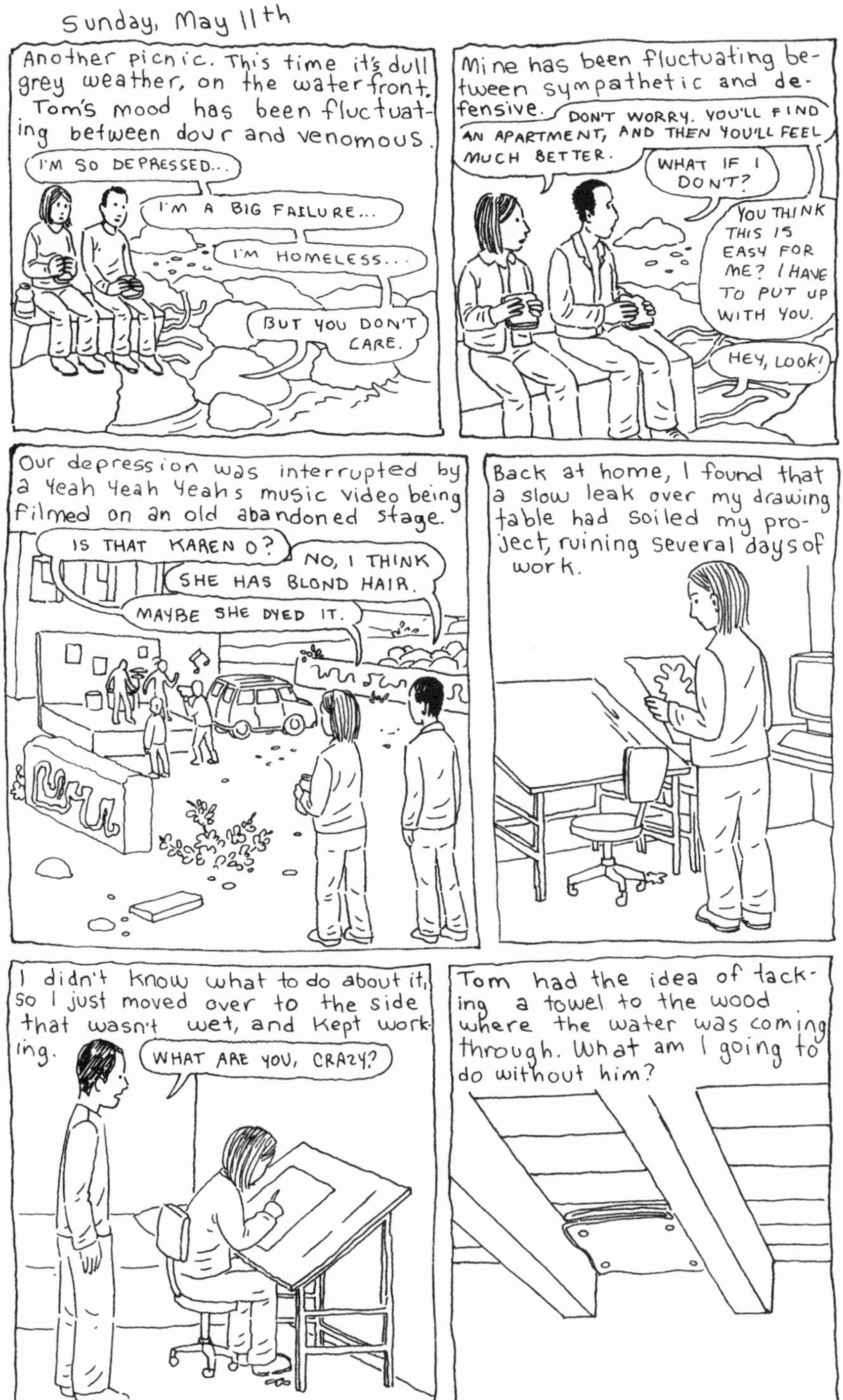
Sunday, May 11th
Another picnic. This time it's dull grey weather, on the waterfront. Tom's mood has been fluctuating between dour and venomous.
I'M SO DEPRESSED...
I'M A BIG FAILURE...
I'M HOMELESS...
BUT YOU DON'T CARE.
Mine has been fluctuating between sympathetic and defensive.
DON'T WORRY. YOU'LL FIND AN APARTMENT, AND THEN YOU'LL FEEL MUCH BETTER.
WHAT IF I DON'T?
YOU THINK THIS IS EASY FOR ME? I HAVE TO PUT UP WITH YOU.
HEY, LOOK!
Our depression was interrupted by a Yeah Yeah Yeahs music video being filmed on an old abandoned stage.
IS THAT KAREN O?
NO, I THINK SHE HAS BLOND HAIR.
MAYBE SHE DYED IT.
Back at home, I found that a slow leak over my drawing table had soiled my project, ruining several days of work.
I didn't know what to do about it, so I just moved over to the side that wasn't wet, and kept working.
WHAT ARE YOU, CRAZY?
Tom had the idea of tacking a towel to the wood where the water was coming through. What am I going to do without him?

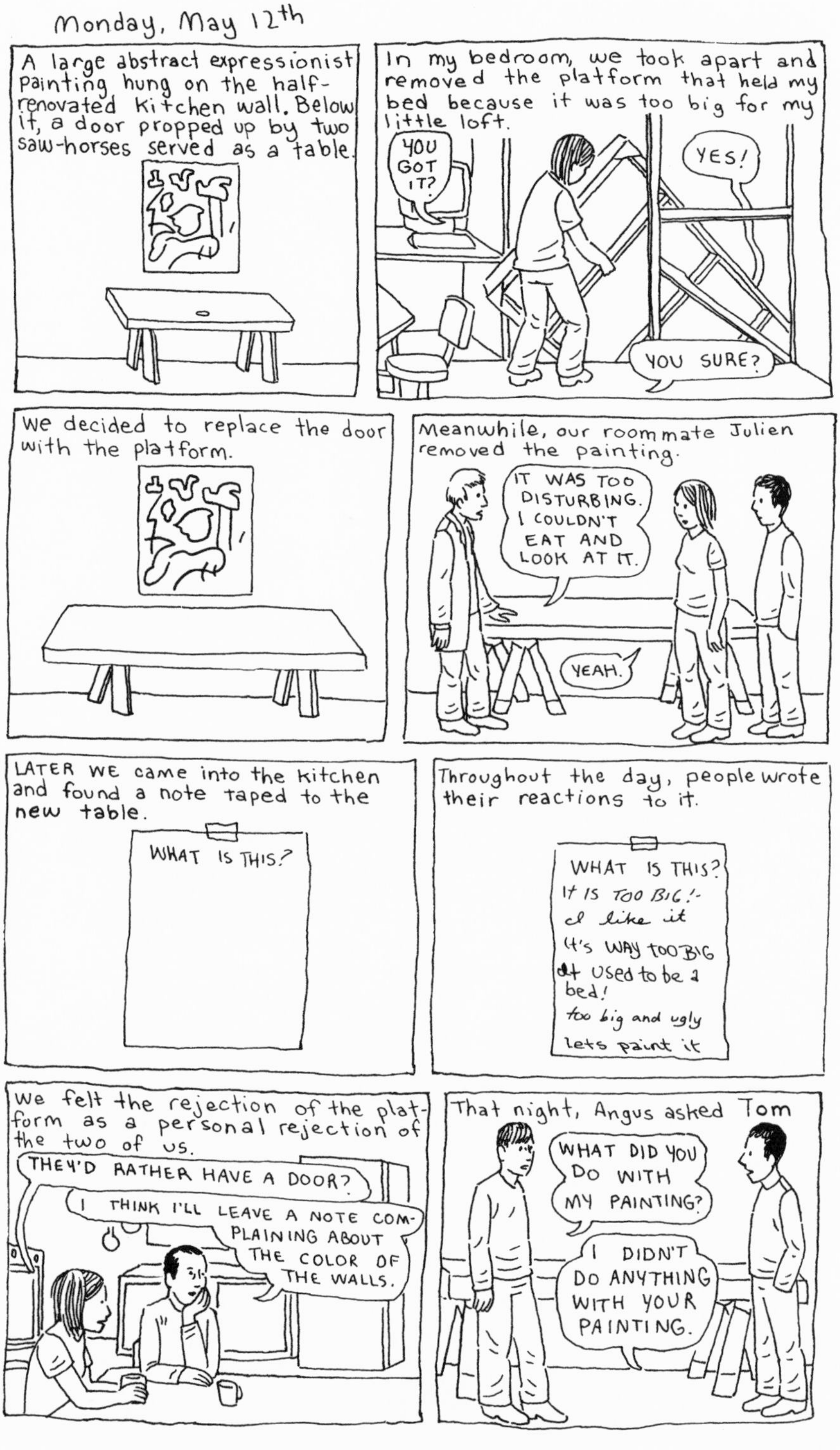
Monday, May 12th
A large abstract expressionist painting hung on the half-renovated kitchen wall. Below it, a door propped up by two saw-horses served as a table.
In my bedroom, we took apart and removed the platform that held my bed because it was too big for my little loft.
YOU GOT IT?
YES!
YOU SURE?
We decided to replace the door with the platform.
Meanwhile, our roommate Julien removed the painting.
IT WAS TOO DISTURBING. I COULDN'T EAT AND LOOK AT IT.
YEAH.
LATER WE came into the kitchen and found a note taped to the new table.
WHAT IS THIS?
Throughout the day, people wrote their reactions to it.
WHAT IS THIS?
It IS TOO BIG!-
I like it
It's WAY TOO BIG
It used to be a bed!
too big and ugly
lets paint it
We felt the rejection of the platform as a personal rejection of the two of us.
THEY'D RATHER HAVE A DOOR?
I THINK I'LL LEAVE A NOTE COMPLAINING ABOUT THE COLOR OF THE WALLS.
That night, Angus asked Tom
WHAT DID YOU DO WITH MY PAINTING?
I DIDN'T DO ANYTHING WITH YOUR PAINTING.

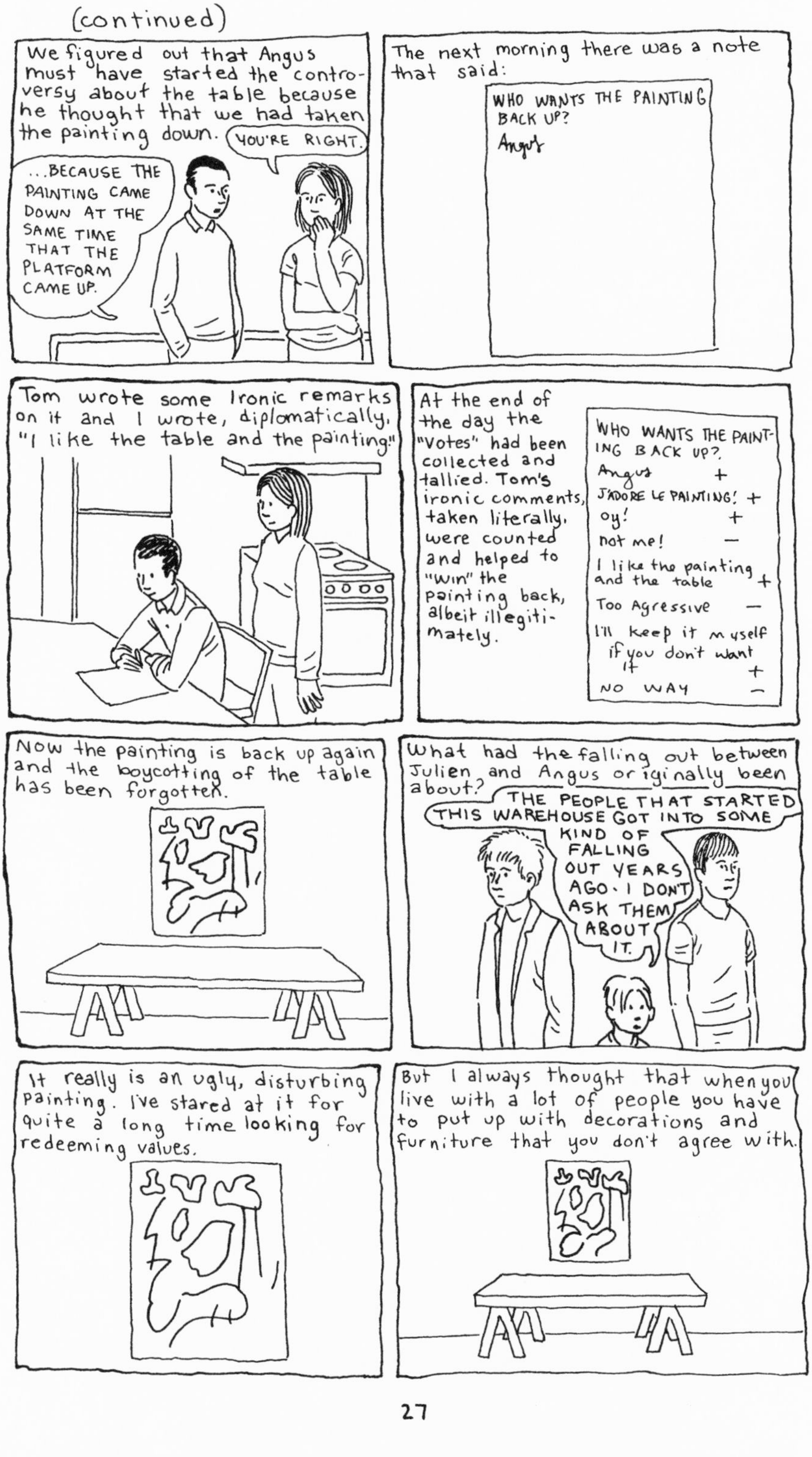
(continued)
We figured out that Angus must have started the controversy about the table because he thought that we had taken the painting down.
YOU'RE RIGHT.
...BECAUSE THE PAINTING CAME DOWN AT THE SAME TIME THAT THE PLATFORM CAME UP.
The next morning there was a note that said:
WHO WANTS THE PAINTING BACK UP?
Angus
Tom wrote some Ironic remarks on it and I wrote, diplomatically, "I like the table and the painting."
At the end of the day the "votes" had been collected and tallied. Tom's ironic comments, taken literally, were counted and helped to "win" the painting back, albeit illegitimately.
WHO WANTS THE PAINTING BACK UP?
Angus +
J'ADORE LE PAINTING! +
oy! +
not me! −
I like the painting and the table +
Too Agressive −
I'll keep it myself if you don't want it +
NO WAY −
Now the painting is back up again and the boycotting of the table has been forgotten.
What had the falling out between Julien and Angus originally been about?
THE PEOPLE THAT STARTED THIS WAREHOUSE GOT INTO SOME KIND OF FALLING OUT YEARS AGO. I DON'T ASK THEM ABOUT IT.
It really is an ugly, disturbing painting. I've stared at it for quite a long time looking for redeeming values.
But I always thought that when you live with a lot of people you have to put up with decorations and furniture that you don't agree with.

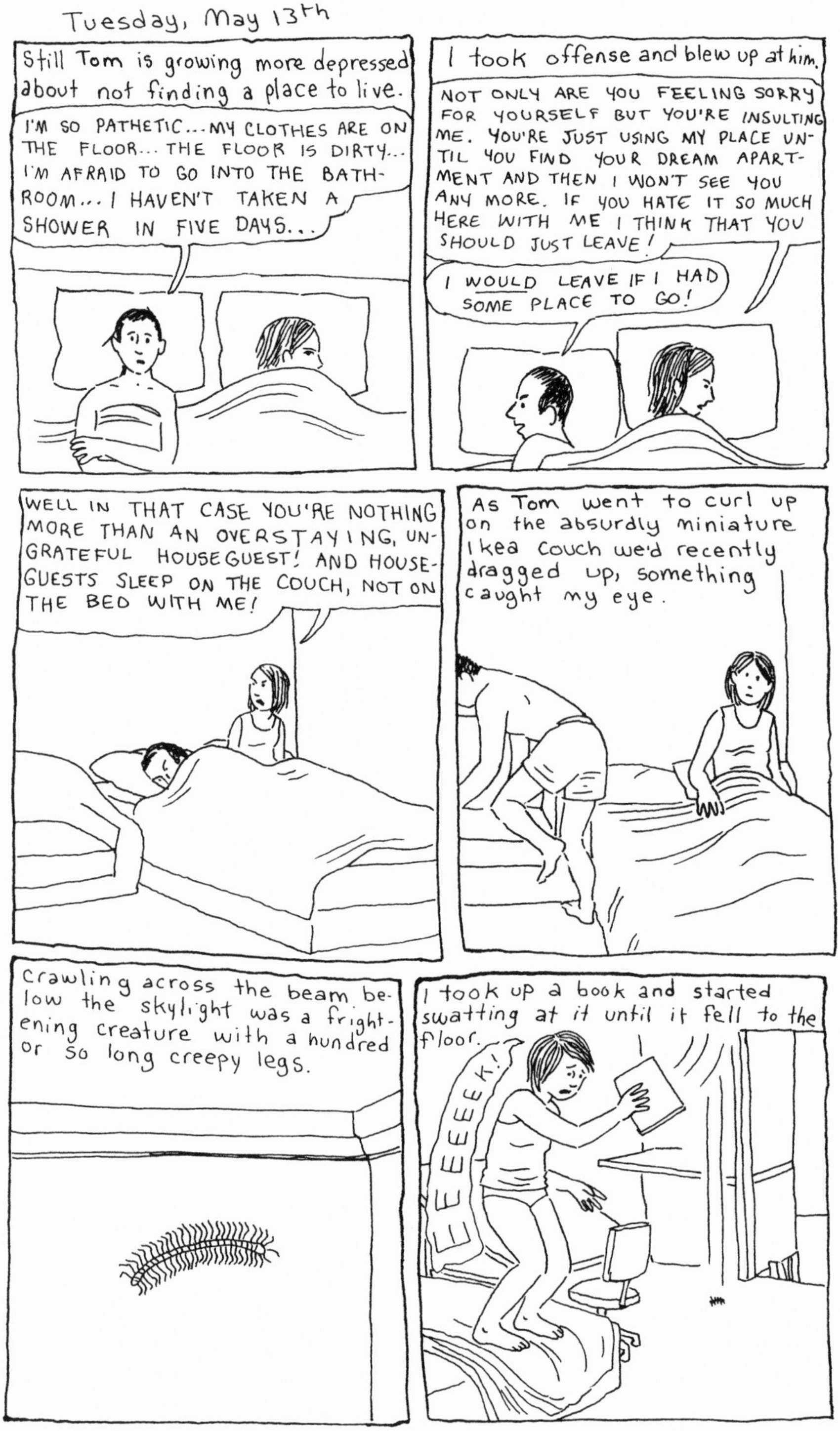
Tuesday, May 13th
Still Tom is growing more depressed about not finding a place to live.
I'M SO PATHETIC... MY CLOTHES ARE ON THE FLOOR... THE FLOOR IS DIRTY... I'M AFRAID TO GO INTO THE BATHROOM... I HAVEN'T TAKEN A SHOWER IN FIVE DAYS...
I took offense and blew up at him.
NOT ONLY ARE YOU FEELING SORRY FOR YOURSELF BUT YOU'RE INSULTING ME. YOU'RE JUST USING MY PLACE UNTIL YOU FIND YOUR DREAM APARTMENT AND THEN I WON'T SEE YOU ANY MORE. IF YOU HATE IT SO MUCH HERE WITH ME I THINK THAT YOU SHOULD JUST LEAVE!
I WOULD LEAVE IF I HAD SOME PLACE TO GO!
WELL IN THAT CASE YOU'RE NOTHING MORE THAN AN OVERSTAYING, UNGRATEFUL HOUSEGUEST! AND HOUSEGUESTS SLEEP ON THE COUCH, NOT ON THE BED WITH ME!
As Tom went to curl up on the absurdly miniature Ikea couch we'd recently dragged up, something caught my eye.
Crawling across the beam below the skylight was a frightening creature with a hundred or so long creepy legs.
I took up a book and started swatting at it until it fell to the floor.
EEEEEEEK!

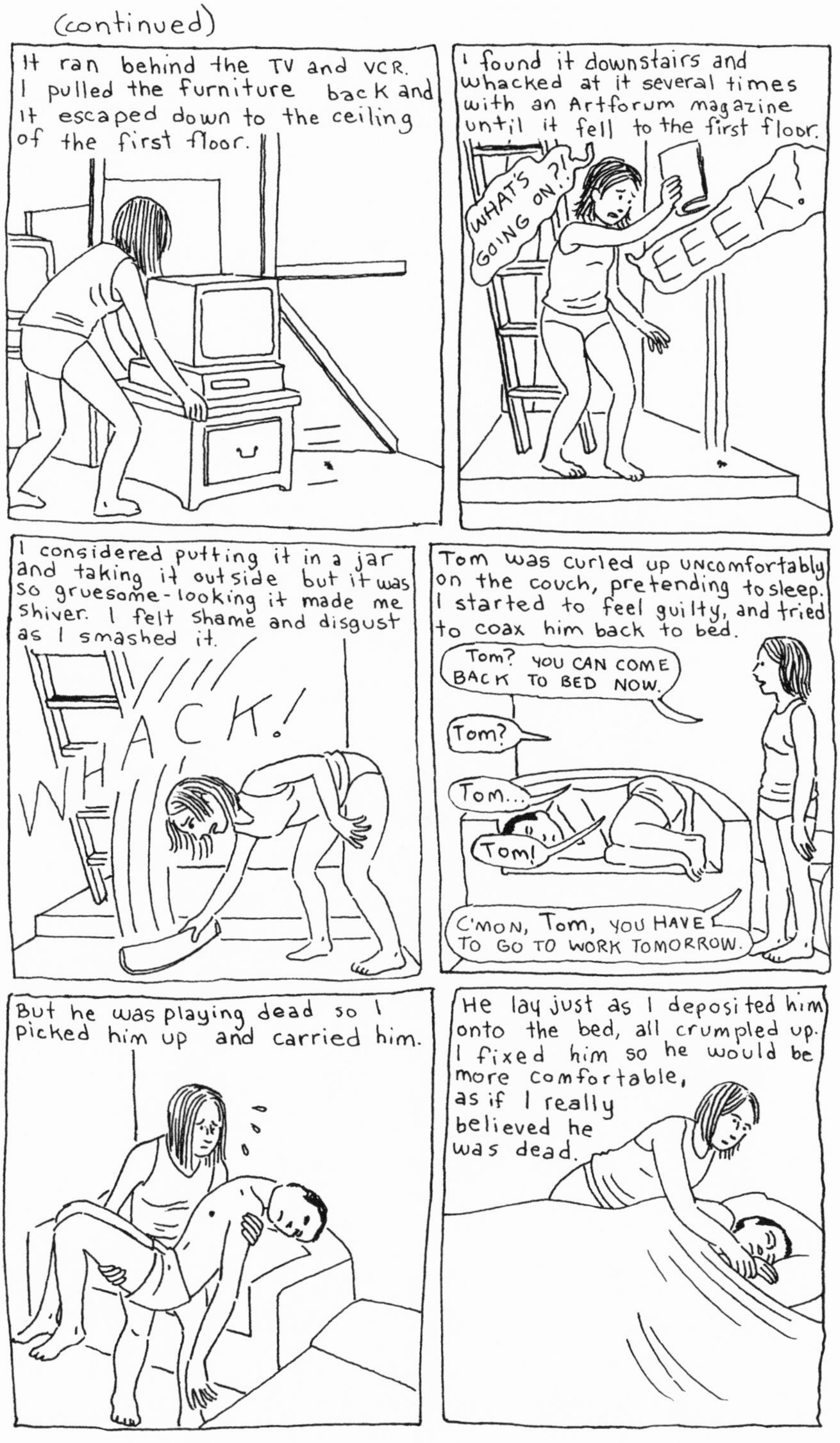
(continued)
It ran behind the TV and VCR. I pulled the furniture back and it escaped down to the ceiling of the first floor.
I found it downstairs and whacked at it several times with an Artforum magazine until it fell to the first floor.
WHAT'S GOING ON?!
EEEK!
I considered putting it in a jar and taking it outside but it was so gruesome-looking it made me shiver. I felt shame and disgust as I smashed it.
WHACK!
Tom was curled up uncomfortably on the couch, pretending to sleep. I started to feel guilty, and tried to coax him back to bed.
Tom? YOU CAN COME BACK TO BED NOW.
Tom?
Tom...
Tom!
C'MON, Tom, YOU HAVE TO GO TO WORK TOMORROW.
But he was playing dead so I picked him up and carried him.
He lay just as I deposited him onto the bed, all crumpled up. I fixed him so he would be more comfortable, as if I really believed he was dead.

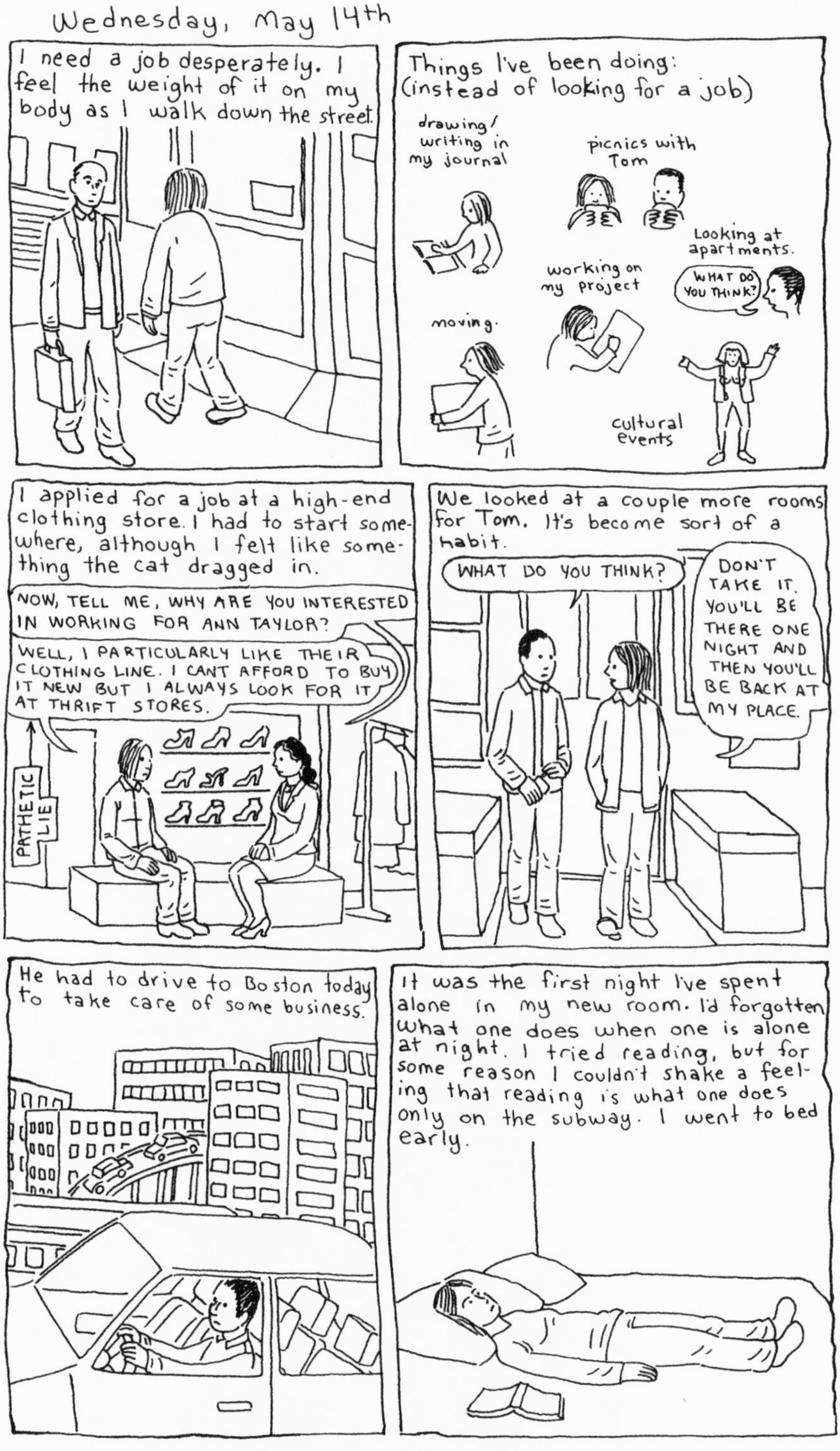
Wednesday, May 14th
I need a job desperately. I feel the weight of it on my body as I walk down the street.
Things I've been doing: (instead of looking for a job)
drawing/ writing in my journal
picnics with Tom
Looking at apartments.
WHAT DO YOU THINK?
working on my project
moving.
cultural events
I applied for a job at a high-end clothing store. I had to start somewhere, although I felt like something the cat dragged in.
NOW, TELL ME, WHY ARE YOU INTERESTED IN WORKING FOR ANN TAYLOR?
WELL, I PARTICULARLY LIKE THEIR CLOTHING LINE. I CANT AFFORD TO BUY IT NEW BUT I ALWAYS LOOK FOR IT AT THRIFT STORES.
PATHETIC LIE
We looked at a couple more rooms for Tom. It's become sort of a habit.
WHAT DO YOU THINK?
DON'T TAKE IT. YOU'LL BE THERE ONE NIGHT AND THEN YOU'LL BE BACK AT MY PLACE.
He had to drive to Boston today to take care of some business.
It was the first night I've spent alone in my new room. I'd forgotten what one does when one is alone at night. I tried reading, but for some reason I couldn't shake a feeling that reading is what one does only on the subway. I went to bed early.

Friday, May 16th

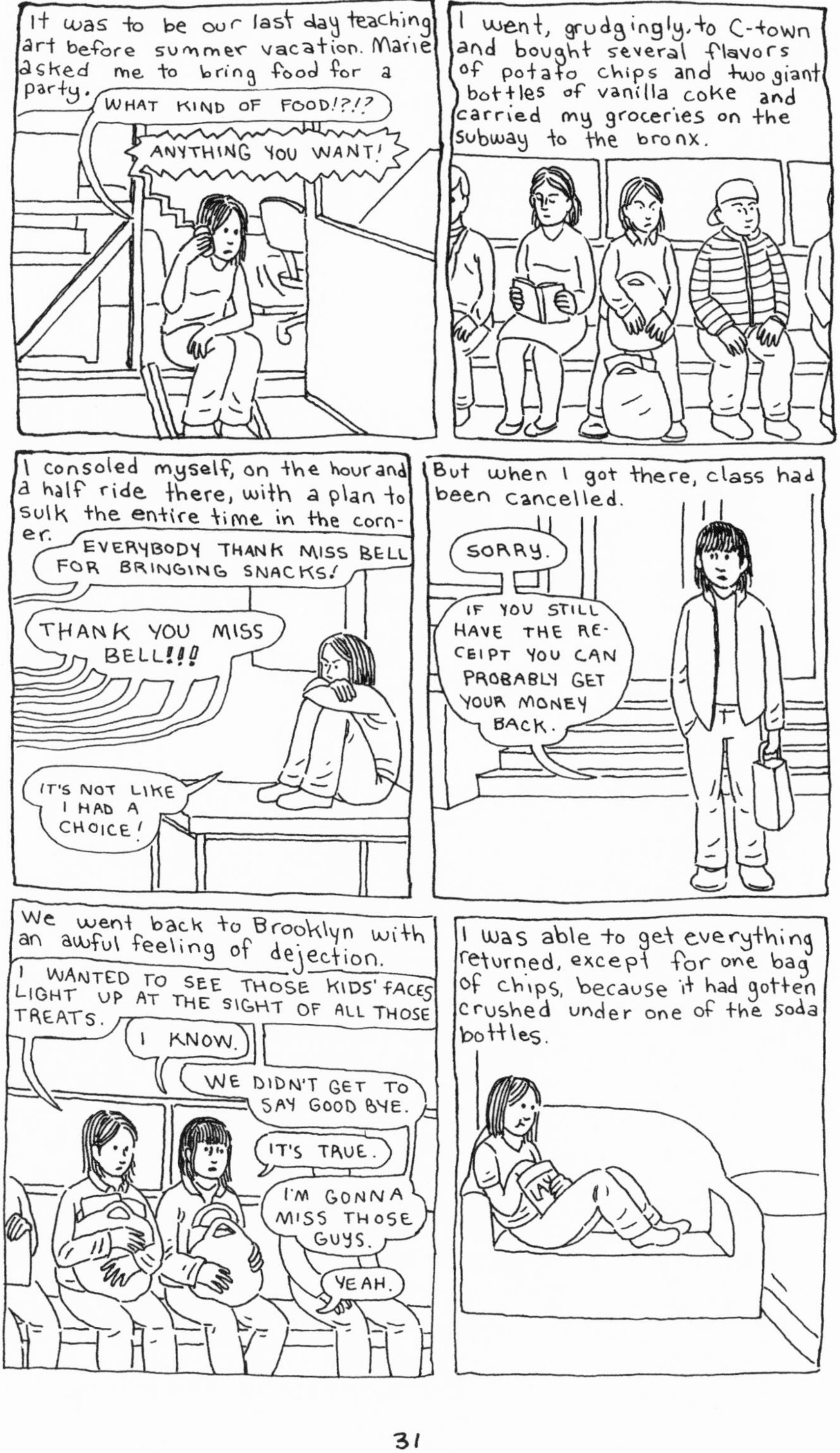
It was to be our last day teaching art before summer vacation. Marie asked me to bring food for a party.
WHAT KIND OF FOOD!?!?
ANYTHING YOU WANT!
I went, grudgingly, to C-town and bought several flavors of potato chips and two giant bottles of vanilla coke and carried my groceries on the subway to the bronx.
I consoled myself, on the hour and a half ride there, with a plan to sulk the entire time in the corner.
EVERYBODY THANK MISS BELL FOR BRINGING SNACKS!
THANK YOU MISS BELL!!!
IT'S NOT LIKE I HAD A CHOICE!
But when I got there, class had been cancelled.
SORRY.
IF YOU STILL HAVE THE RECEIPT YOU CAN PROBABLY GET YOUR MONEY BACK.
We went back to Brooklyn with an awful feeling of dejection.
I WANTED TO SEE THOSE KIDS' FACES LIGHT UP AT THE SIGHT OF ALL THOSE TREATS.
I KNOW.
WE DIDN'T GET TO SAY GOOD BYE.
IT'S TRUE.
I'M GONNA MISS THOSE GUYS.
YEAH.
I was able to get everything returned, except for one bag of chips, because it had gotten crushed under one of the soda bottles.
LAY

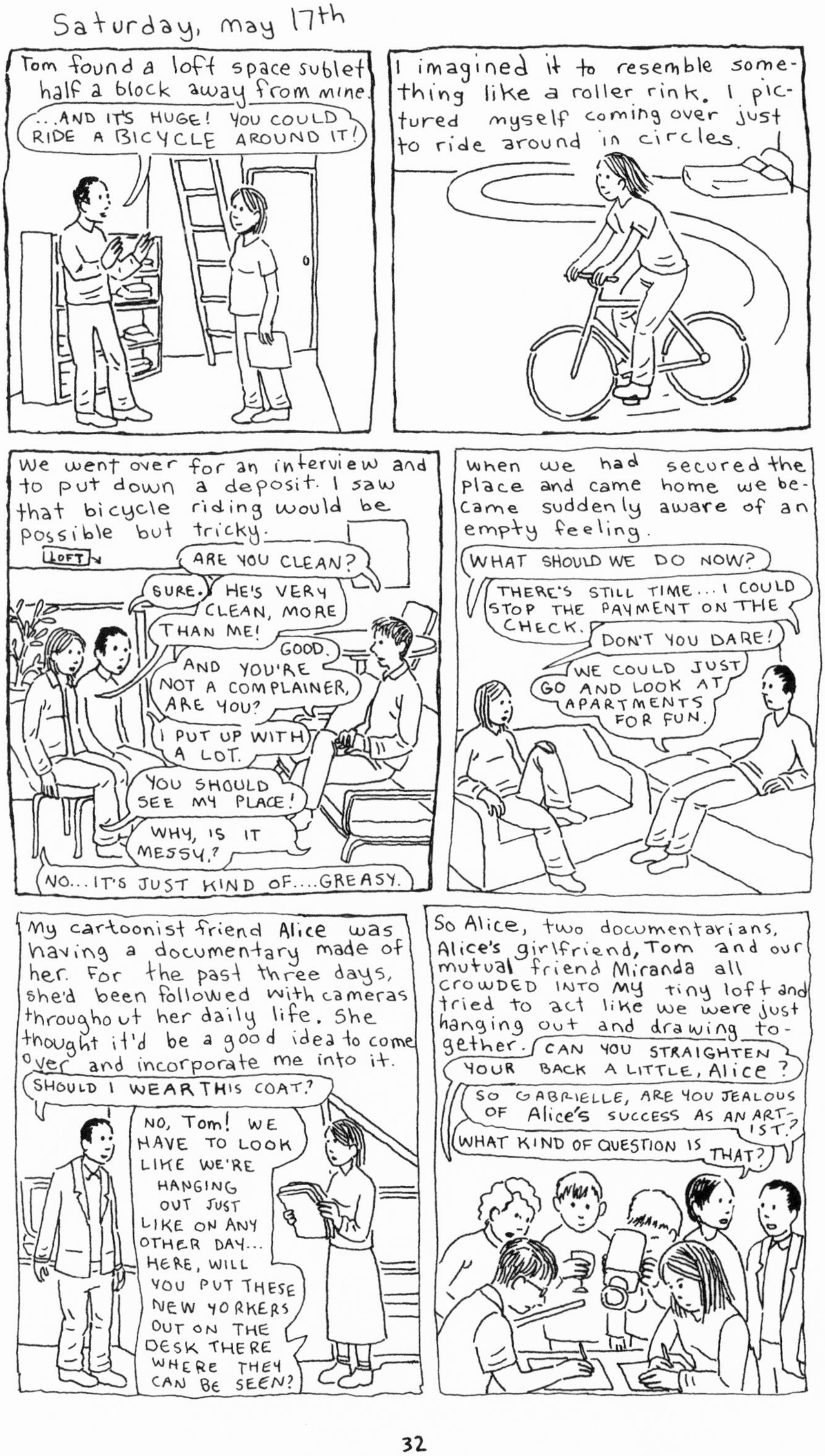
Saturday, may 17th
Tom found a loft space sublet half a block away from mine.
...AND IT'S HUGE! YOU COULD RIDE A BICYCLE AROUND IT!
I imagined it to resemble something like a roller rink. I pictured myself coming over just to ride around in circles.
We went over for an interview and to put down a deposit. I saw that bicycle riding would be possible but tricky.
LOFT
ARE YOU CLEAN?
SURE.
HE'S VERY CLEAN, MORE THAN ME!
GOOD.
AND YOU'RE NOT A COMPLAINER, ARE YOU?
I PUT UP WITH A LOT.
YOU SHOULD SEE MY PLACE!
WHY, IS IT MESSY?
NO... IT'S JUST KIND OF.... GREASY.
When we had secured the place and came home we became suddenly aware of an empty feeling.
WHAT SHOULD WE DO NOW?
THERE'S STILL TIME... I COULD STOP THE PAYMENT ON THE CHECK.
DON'T YOU DARE!
WE COULD JUST GO AND LOOK AT APARTMENTS FOR FUN.
My cartoonist friend Alice was having a documentary made of her. For the past three days, she'd been followed with cameras throughout her daily life. She thought it'd be a good idea to come over and incorporate me into it.
SHOULD I WEAR THIS COAT?
NO, Tom! WE HAVE TO LOOK LIKE WE'RE HANGING OUT JUST LIKE ON ANY OTHER DAY... HERE, WILL YOU PUT THESE NEW YORKERS OUT ON THE DESK THERE WHERE THEY CAN BE SEEN?
So Alice, two documentarians, Alice's girlfriend, Tom and our mutual friend Miranda all crowded into my tiny loft and tried to act like we were just hanging out and drawing together.
CAN YOU STRAIGHTEN YOUR BACK A LITTLE, Alice?
SO GABRIELLE, ARE YOU JEALOUS OF Alice's SUCCESS AS AN ARTIST?
WHAT KIND OF QUESTION IS THAT?

(continued)

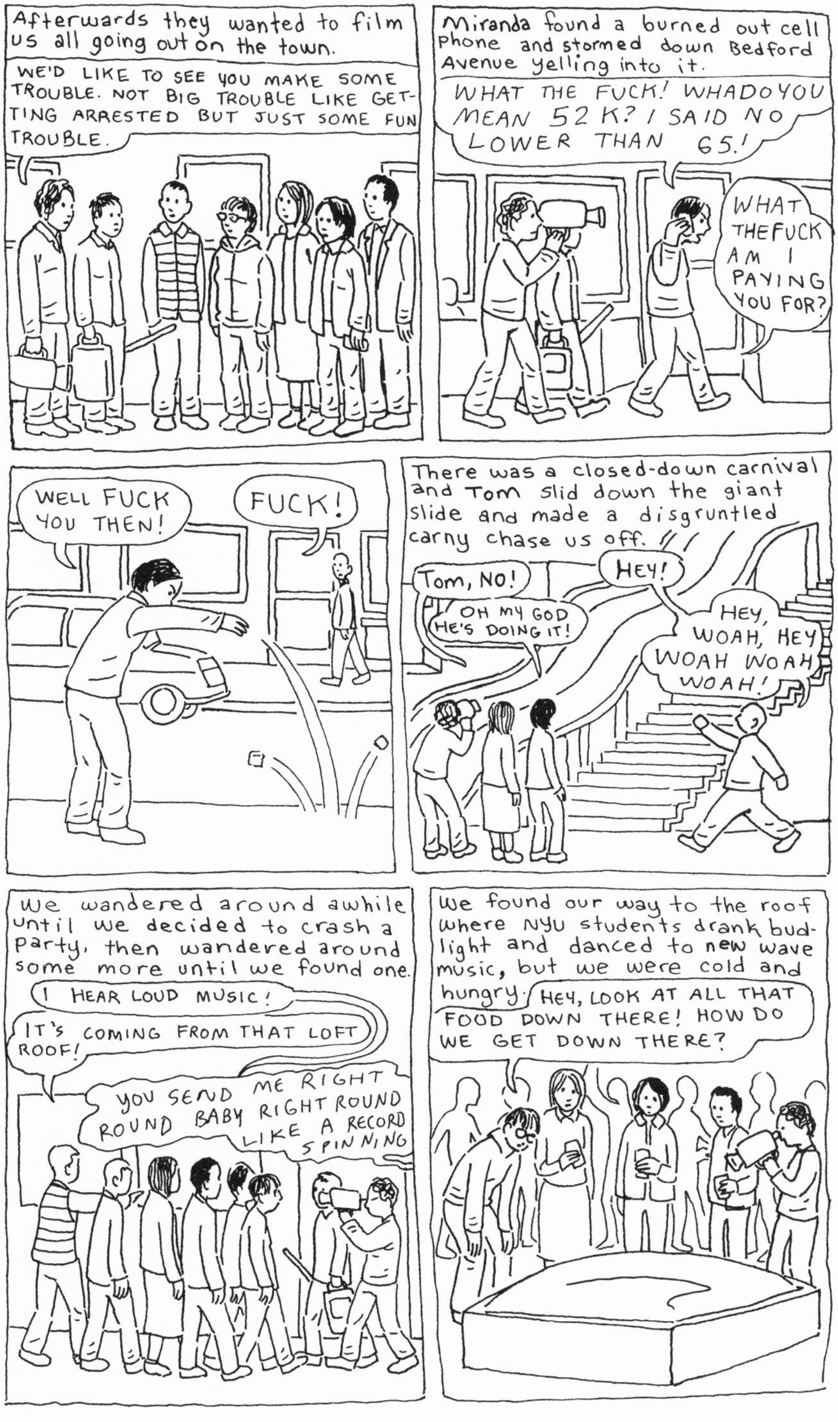

Afterwards they wanted to film us all going out on the town.
WE'D LIKE TO SEE YOU MAKE SOME TROUBLE. NOT BIG TROUBLE LIKE GETTING ARRESTED BUT JUST SOME FUN TROUBLE.
Miranda found a burned out cell phone and stormed down Bedford Avenue yelling into it.
WHAT THE FUCK! WHADOYOU MEAN 52 K? I SAID NO LOWER THAN 65!
WHAT THE FUCK AM I PAYING YOU FOR?
WELL FUCK YOU THEN!
FUCK!
There was a closed-down carnival and Tom slid down the giant slide and made a disgruntled carny chase us off.
Tom, NO!
OH MY GOD HE'S DOING IT!
HEY!
HEY, WOAH, HEY WOAH WOAH WOAH!
We wandered around awhile until we decided to crash a party, then wandered around some more until we found one.
I HEAR LOUD MUSIC!
IT'S COMING FROM THAT LOFT ROOF!
YOU SEND ME RIGHT ROUND BABY RIGHT ROUND LIKE A RECORD SPINNING
We found our way to the roof where NYU students drank bud-light and danced to new wave music, but we were cold and hungry.
HEY, LOOK AT ALL THAT FOOD DOWN THERE! HOW DO WE GET DOWN THERE?

(continued)

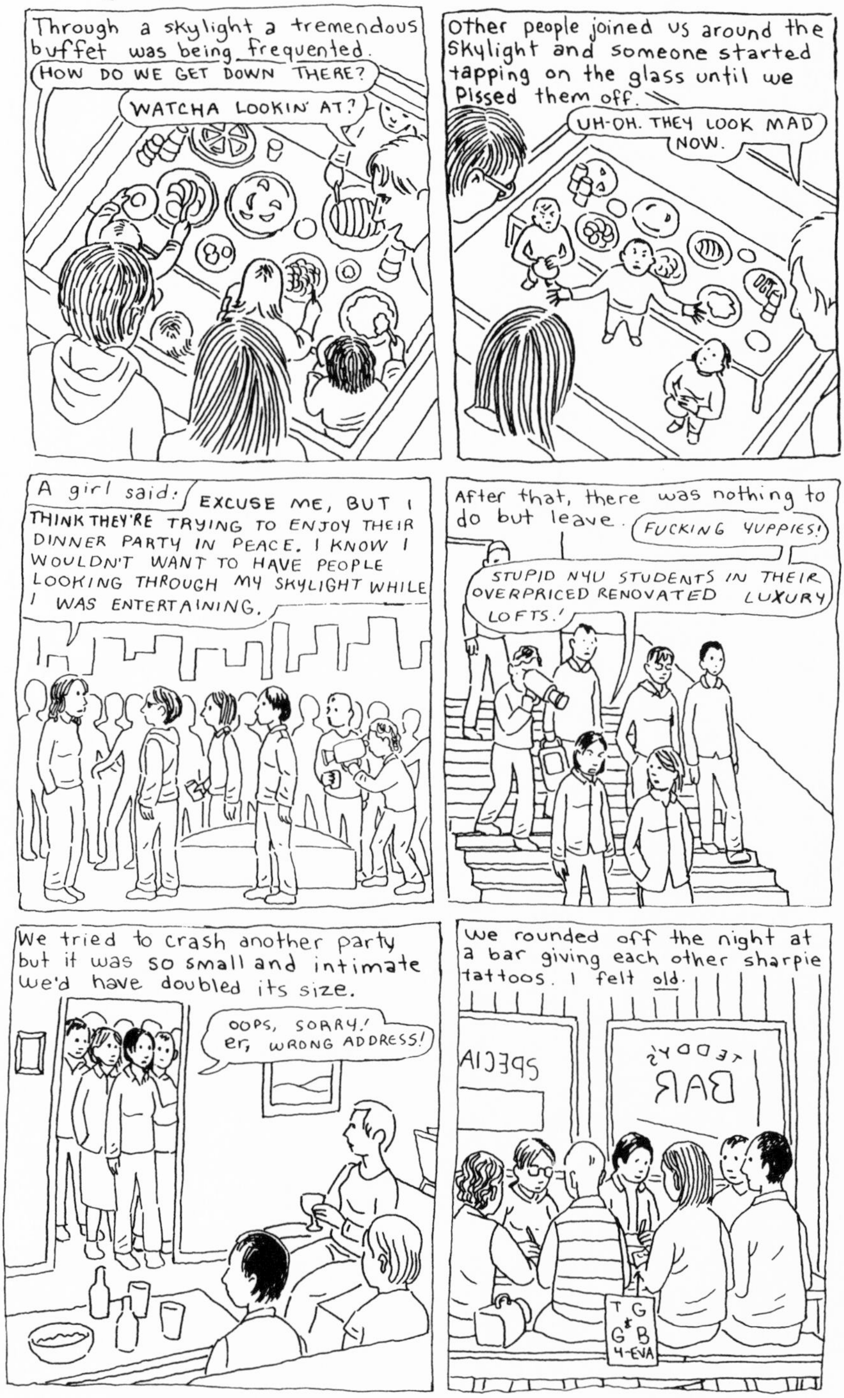
Through a skylight a tremendous buffet was being frequented.
HOW DO WE GET DOWN THERE?
WATCHA LOOKIN' AT?
Other people joined us around the skylight and someone started tapping on the glass until we pissed them off.
UH-OH. THEY LOOK MAD NOW.
A girl said:
EXCUSE ME, BUT I THINK THEY'RE TRYING TO ENJOY THEIR DINNER PARTY IN PEACE. I KNOW I WOULDN'T WANT TO HAVE PEOPLE LOOKING THROUGH MY SKYLIGHT WHILE I WAS ENTERTAINING.
After that, there was nothing to do but leave.
FUCKING YUPPIES!
STUPID NYU STUDENTS IN THEIR OVERPRICED RENOVATED LUXURY LOFTS!
We tried to crash another party but it was so small and intimate we'd have doubled its size.
OOPS, SORRY! er, WRONG ADDRESS!
We rounded off the night at a bar giving each other sharpie tattoos. I felt old.
T G & G B 4-EVA

## Monday, May 19th

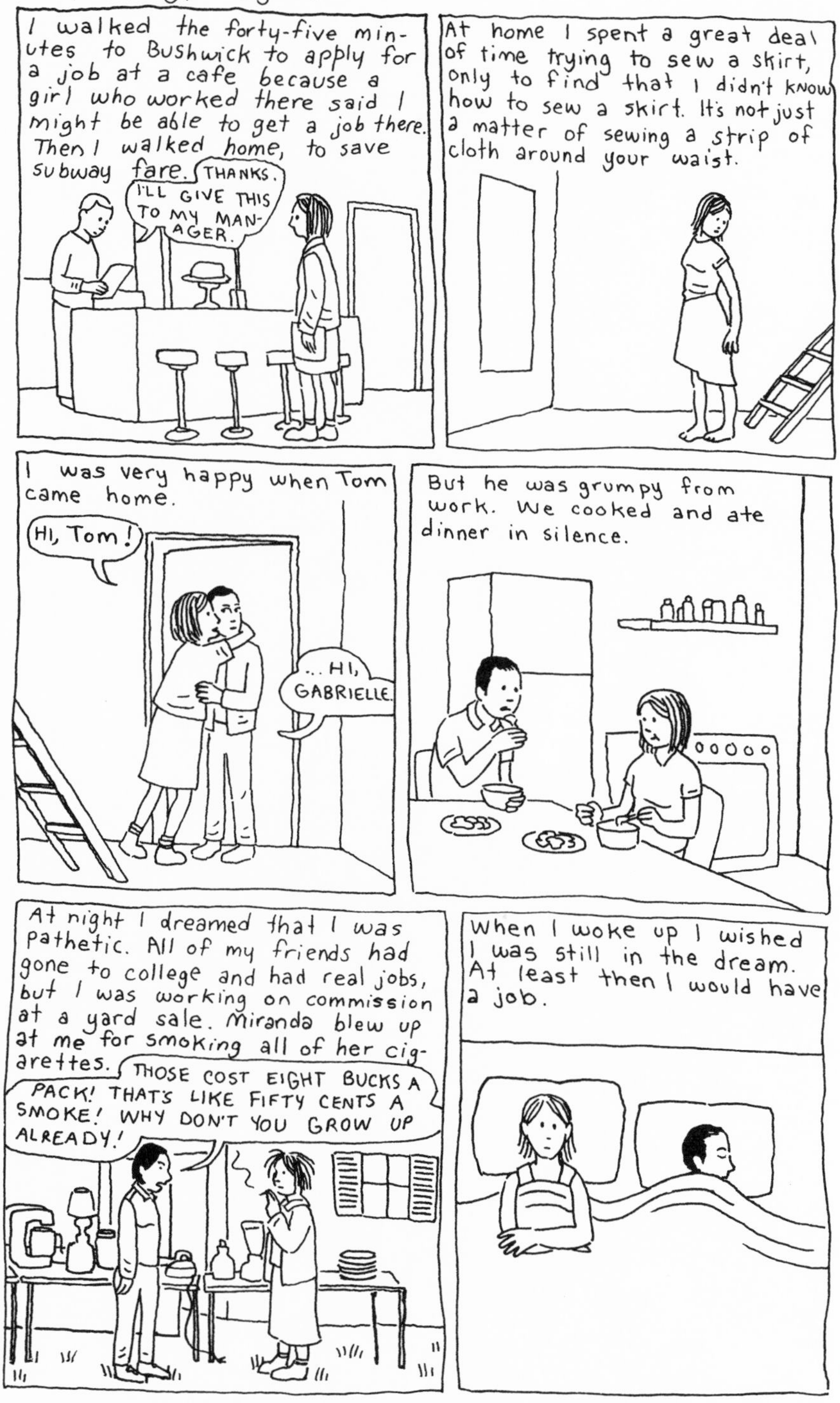
I walked the forty-five minutes to Bushwick to apply for a job at a cafe because a girl who worked there said I might be able to get a job there. Then I walked home, to save subway fare.
THANKS. I'LL GIVE THIS TO MY MANAGER.
At home I spent a great deal of time trying to sew a skirt, only to find that I didn't know how to sew a skirt. It's not just a matter of sewing a strip of cloth around your waist.
I was very happy when Tom came home.
HI, Tom!
...HI, GABRIELLE.
But he was grumpy from work. We cooked and ate dinner in silence.
At night I dreamed that I was pathetic. All of my friends had gone to college and had real jobs, but I was working on commission at a yard sale. Miranda blew up at me for smoking all of her cigarettes.
THOSE COST EIGHT BUCKS A PACK! THAT'S LIKE FIFTY CENTS A SMOKE! WHY DON'T YOU GROW UP ALREADY!
When I woke up I wished I was still in the dream. At least then I would have a job.

Wednesday, May 21st

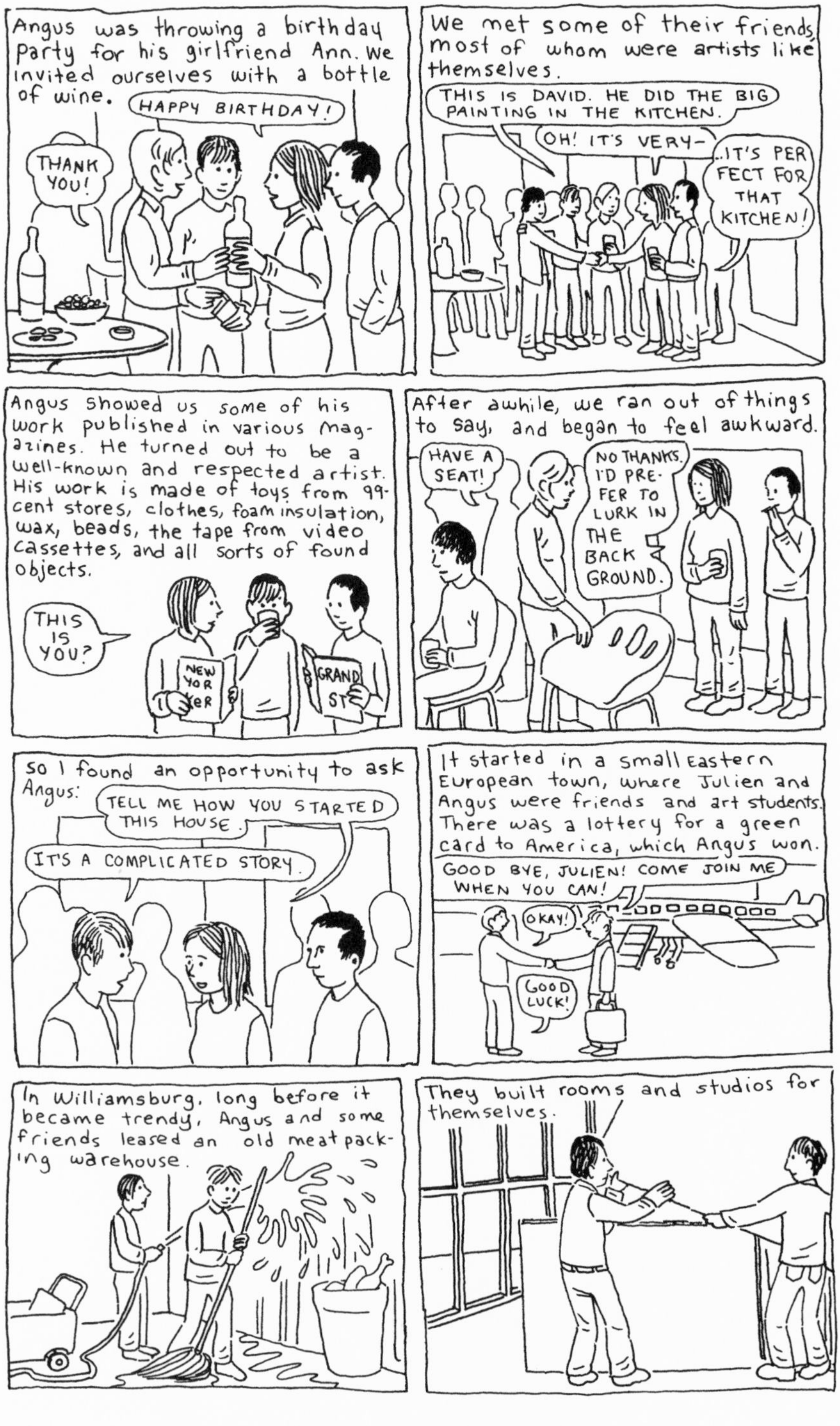

Angus was throwing a birthday party for his girlfriend Ann. We invited ourselves with a bottle of wine.
HAPPY BIRTHDAY!
THANK YOU!
We met some of their friends, most of whom were artists like themselves.
THIS IS DAVID. HE DID THE BIG PAINTING IN THE KITCHEN.
OH! IT'S VERY-
..IT'S PERFECT FOR THAT KITCHEN!
Angus showed us some of his work published in various magazines. He turned out to be a well-known and respected artist. His work is made of toys from 99-cent stores, clothes, foam insulation, wax, beads, the tape from video cassettes, and all sorts of found objects.
THIS IS YOU?
NEW YOR KER
GRAND ST
After awhile, we ran out of things to say, and began to feel awkward.
HAVE A SEAT!
NO THANKS. I'D PREFER TO LURK IN THE BACKGROUND.
So I found an opportunity to ask Angus:
TELL ME HOW YOU STARTED THIS HOUSE.
IT'S A COMPLICATED STORY.
It started in a small Eastern European town, where Julien and Angus were friends and art students. There was a lottery for a green card to America, which Angus won.
GOOD BYE, JULIEN! COME JOIN ME WHEN YOU CAN!
OKAY!
GOOD LUCK!
In Williamsburg, long before it became trendy, Angus and some friends leased an old meatpacking warehouse.
They built rooms and studios for themselves.

(continued)

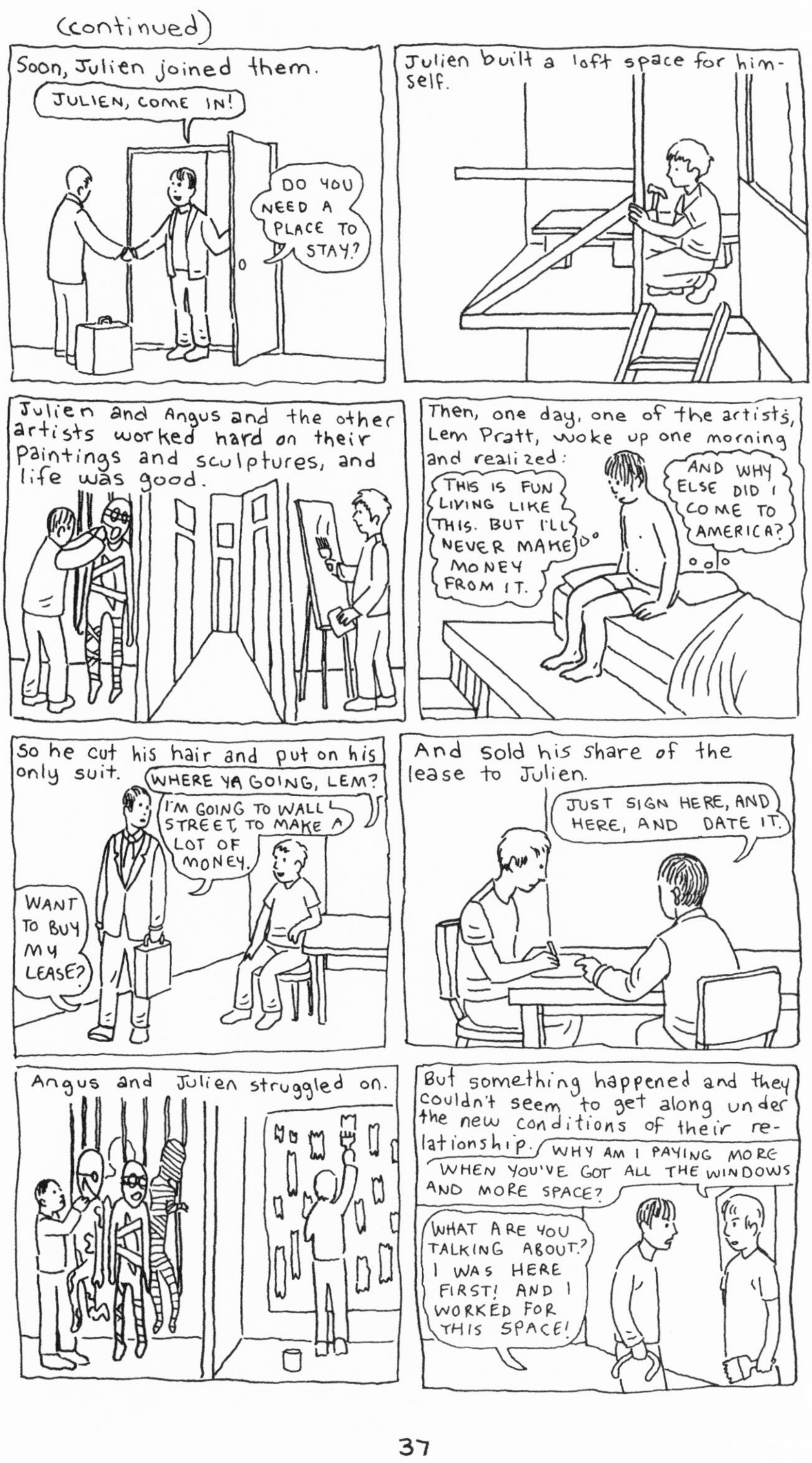
Soon, Julien joined them.
JULIEN, COME IN!
DO YOU NEED A PLACE TO STAY?
Julien built a loft space for him-self.
Julien and Angus and the other artists worked hard on their paintings and sculptures, and life was good.
Then, one day, one of the artists, Lem Pratt, woke up one morning and realized:
THIS IS FUN LIVING LIKE THIS. BUT I'LL NEVER MAKE MONEY FROM IT.
AND WHY ELSE DID I COME TO AMERICA?
So he cut his hair and put on his only suit.
WHERE YA GOING, LEM?
I'M GOING TO WALL STREET, TO MAKE A LOT OF MONEY.
WANT TO BUY MY LEASE?
And sold his share of the lease to Julien.
JUST SIGN HERE, AND HERE, AND DATE IT.
Angus and Julien struggled on.
But something happened and they couldn't seem to get along under the new conditions of their re-lationship.
WHY AM I PAYING MORE WHEN YOU'VE GOT ALL THE WINDOWS AND MORE SPACE?
WHAT ARE YOU TALKING ABOUT? I WAS HERE FIRST! AND I WORKED FOR THIS SPACE!

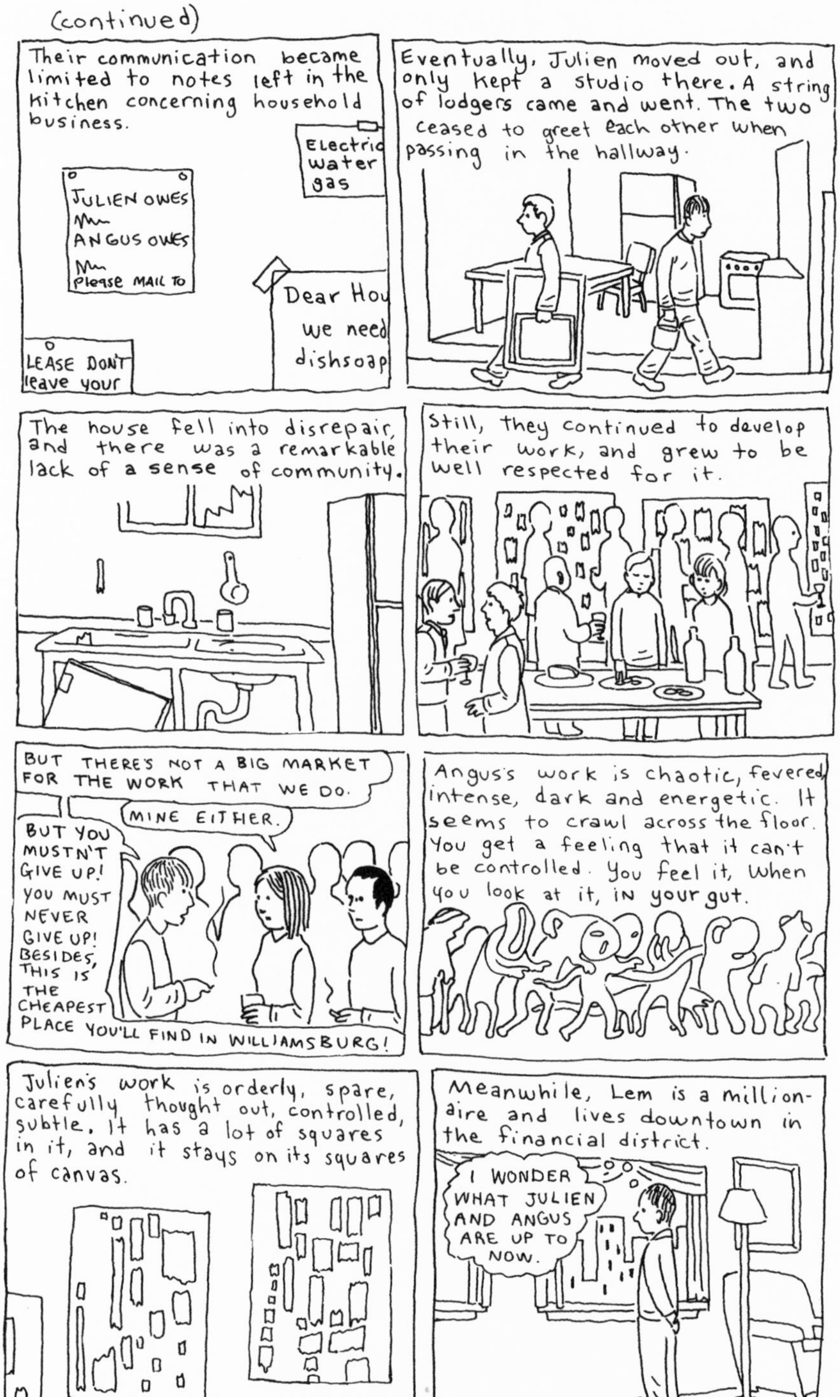
(continued)
Their communication became limited to notes left in the kitchen concerning household business.
JULIEN OWES
ANGUS OWES
Please MAIL TO
Electric
water
gas
Dear Hou
we need
dishsoap
LEASE DON'T
leave your
Eventually, Julien moved out, and only kept a studio there. A string of lodgers came and went. The two ceased to greet each other when passing in the hallway.
The house fell into disrepair, and there was a remarkable lack of a sense of community.
Still, they continued to develop their work, and grew to be well respected for it.
BUT THERE'S NOT A BIG MARKET FOR THE WORK THAT WE DO.
MINE EITHER.
BUT YOU MUSTN'T GIVE UP! YOU MUST NEVER GIVE UP! BESIDES, THIS IS THE CHEAPEST PLACE YOU'LL FIND IN WILLIAMSBURG!
Angus's work is chaotic, fevered, intense, dark and energetic. It seems to crawl across the floor. You get a feeling that it can't be controlled. You feel it, when you look at it, in your gut.
Julien's work is orderly, spare, carefully thought out, controlled, subtle. It has a lot of squares in it, and it stays on its squares of canvas.
Meanwhile, Lem is a millionaire and lives downtown in the financial district.
I WONDER WHAT JULIEN AND ANGUS ARE UP TO NOW.

Friday, May 23rd

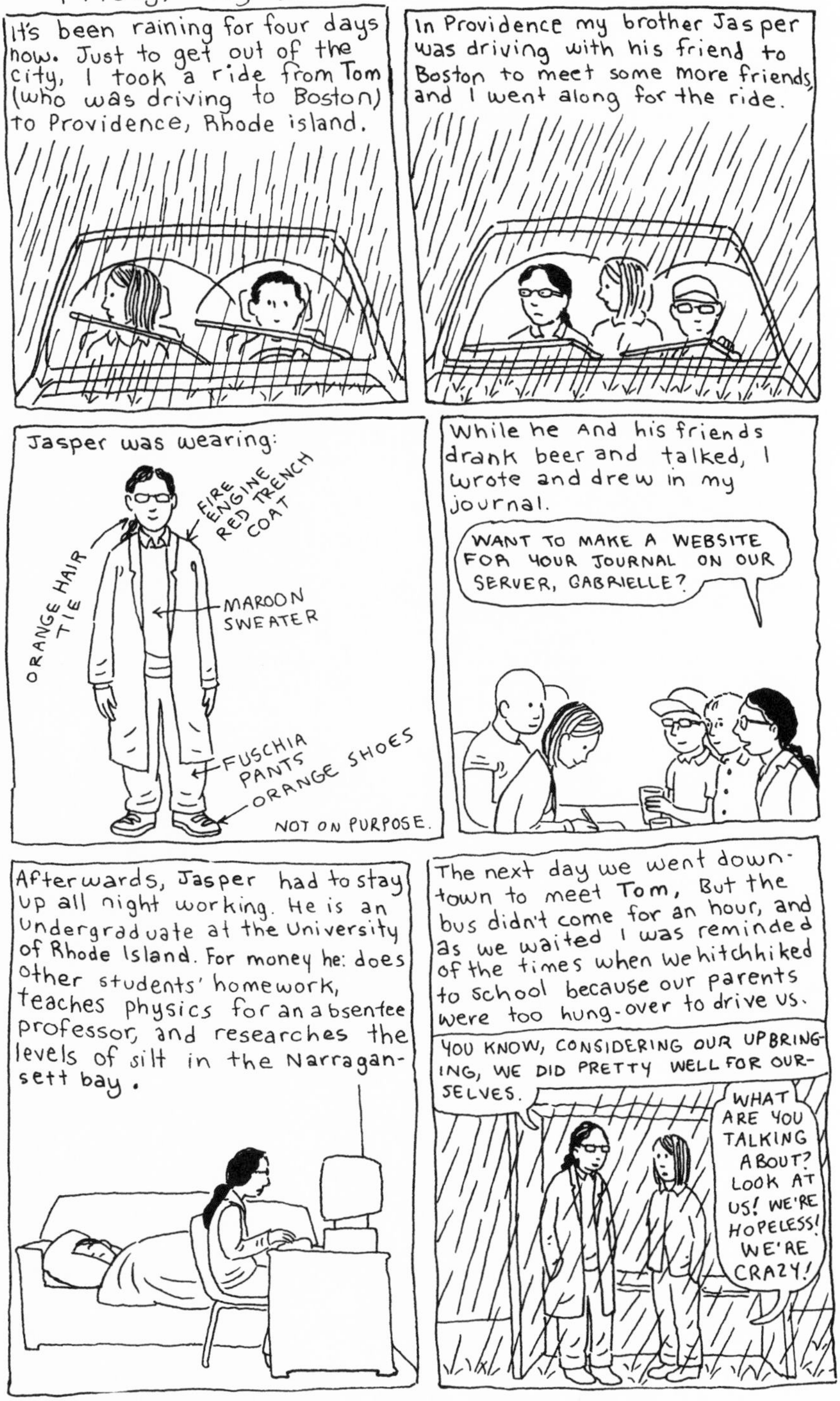
It's been raining for four days now. Just to get out of the city, I took a ride from Tom (who was driving to Boston) to Providence, Rhode island.
In Providence my brother Jasper was driving with his friend to Boston to meet some more friends, and I went along for the ride.
Jasper was wearing:
FIRE ENGINE RED TRENCH COAT
ORANGE HAIR TIE
MAROON SWEATER
FUSCHIA PANTS
ORANGE SHOES
NOT ON PURPOSE.
While he and his friends drank beer and talked, I wrote and drew in my journal.
WANT TO MAKE A WEBSITE FOR YOUR JOURNAL ON OUR SERVER, GABRIELLE?
Afterwards, Jasper had to stay up all night working. He is an undergraduate at the University of Rhode Island. For money he: does other students' homework, teaches physics for an absentee professor, and researches the levels of silt in the Narragansett bay.
The next day we went downtown to meet Tom, But the bus didn't come for an hour, and as we waited I was reminded of the times when we hitchhiked to school because our parents were too hung-over to drive us.
YOU KNOW, CONSIDERING OUR UPBRINGING, WE DID PRETTY WELL FOR OURSELVES.
WHAT ARE YOU TALKING ABOUT? LOOK AT US! WE'RE HOPELESS! WE'RE CRAZY!

Monday, May 26th

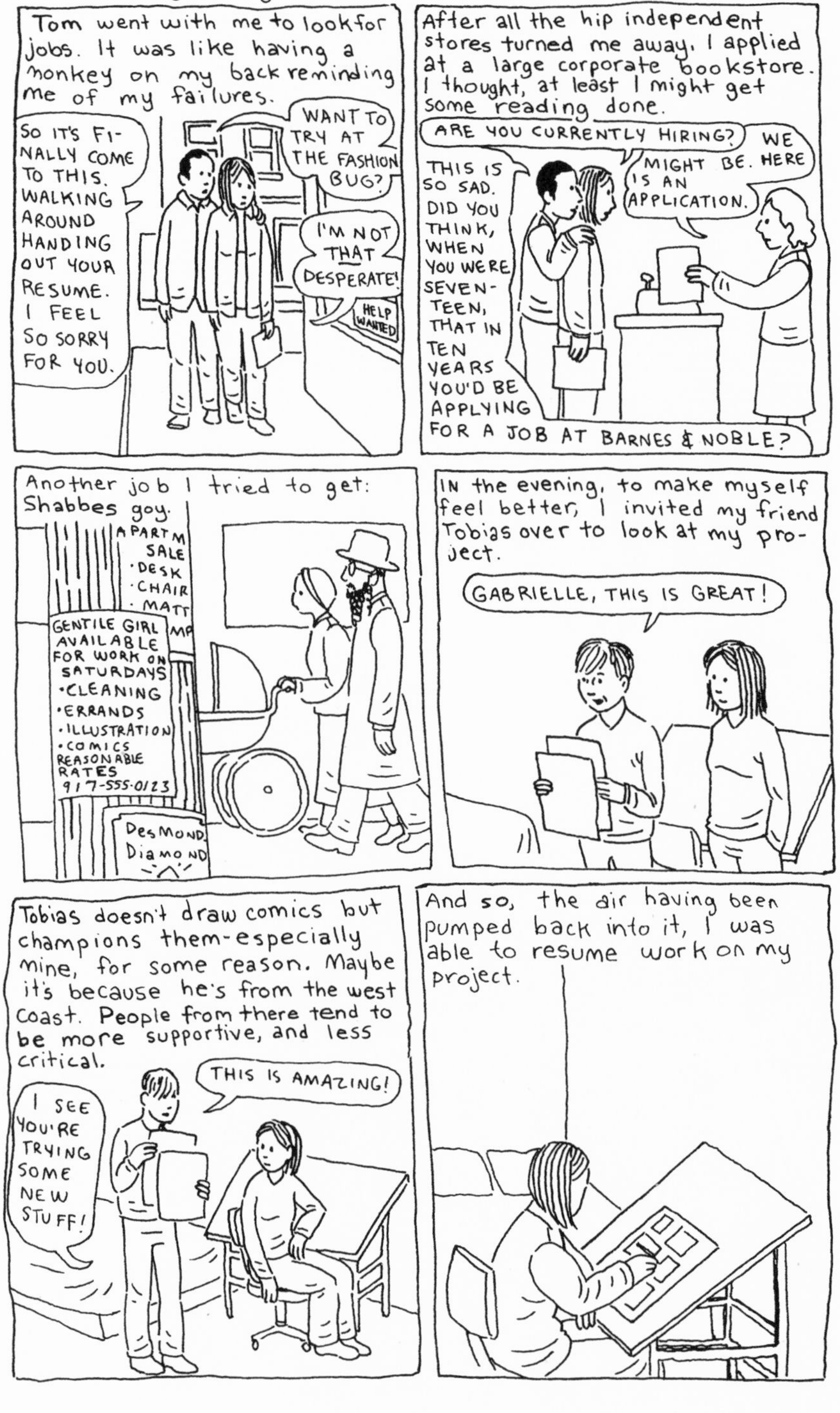
Tom went with me to look for jobs. It was like having a monkey on my back reminding me of my failures.
So it's finally come to this. Walking around handing out your resume. I feel so sorry for you.
Want to try at the Fashion Bug?
I'm not THAT desperate!
HELP WANTED
After all the hip independent stores turned me away, I applied at a large corporate bookstore. I thought, at least I might get some reading done.
Are you currently hiring?
This is so sad. Did you think, when you were seventeen, that in ten years you'd be applying for a job at Barnes & Noble?
We might be. Here is an application.
Another job I tried to get: Shabbes goy.
APARTM SALE ·DESK ·CHAIR ·MATT
GENTILE GIRL AVAILABLE FOR WORK ON SATURDAYS ·CLEANING ·ERRANDS ·ILLUSTRATION ·COMICS REASONABLE RATES 917-555-0123
Desmond Diamond
In the evening, to make myself feel better, I invited my friend Tobias over to look at my project.
Gabrielle, this is great!
Tobias doesn't draw comics but champions them-especially mine, for some reason. Maybe it's because he's from the west coast. People from there tend to be more supportive, and less critical.
This is amazing!
I see you're trying some new stuff!
And so, the air having been pumped back into it, I was able to resume work on my project.

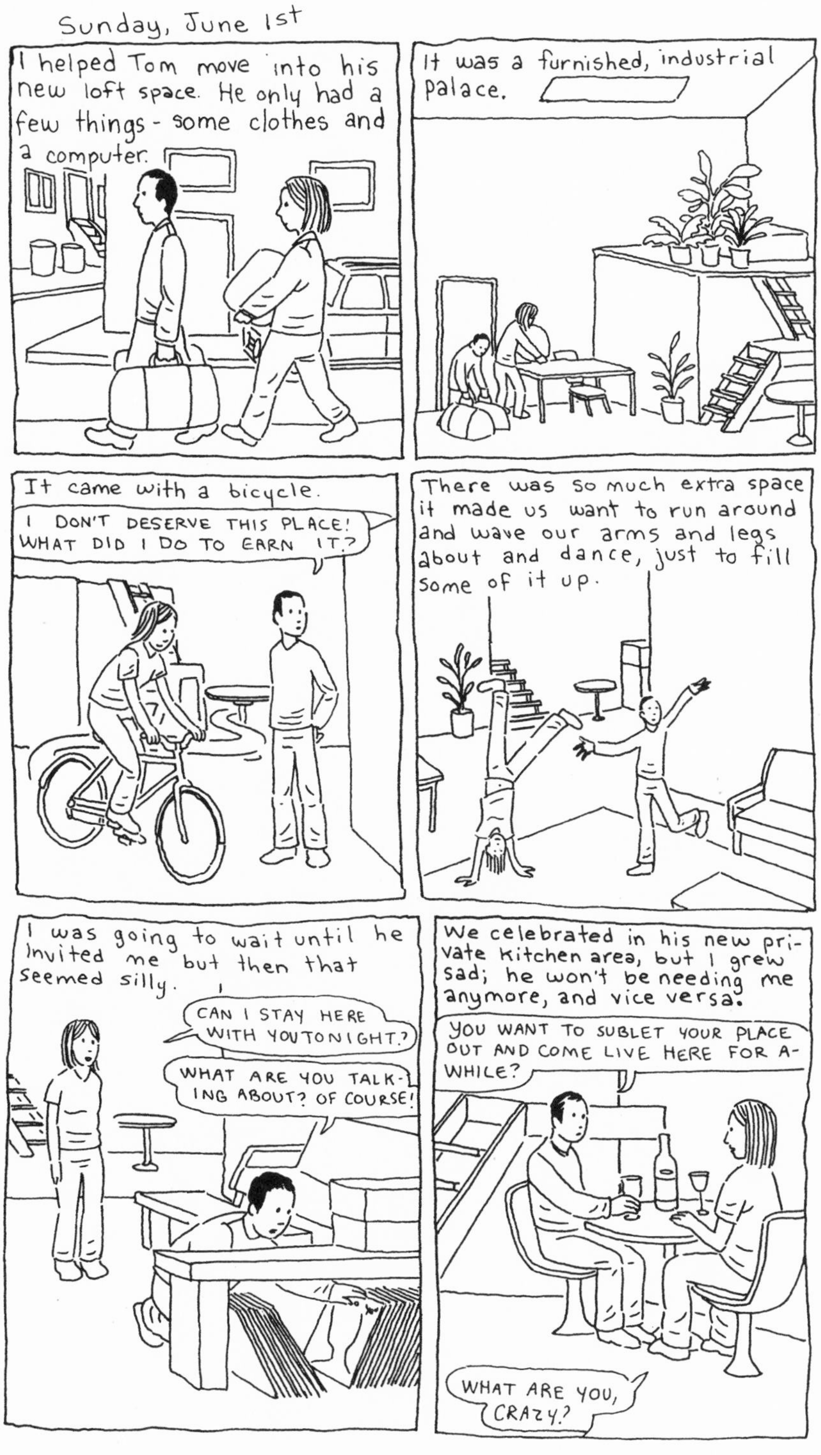
Sunday, June 1st
I helped Tom move into his new loft space. He only had a few things - some clothes and a computer.
It was a furnished, industrial palace.
It came with a bicycle.
I DON'T DESERVE THIS PLACE! WHAT DID I DO TO EARN IT?
There was so much extra space it made us want to run around and wave our arms and legs about and dance, just to fill some of it up.
I was going to wait until he invited me but then that seemed silly.
CAN I STAY HERE WITH YOU TONIGHT?
WHAT ARE YOU TALKING ABOUT? OF COURSE!
We celebrated in his new private kitchen area, but I grew sad; he won't be needing me anymore, and vice versa.
YOU WANT TO SUBLET YOUR PLACE OUT AND COME LIVE HERE FOR A-WHILE?
WHAT ARE YOU, CRAZY?

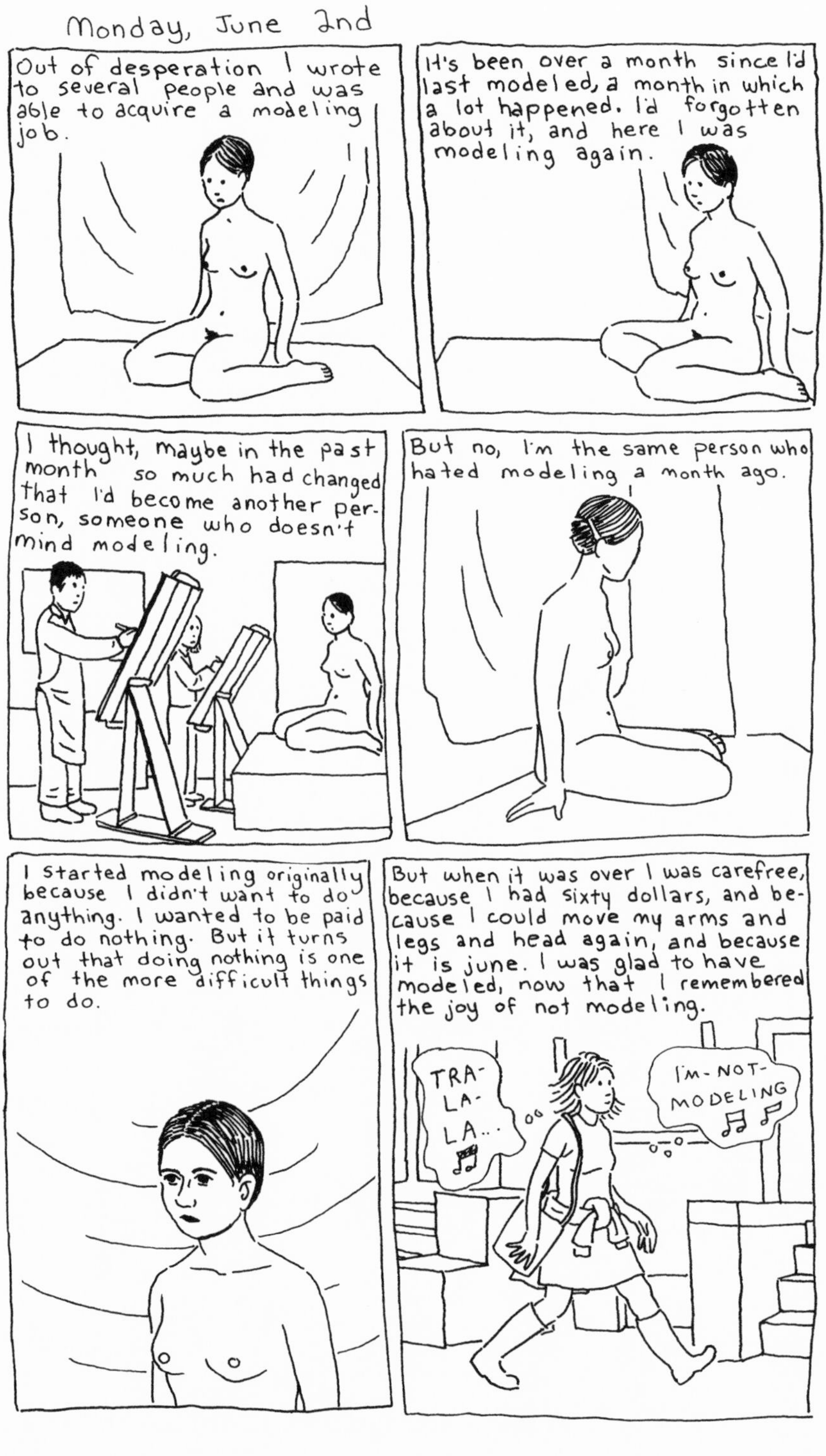
Monday, June 2nd
Out of desperation I wrote to several people and was able to acquire a modeling job.
It's been over a month since I'd last modeled, a month in which a lot happened. I'd forgotten about it, and here I was modeling again.
I thought, maybe in the past month so much had changed that I'd become another person, someone who doesn't mind modeling.
But no, I'm the same person who hated modeling a month ago.
I started modeling originally because I didn't want to do anything. I wanted to be paid to do nothing. But it turns out that doing nothing is one of the more difficult things to do.
But when it was over I was carefree, because I had sixty dollars, and because I could move my arms and legs and head again, and because it is june. I was glad to have modeled, now that I remembered the joy of not modeling.
TRA-LA-LA...
I'M-NOT-MODELING

Lucky # 2 (September 2003)

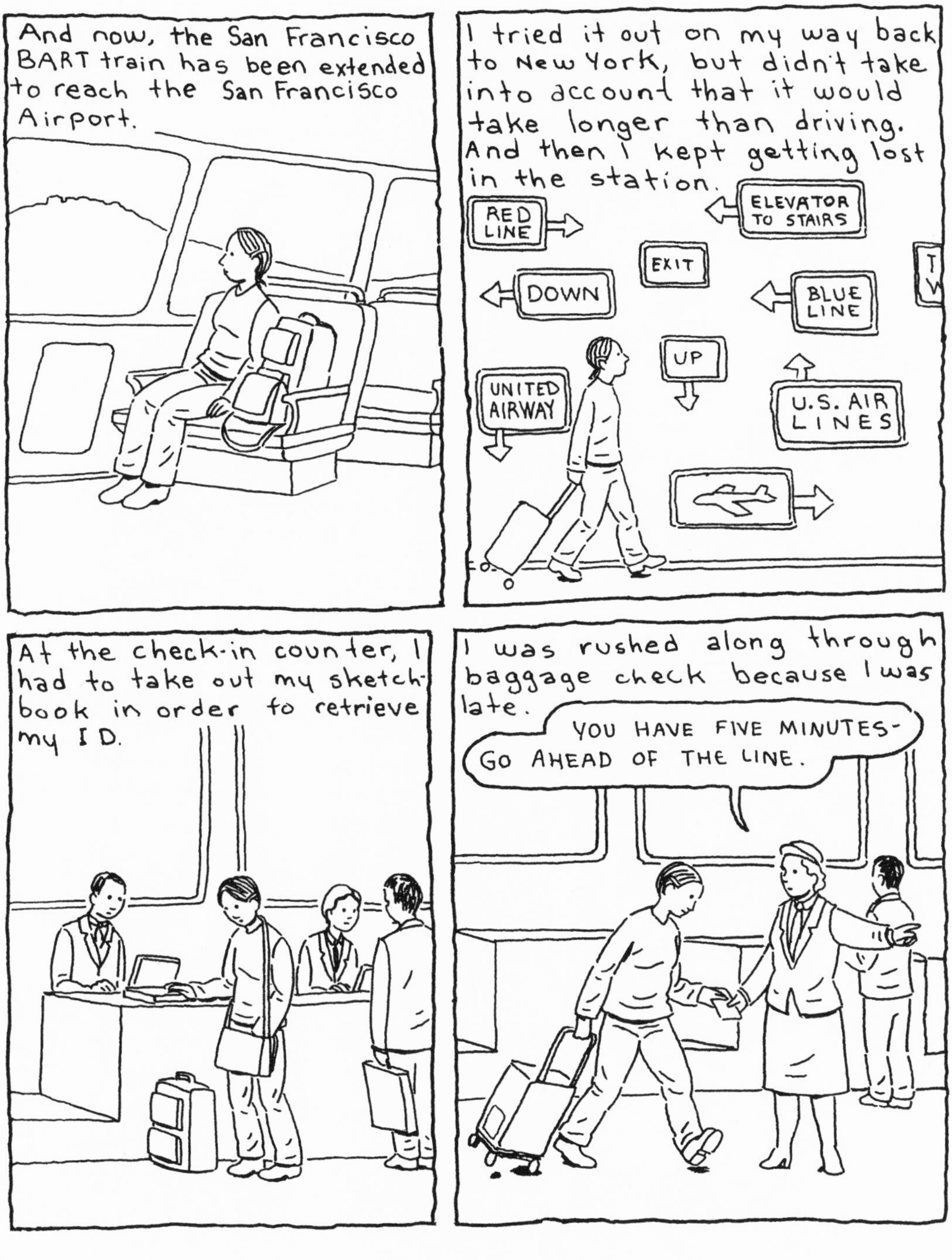
And now, the San Francisco BART train has been extended to reach the San Francisco Airport.
I tried it out on my way back to New York, but didn't take into account that it would take longer than driving. And then I kept getting lost in the station.
RED LINE
ELEVATOR TO STAIRS
EXIT
DOWN
BLUE LINE
UP
UNITED AIRWAY
U.S. AIR LINES
At the check-in counter, I had to take out my sketch-book in order to retrieve my I D.
I was rushed along through baggage check because I was late.
YOU HAVE FIVE MINUTES- GO AHEAD OF THE LINE.

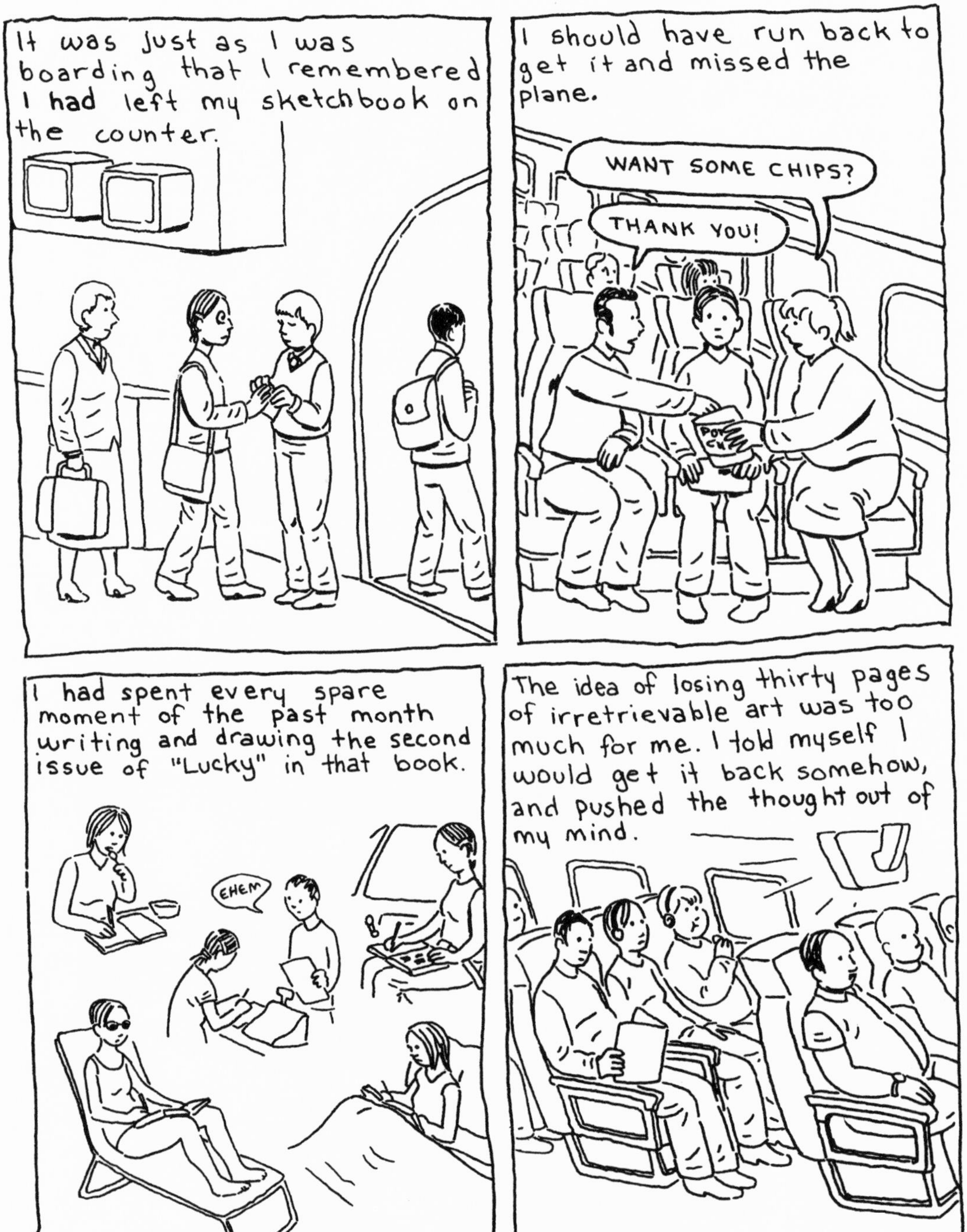
It was just as I was boarding that I remembered I had left my sketchbook on the counter.
I should have run back to get it and missed the plane.
WANT SOME CHIPS?
THANK YOU!
I had spent every spare moment of the past month writing and drawing the second issue of "Lucky" in that book.
EHEM
The idea of losing thirty pages of irretrievable art was too much for me. I told myself I would get it back somehow, and pushed the thought out of my mind.

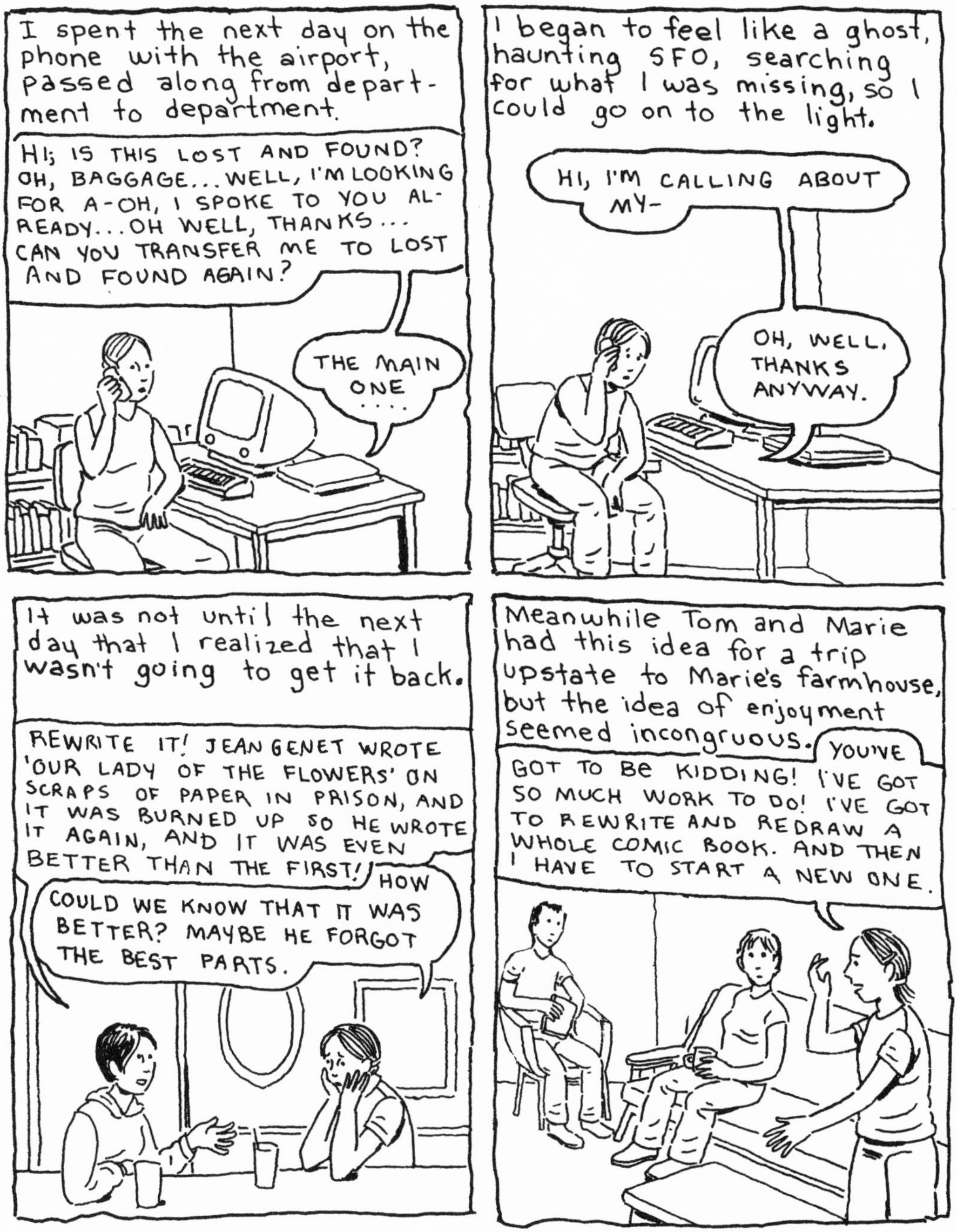
I spent the next day on the phone with the airport, passed along from department to department.
HI; IS THIS LOST AND FOUND? OH, BAGGAGE... WELL, I'M LOOKING FOR A-OH, I SPOKE TO YOU ALREADY... OH WELL, THANKS... CAN YOU TRANSFER ME TO LOST AND FOUND AGAIN?
THE MAIN ONE ....
I began to feel like a ghost, haunting SFO, searching for what I was missing, so I could go on to the light.
HI, I'M CALLING ABOUT MY-
OH, WELL. THANKS ANYWAY.
It was not until the next day that I realized that I wasn't going to get it back.
REWRITE IT! JEAN GENET WROTE 'OUR LADY OF THE FLOWERS' ON SCRAPS OF PAPER IN PRISON, AND IT WAS BURNED UP SO HE WROTE IT AGAIN, AND IT WAS EVEN BETTER THAN THE FIRST!
HOW COULD WE KNOW THAT IT WAS BETTER? MAYBE HE FORGOT THE BEST PARTS.
Meanwhile Tom and Marie had this idea for a trip upstate to Marie's farmhouse, but the idea of enjoyment seemed incongruous.
YOU'VE GOT TO BE KIDDING! I'VE GOT SO MUCH WORK TO DO! I'VE GOT TO REWRITE AND REDRAW A WHOLE COMIC BOOK. AND THEN I HAVE TO START A NEW ONE.

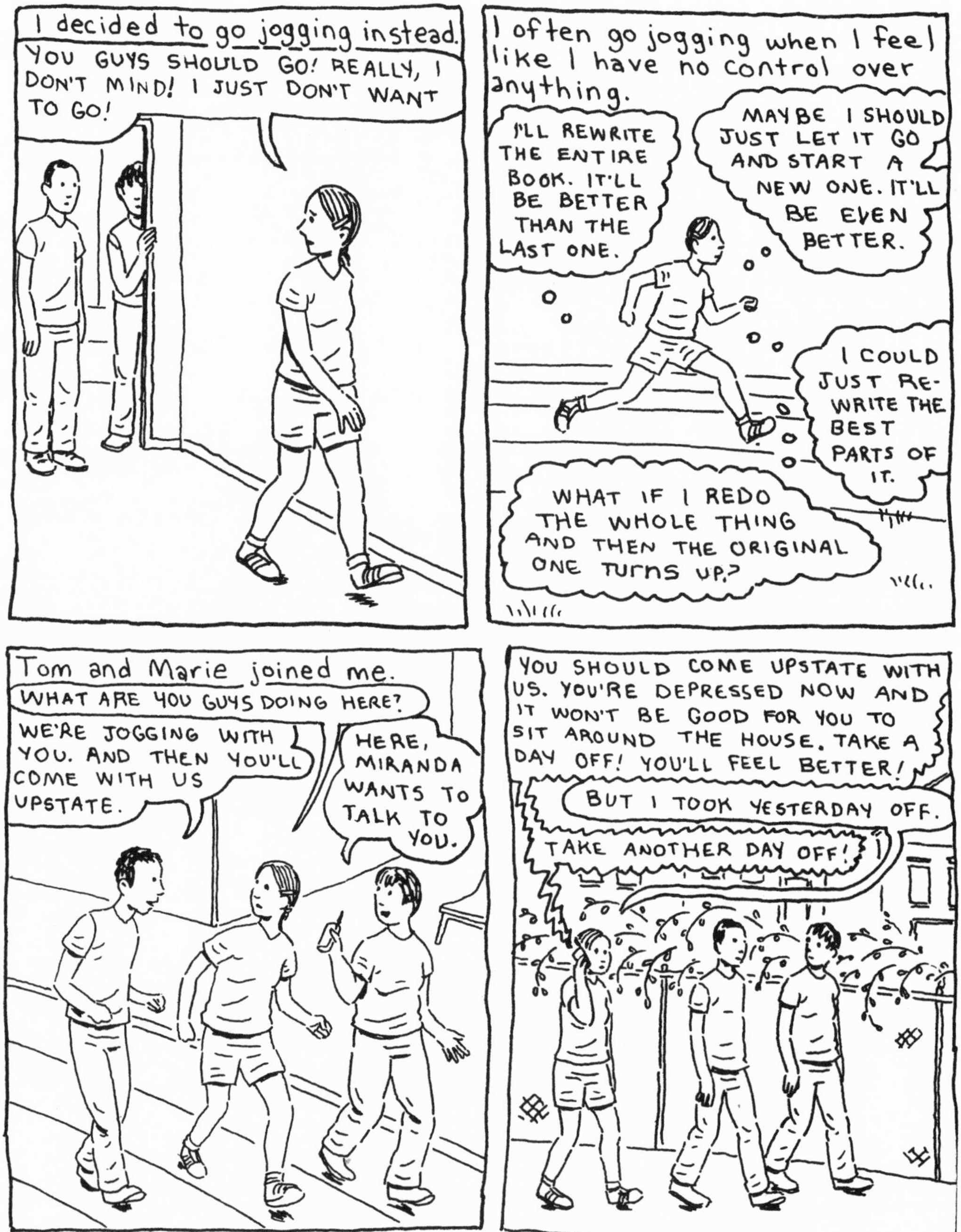

I decided to go jogging instead.
YOU GUYS SHOULD GO! REALLY, I DON'T MIND! I JUST DON'T WANT TO GO!
I often go jogging when I feel like I have no control over anything.
I'LL REWRITE THE ENTIRE BOOK. IT'LL BE BETTER THAN THE LAST ONE.
MAYBE I SHOULD JUST LET IT GO AND START A NEW ONE. IT'LL BE EVEN BETTER.
I COULD JUST RE-WRITE THE BEST PARTS OF IT.
WHAT IF I REDO THE WHOLE THING AND THEN THE ORIGINAL ONE TURNS UP?
Tom and Marie joined me.
WHAT ARE YOU GUYS DOING HERE?
WE'RE JOGGING WITH YOU. AND THEN YOU'LL COME WITH US UPSTATE.
HERE, MIRANDA WANTS TO TALK TO YOU.
YOU SHOULD COME UPSTATE WITH US. YOU'RE DEPRESSED NOW AND IT WON'T BE GOOD FOR YOU TO SIT AROUND THE HOUSE. TAKE A DAY OFF! YOU'LL FEEL BETTER!
BUT I TOOK YESTERDAY OFF.
TAKE ANOTHER DAY OFF!

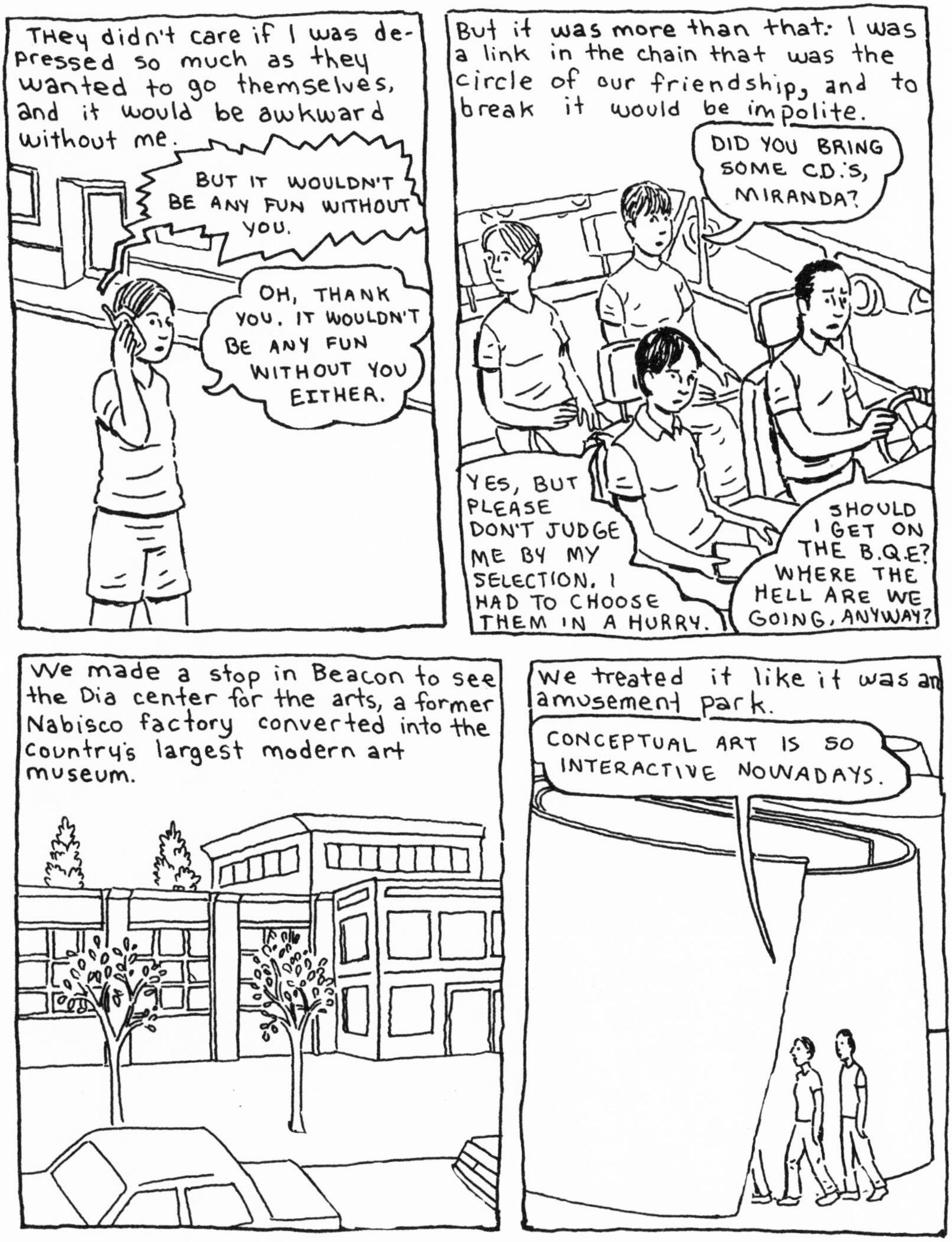
They didn't care if I was depressed so much as they wanted to go themselves, and it would be awkward without me.
BUT IT WOULDN'T BE ANY FUN WITHOUT YOU.
OH, THANK YOU. IT WOULDN'T BE ANY FUN WITHOUT YOU EITHER.
But it was more than that: I was a link in the chain that was the circle of our friendship, and to break it would be impolite.
DID YOU BRING SOME C.D.'S, MIRANDA?
YES, BUT PLEASE DON'T JUDGE ME BY MY SELECTION. I HAD TO CHOOSE THEM IN A HURRY.
SHOULD I GET ON THE B.Q.E? WHERE THE HELL ARE WE GOING, ANYWAY?
We made a stop in Beacon to see the Dia center for the arts, a former Nabisco factory converted into the country's largest modern art museum.
We treated it like it was an amusement park.
CONCEPTUAL ART IS SO INTERACTIVE NOWADAYS.

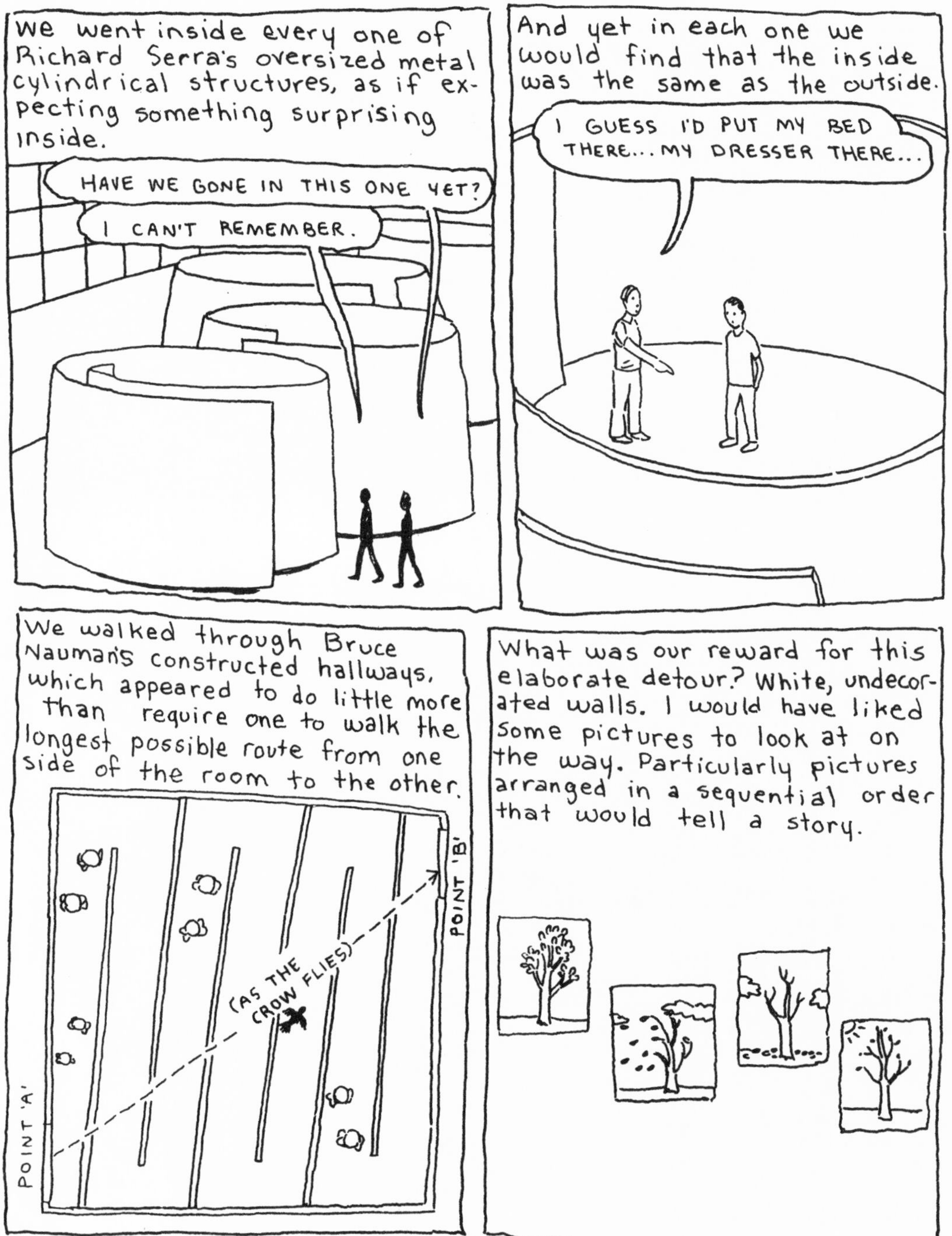
We went inside every one of Richard Serra's oversized metal cylindrical structures, as if expecting something surprising inside.
HAVE WE GONE IN THIS ONE YET?
I CAN'T REMEMBER.
And yet in each one we would find that the inside was the same as the outside.
I GUESS I'D PUT MY BED THERE... MY DRESSER THERE...
We walked through Bruce Nauman's constructed hallways, which appeared to do little more than require one to walk the longest possible route from one side of the room to the other.
POINT 'B'
(AS THE CROW FLIES)
POINT 'A'
What was our reward for this elaborate detour? White, undecorated walls. I would have liked some pictures to look at on the way. Particularly pictures arranged in a sequential order that would tell a story.

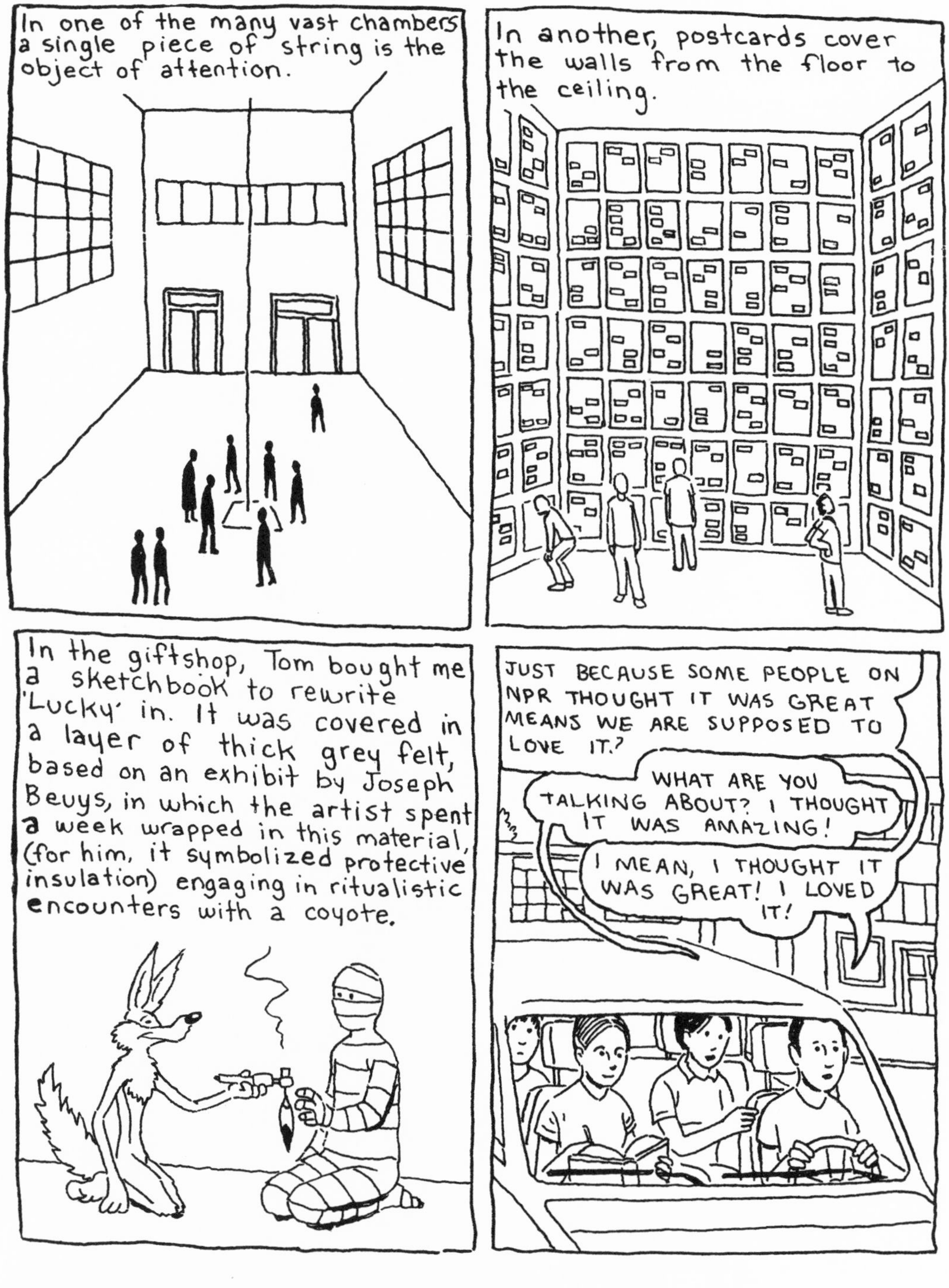
In one of the many vast chambers a single piece of string is the object of attention.
In another, postcards cover the walls from the floor to the ceiling.
In the giftshop, Tom bought me a sketchbook to rewrite 'Lucky' in. It was covered in a layer of thick grey felt, based on an exhibit by Joseph Beuys, in which the artist spent a week wrapped in this material, (for him, it symbolized protective insulation) engaging in ritualistic encounters with a coyote.
JUST BECAUSE SOME PEOPLE ON NPR THOUGHT IT WAS GREAT MEANS WE ARE SUPPOSED TO LOVE IT.?
WHAT ARE YOU TALKING ABOUT? I THOUGHT IT WAS AMAZING!
I MEAN, I THOUGHT IT WAS GREAT! I LOVED IT!

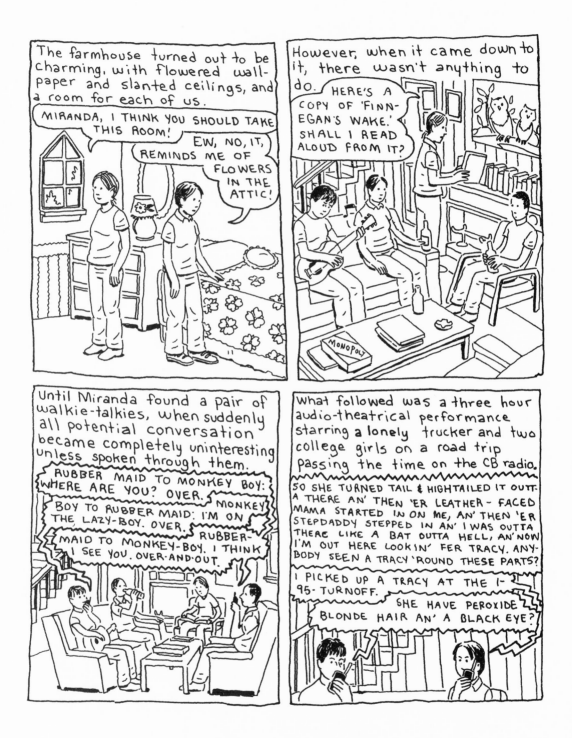

The farmhouse turned out to be charming, with flowered wall-paper and slanted ceilings, and a room for each of us.

MIRANDA, I THINK YOU SHOULD TAKE THIS ROOM!

EW, NO, IT, REMINDS ME OF FLOWERS IN THE ATTIC!

However, when it came down to it, there wasn't anything to do.

HERE'S A COPY OF 'FINN-EGAN'S WAKE.' SHALL I READ ALOUD FROM IT?

Until Miranda found a pair of walkie-talkies, when suddenly all potential conversation became completely uninteresting unless spoken through them.

RUBBER MAID TO MONKEY BOY: WHERE ARE YOU? OVER.

MONKEY BOY TO RUBBER MAID: I'M ON THE LAZY-BOY. OVER.

RUBBER-MAID TO MONKEY-BOY. I THINK I SEE YOU. OVER-AND-OUT.

What followed was a three hour audio-theatrical performance starring a lonely trucker and two college girls on a road trip passing the time on the CB radio.

SO SHE TURNED TAIL & HIGHTAILED IT OUTT-A THERE AN' THEN 'ER LEATHER - FACED MAMA STARTED IN ON ME, AN' THEN 'ER STEPDADDY STEPPED IN AN' I WAS OUTTA THERE LIKE A BAT OUTTA HELL, AN' NOW I'M OUT HERE LOOKIN' FER TRACY. ANY-BODY SEEN A TRACY 'ROUND THESE PARTS?

I PICKED UP A TRACY AT THE I-95- TURNOFF.

SHE HAVE PEROXIDE BLONDE HAIR AN' A BLACK EYE?

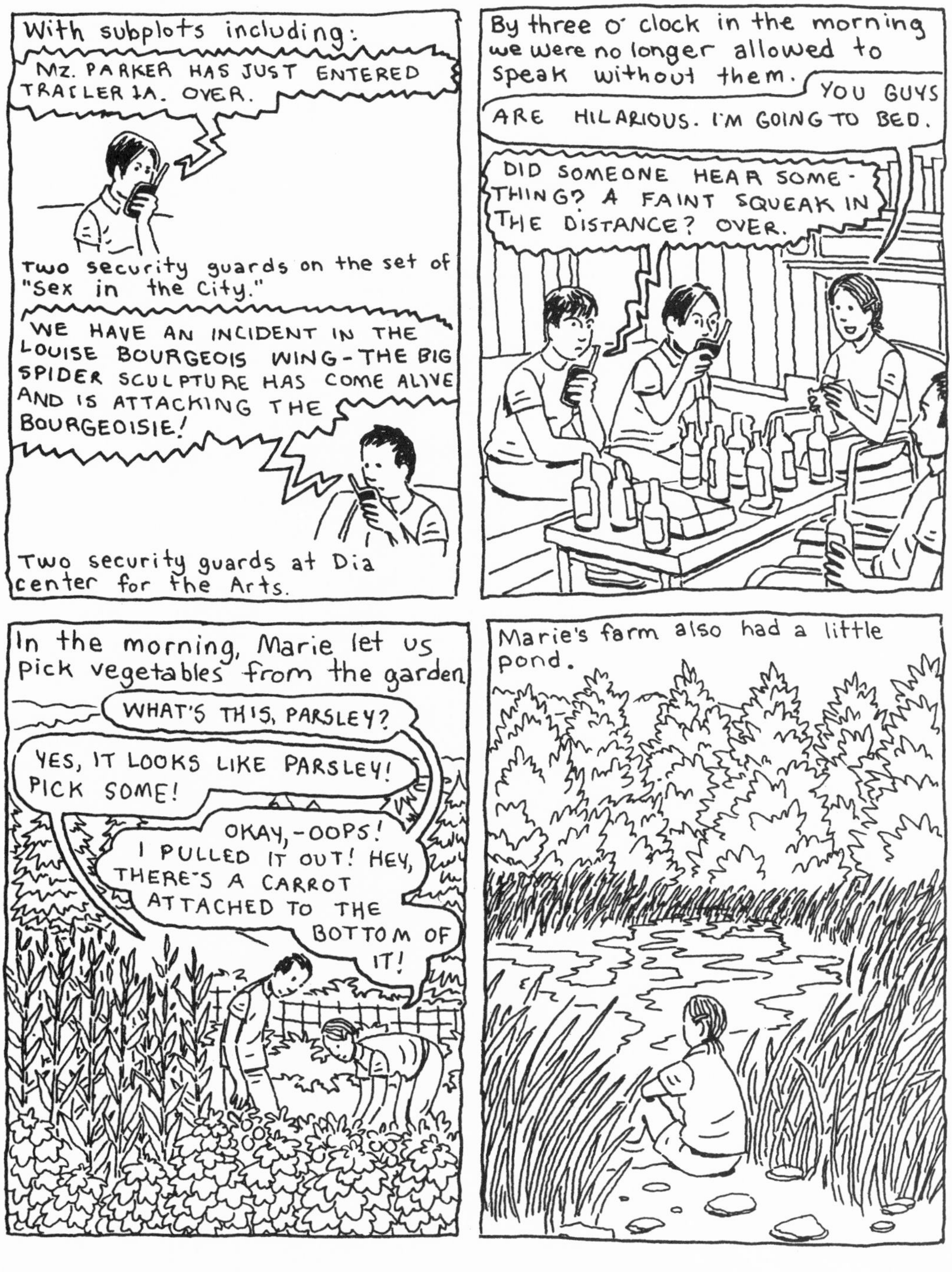

With subplots including:
MZ. PARKER HAS JUST ENTERED TRAILER 1A. OVER.
Two security guards on the set of "Sex in the City."
WE HAVE AN INCIDENT IN THE LOUISE BOURGEOIS WING - THE BIG SPIDER SCULPTURE HAS COME ALIVE AND IS ATTACKING THE BOURGEOISIE!
Two security guards at Dia center for the Arts.
By three o' clock in the morning we were no longer allowed to speak without them.
YOU GUYS ARE HILARIOUS. I'M GOING TO BED.
DID SOMEONE HEAR SOMETHING? A FAINT SQUEAK IN THE DISTANCE? OVER.
In the morning, Marie let us pick vegetables from the garden
WHAT'S THIS, PARSLEY?
YES, IT LOOKS LIKE PARSLEY! PICK SOME!
OKAY, -OOPS! I PULLED IT OUT! HEY, THERE'S A CARROT ATTACHED TO THE BOTTOM OF IT!
Marie's farm also had a little pond.

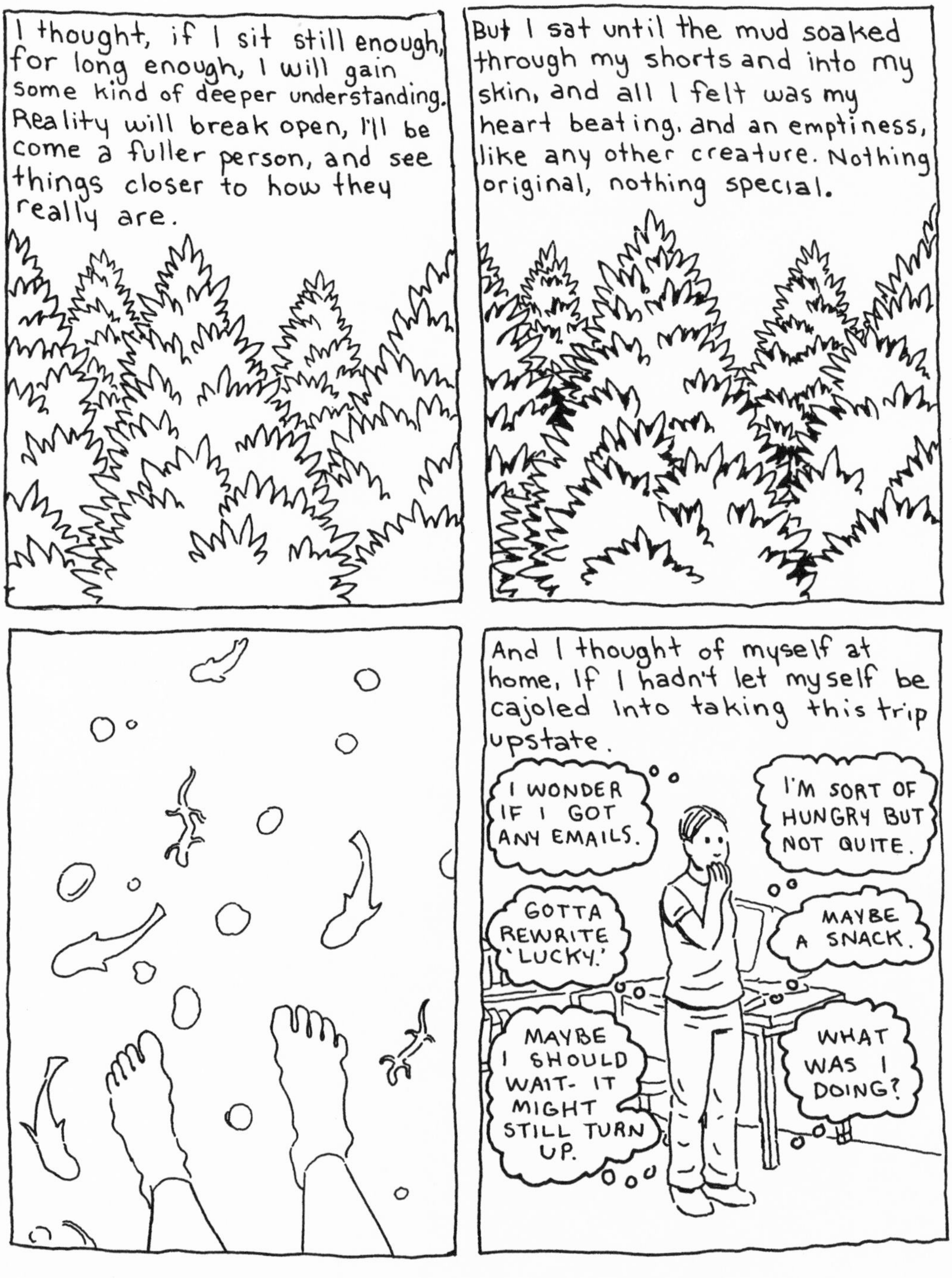
I thought, if I sit still enough, for long enough, I will gain some kind of deeper understanding. Reality will break open, I'll be come a fuller person, and see things closer to how they really are.
But I sat until the mud soaked through my shorts and into my skin, and all I felt was my heart beating. and an emptiness, like any other creature. Nothing original, nothing special.
And I thought of myself at home, If I hadn't let myself be cajoled into taking this trip upstate.
I WONDER IF I GOT ANY EMAILS.
I'M SORT OF HUNGRY BUT NOT QUITE.
GOTTA REWRITE 'LUCKY.'
MAYBE A SNACK.
MAYBE I SHOULD WAIT- IT MIGHT STILL TURN UP.
WHAT WAS I DOING?

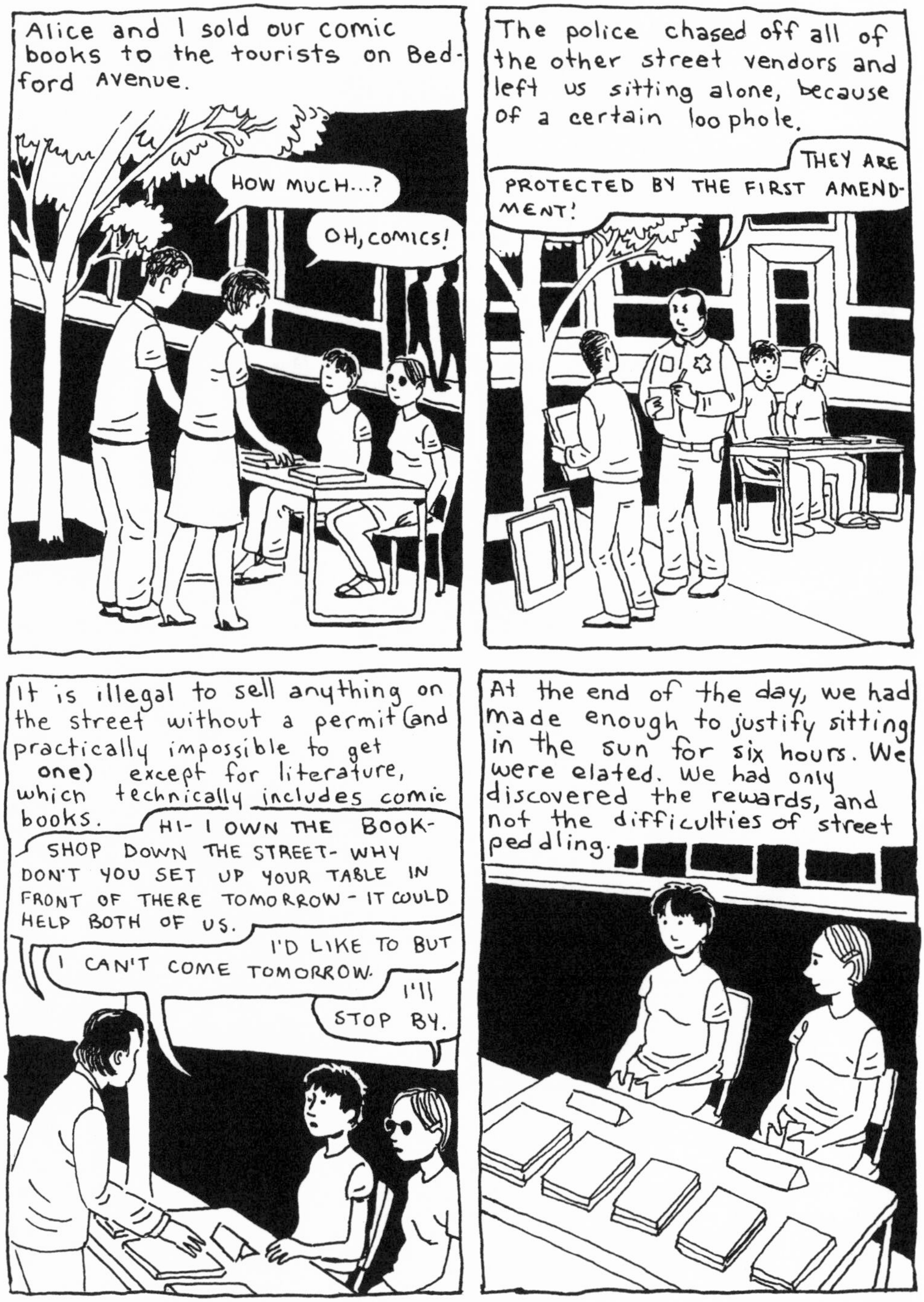
Alice and I sold our comic books to the tourists on Bedford Avenue.
HOW MUCH...?
OH, COMICS!
The police chased off all of the other street vendors and left us sitting alone, because of a certain loophole.
THEY ARE PROTECTED BY THE FIRST AMENDMENT!
It is illegal to sell anything on the street without a permit (and practically impossible to get one) except for literature, which technically includes comic books.
HI- I OWN THE BOOKSHOP DOWN THE STREET- WHY DON'T YOU SET UP YOUR TABLE IN FRONT OF THERE TOMORROW - IT COULD HELP BOTH OF US.
I'D LIKE TO BUT I CAN'T COME TOMORROW.
I'LL STOP BY.
At the end of the day, we had made enough to justify sitting in the sun for six hours. We were elated. We had only discovered the rewards, and not the difficulties of street peddling.

The next day, I was so excited about selling comics, I kept forgetting myself.

I'M GOING TO GO DO LAUNDRY. DO YOU WANT ANYTHING WASHED?

SHOULD I COME HELP YOU?

SURE.

BUT I WANT TO GO SELL COMICS!

After I helped him haul the clothes to the laundromat, Tom helped me with my books. But I was too hasty, and something went wrong.

WATCH IT, GABRIELLE! YOU ALMOST HIT THAT GUY!

YOU KNOW, I CAN DO THIS MYSELF!

FINE.

I set up in front of the bookstore, really prepared this time.

OKS

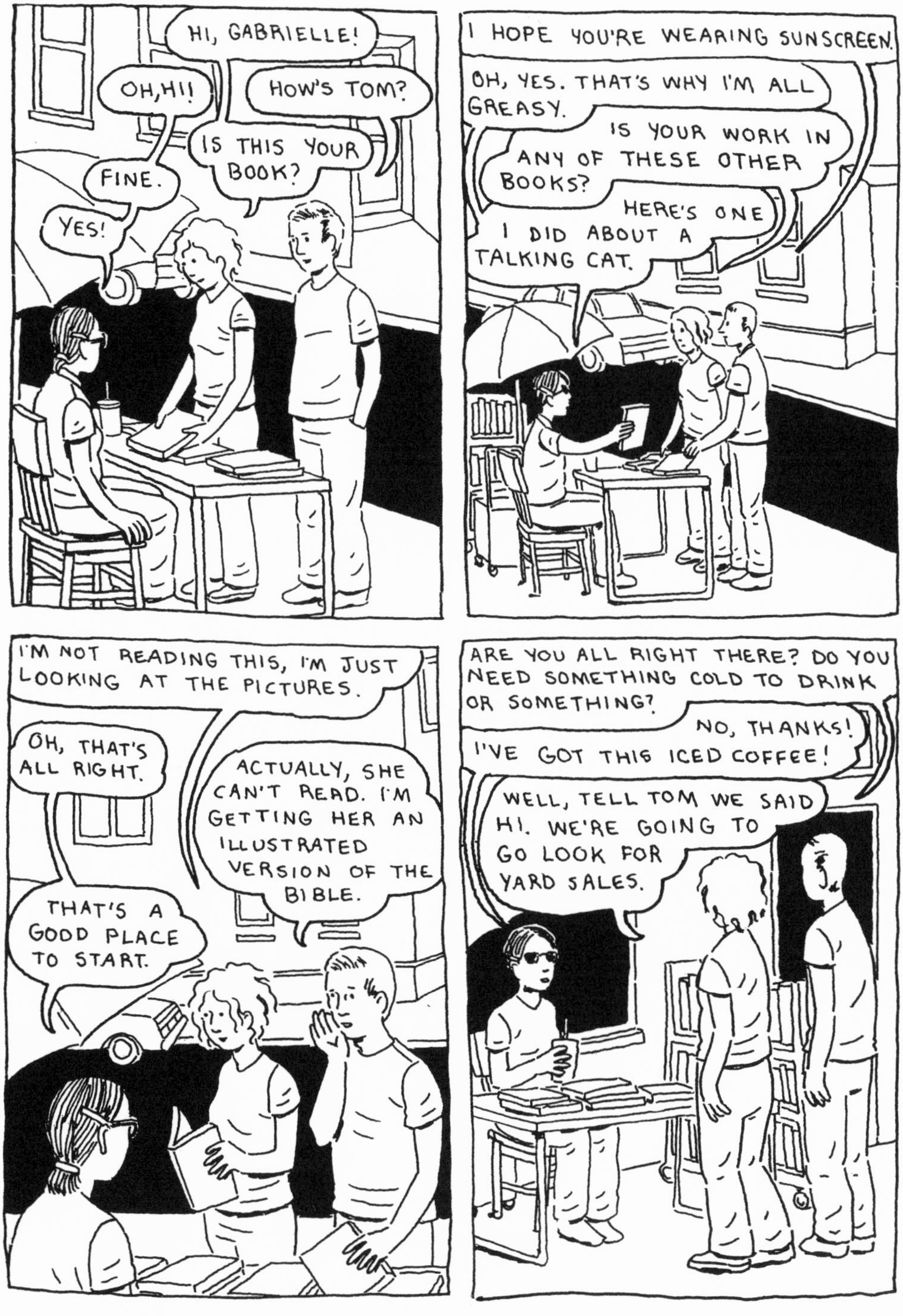
HI, GABRIELLE!
OH, HI!
HOW'S TOM?
FINE.
IS THIS YOUR BOOK?
YES!
I HOPE YOU'RE WEARING SUNSCREEN.
OH, YES. THAT'S WHY I'M ALL GREASY.
IS YOUR WORK IN ANY OF THESE OTHER BOOKS?
HERE'S ONE I DID ABOUT A TALKING CAT.
I'M NOT READING THIS, I'M JUST LOOKING AT THE PICTURES.
OH, THAT'S ALL RIGHT.
ACTUALLY, SHE CAN'T READ. I'M GETTING HER AN ILLUSTRATED VERSION OF THE BIBLE.
THAT'S A GOOD PLACE TO START.
ARE YOU ALL RIGHT THERE? DO YOU NEED SOMETHING COLD TO DRINK OR SOMETHING?
NO, THANKS! I'VE GOT THIS ICED COFFEE!
WELL, TELL TOM WE SAID HI. WE'RE GOING TO GO LOOK FOR YARD SALES.

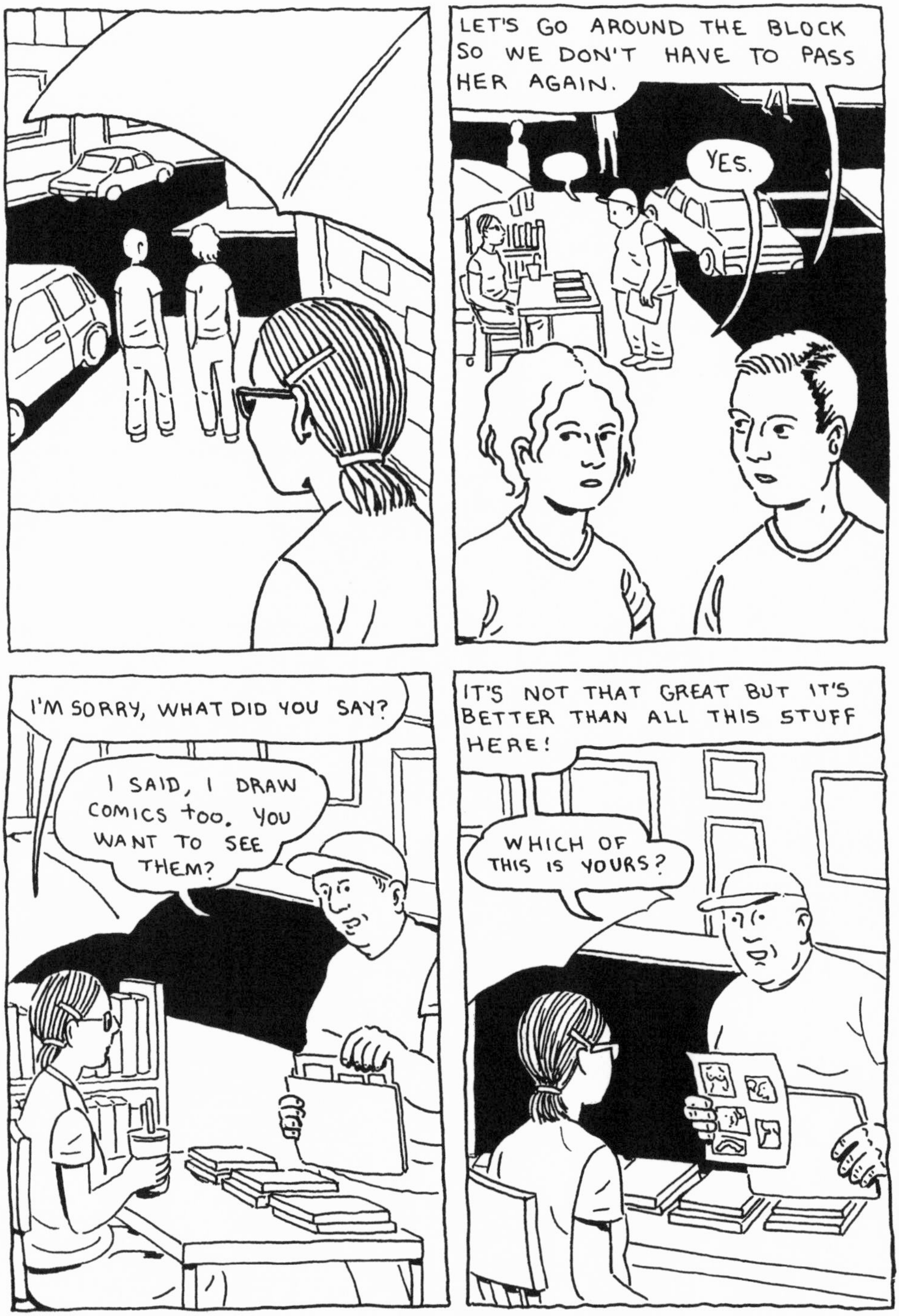
LET'S GO AROUND THE BLOCK SO WE DON'T HAVE TO PASS HER AGAIN.
YES.
I'M SORRY, WHAT DID YOU SAY?
I SAID, I DRAW COMICS too. YOU WANT TO SEE THEM?
IT'S NOT THAT GREAT BUT IT'S BETTER THAN ALL THIS STUFF HERE!
WHICH OF THIS IS YOURS?

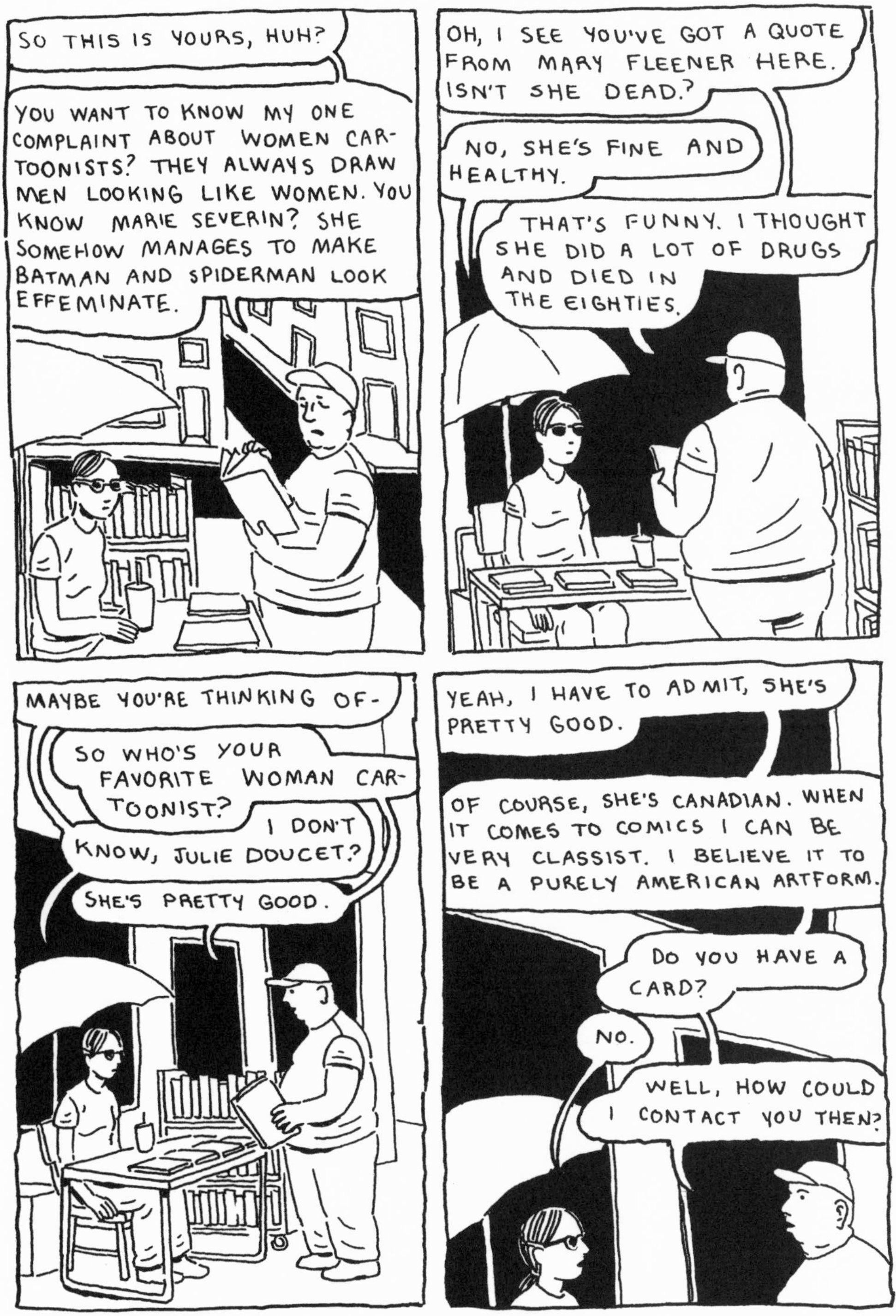

SO THIS IS YOURS, HUH?
YOU WANT TO KNOW MY ONE COMPLAINT ABOUT WOMEN CARTOONISTS? THEY ALWAYS DRAW MEN LOOKING LIKE WOMEN. YOU KNOW MARIE SEVERIN? SHE SOMEHOW MANAGES TO MAKE BATMAN AND SPIDERMAN LOOK EFFEMINATE.
OH, I SEE YOU'VE GOT A QUOTE FROM MARY FLEENER HERE. ISN'T SHE DEAD?
NO, SHE'S FINE AND HEALTHY.
THAT'S FUNNY. I THOUGHT SHE DID A LOT OF DRUGS AND DIED IN THE EIGHTIES.
MAYBE YOU'RE THINKING OF-
SO WHO'S YOUR FAVORITE WOMAN CARTOONIST?
I DON'T KNOW, JULIE DOUCET?
SHE'S PRETTY GOOD.
YEAH, I HAVE TO ADMIT, SHE'S PRETTY GOOD.
OF COURSE, SHE'S CANADIAN. WHEN IT COMES TO COMICS I CAN BE VERY CLASSIST. I BELIEVE IT TO BE A PURELY AMERICAN ARTFORM.
DO YOU HAVE A CARD?
NO.
WELL, HOW COULD I CONTACT YOU THEN?

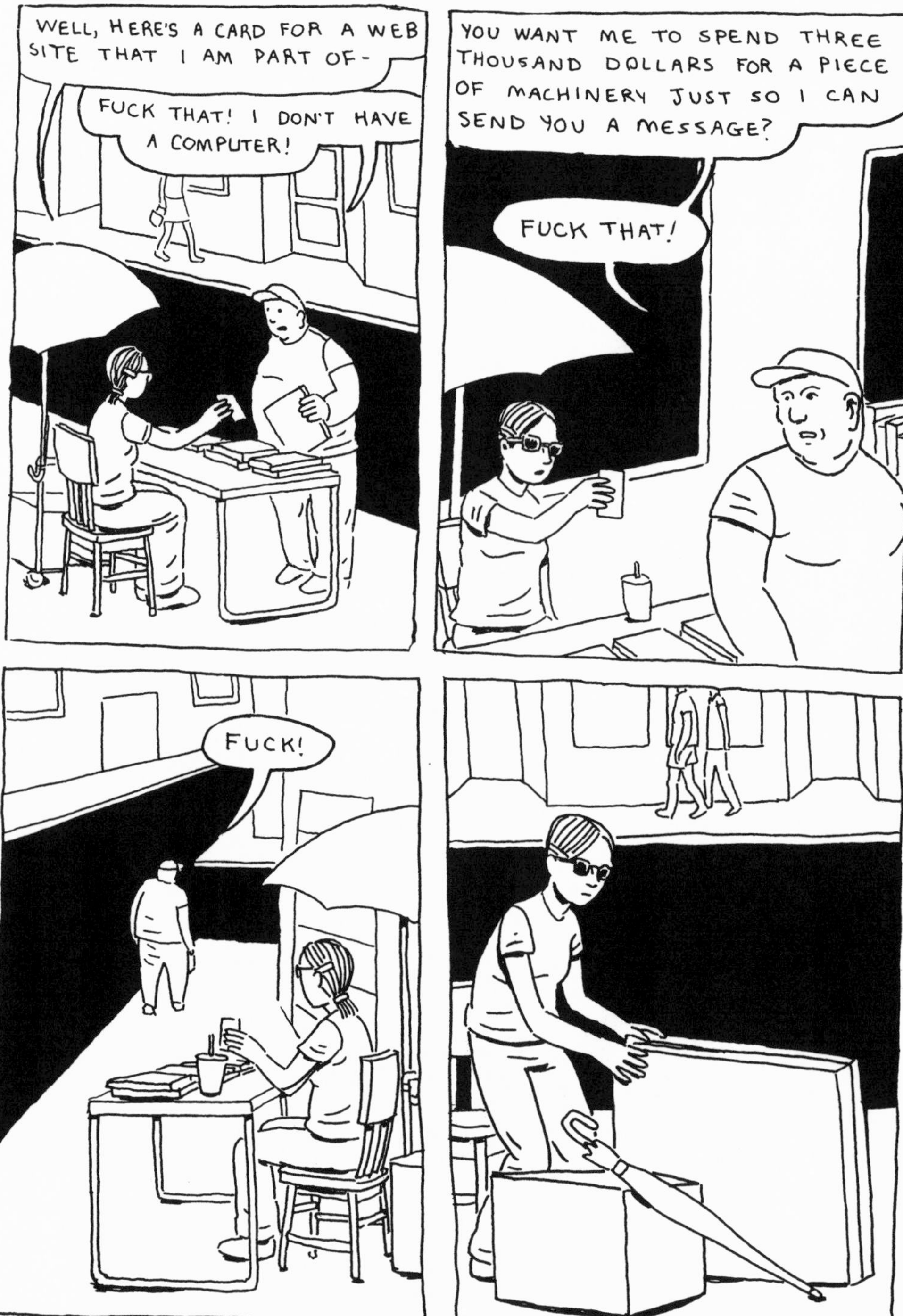
WELL, HERE'S A CARD FOR A WEB SITE THAT I AM PART OF-
FUCK THAT! I DON'T HAVE A COMPUTER!
YOU WANT ME TO SPEND THREE THOUSAND DOLLARS FOR A PIECE OF MACHINERY JUST SO I CAN SEND YOU A MESSAGE?
FUCK THAT!
FUCK!

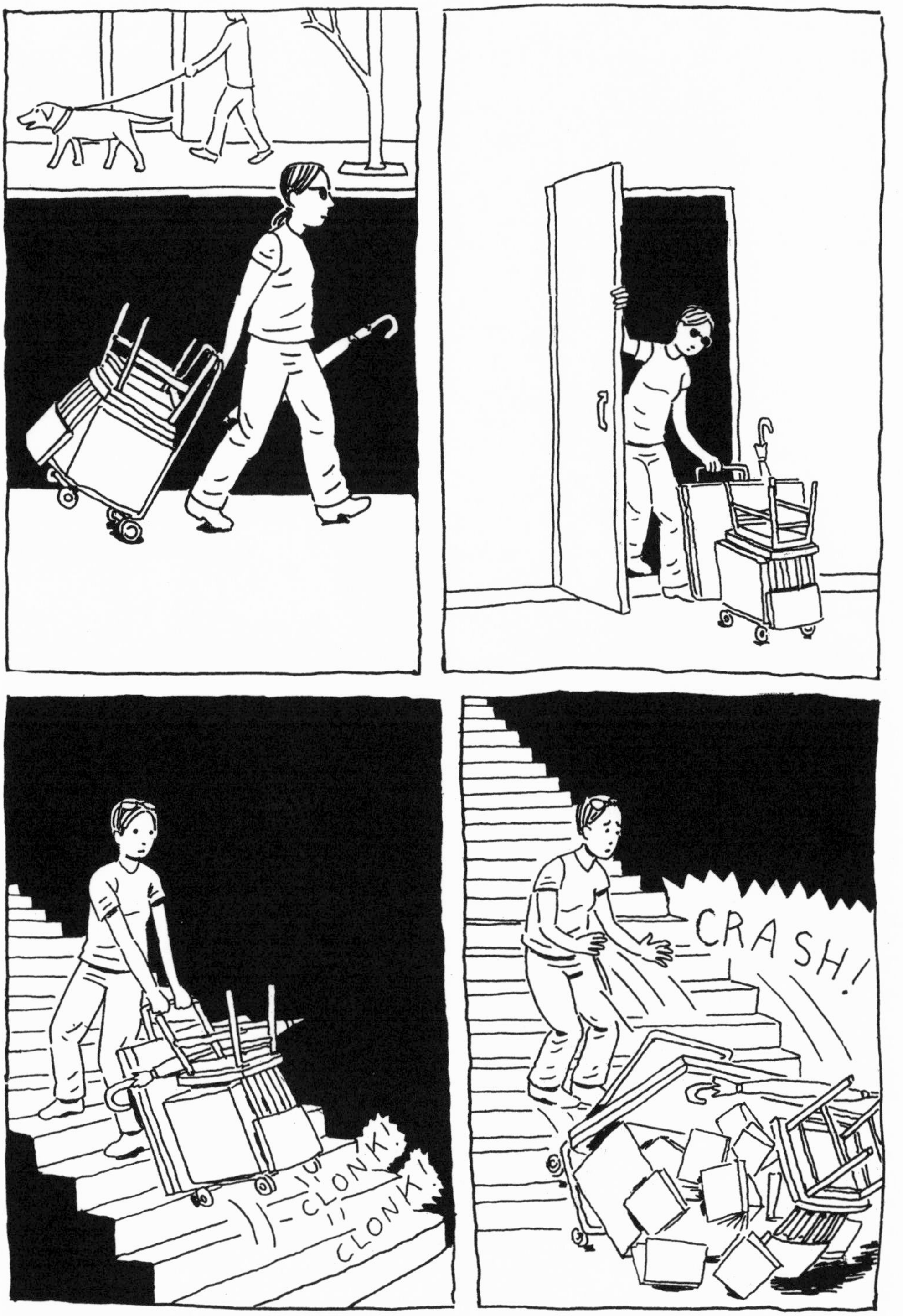
CLONK!
CLONK!
CRASH!

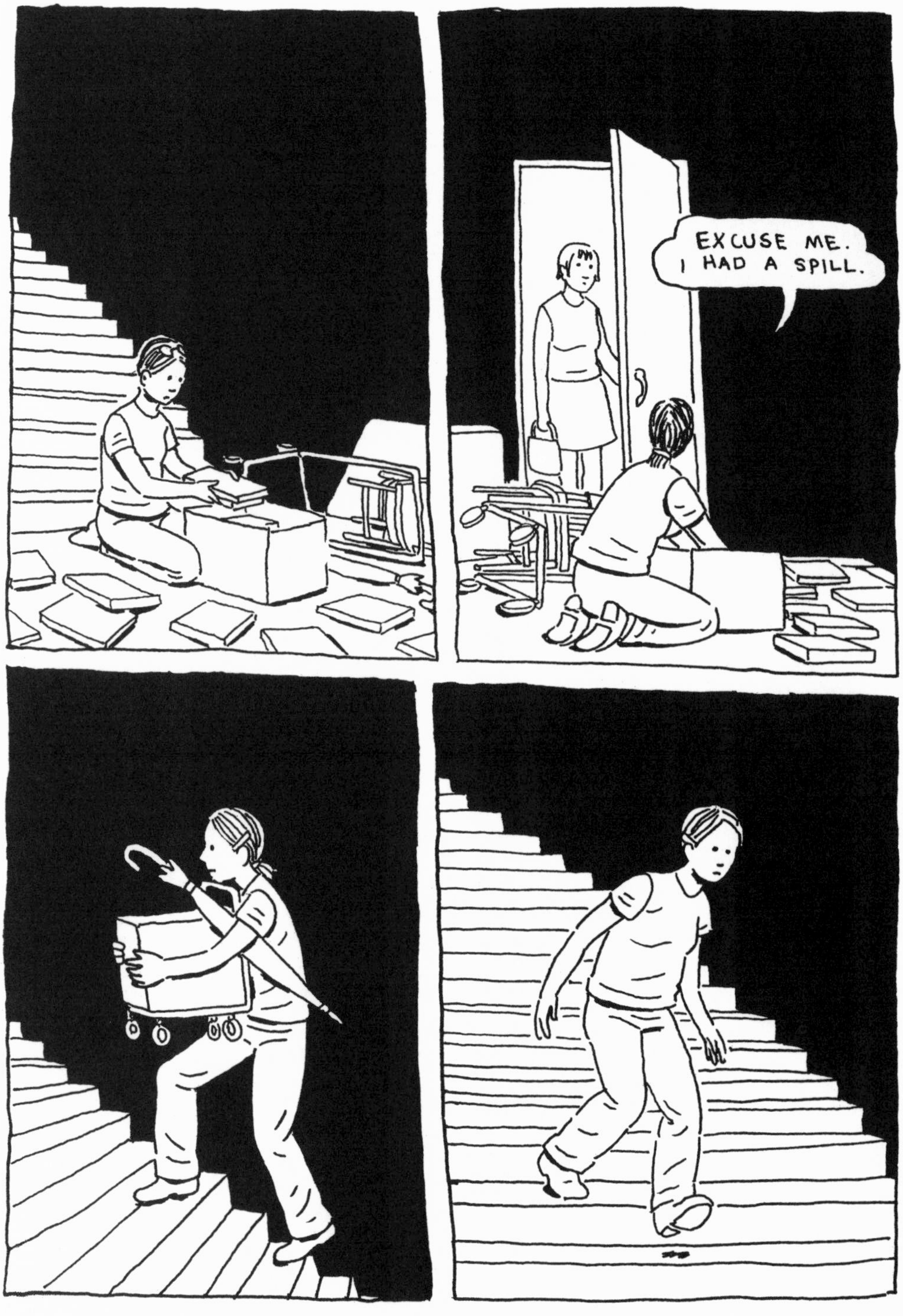
EXCUSE ME.
I HAD A SPILL.

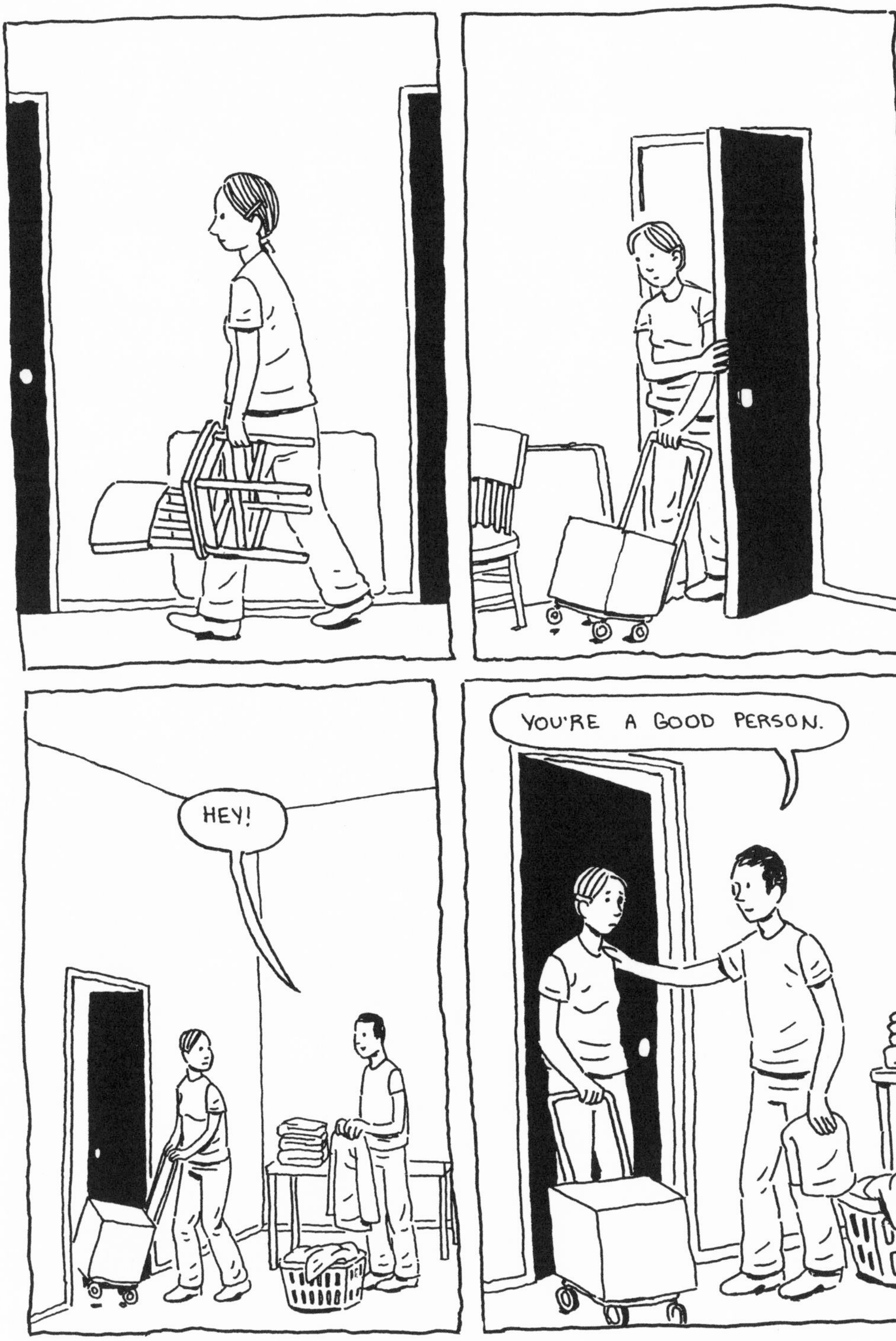
HEY!
YOU'RE A GOOD PERSON.

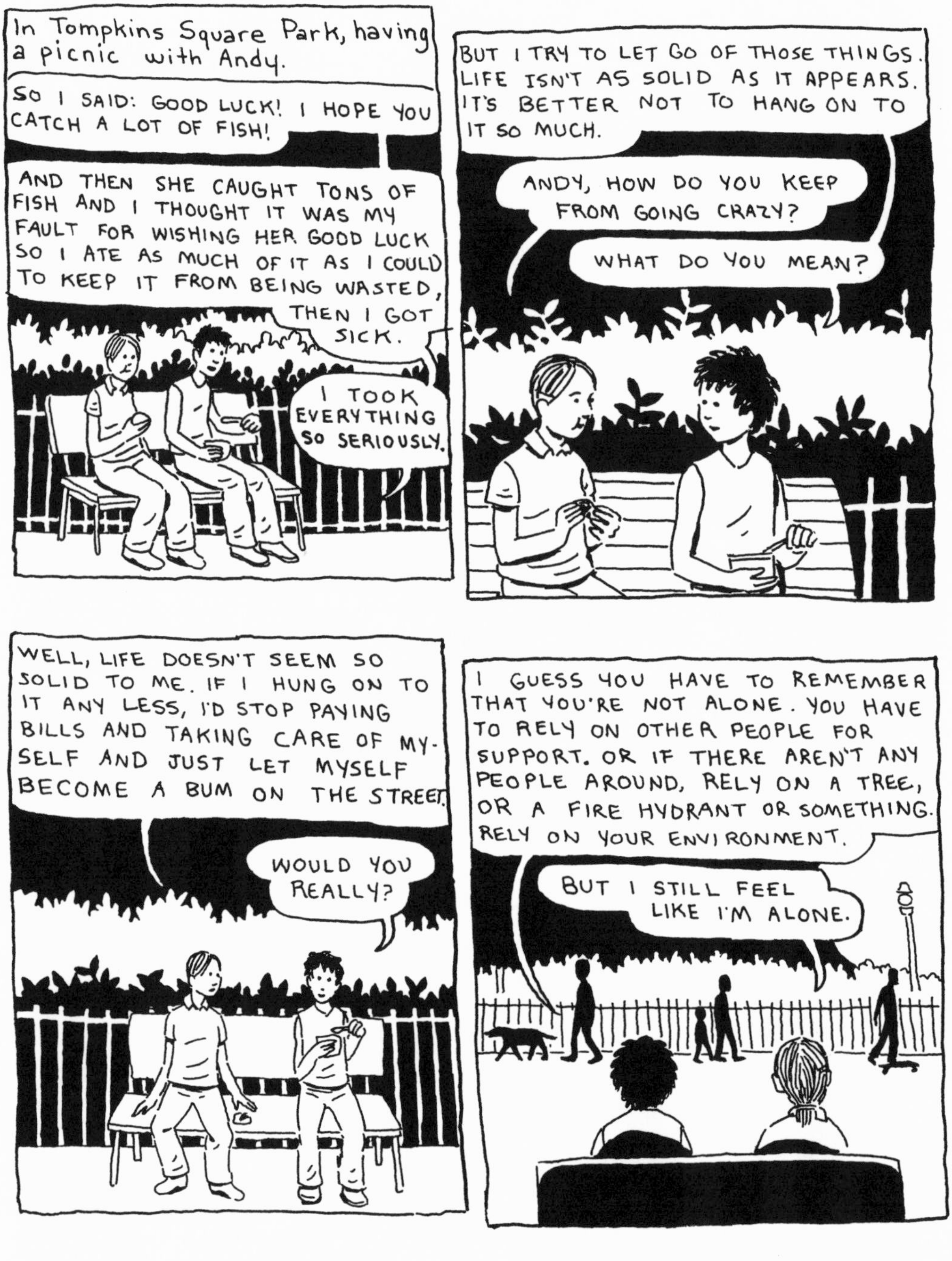
In Tompkins Square Park, having a picnic with Andy.
SO I SAID: GOOD LUCK! I HOPE YOU CATCH A LOT OF FISH!
AND THEN SHE CAUGHT TONS OF FISH AND I THOUGHT IT WAS MY FAULT FOR WISHING HER GOOD LUCK SO I ATE AS MUCH OF IT AS I COULD TO KEEP IT FROM BEING WASTED, THEN I GOT SICK.
I TOOK EVERYTHING SO SERIOUSLY.
BUT I TRY TO LET GO OF THOSE THINGS. LIFE ISN'T AS SOLID AS IT APPEARS. IT'S BETTER NOT TO HANG ON TO IT SO MUCH.
ANDY, HOW DO YOU KEEP FROM GOING CRAZY?
WHAT DO YOU MEAN?
WELL, LIFE DOESN'T SEEM SO SOLID TO ME. IF I HUNG ON TO IT ANY LESS, I'D STOP PAYING BILLS AND TAKING CARE OF MY-SELF AND JUST LET MYSELF BECOME A BUM ON THE STREET.
WOULD YOU REALLY?
I GUESS YOU HAVE TO REMEMBER THAT YOU'RE NOT ALONE. YOU HAVE TO RELY ON OTHER PEOPLE FOR SUPPORT. OR IF THERE AREN'T ANY PEOPLE AROUND, RELY ON A TREE, OR A FIRE HYDRANT OR SOMETHING. RELY ON YOUR ENVIRONMENT.
BUT I STILL FEEL LIKE I'M ALONE.

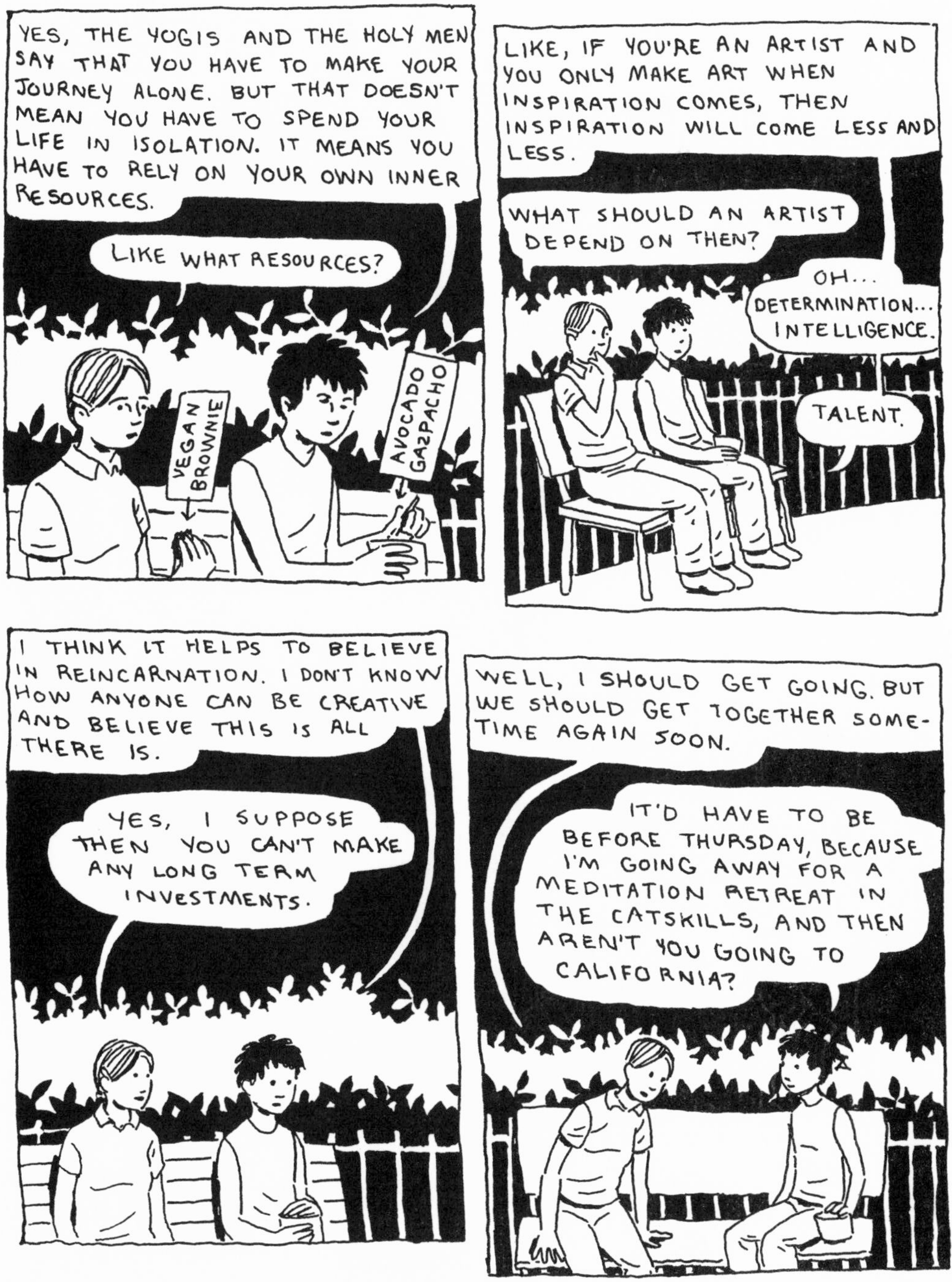
YES, THE YOGIS AND THE HOLY MEN SAY THAT YOU HAVE TO MAKE YOUR JOURNEY ALONE. BUT THAT DOESN'T MEAN YOU HAVE TO SPEND YOUR LIFE IN ISOLATION. IT MEANS YOU HAVE TO RELY ON YOUR OWN INNER RESOURCES.
LIKE WHAT RESOURCES?
VEGAN BROWNIE
AVOCADO GAZPACHO
LIKE, IF YOU'RE AN ARTIST AND YOU ONLY MAKE ART WHEN INSPIRATION COMES, THEN INSPIRATION WILL COME LESS AND LESS.
WHAT SHOULD AN ARTIST DEPEND ON THEN?
OH... DETERMINATION... INTELLIGENCE.
TALENT.
I THINK IT HELPS TO BELIEVE IN REINCARNATION. I DON'T KNOW HOW ANYONE CAN BE CREATIVE AND BELIEVE THIS IS ALL THERE IS.
YES, I SUPPOSE THEN YOU CAN'T MAKE ANY LONG TERM INVESTMENTS.
WELL, I SHOULD GET GOING. BUT WE SHOULD GET TOGETHER SOMETIME AGAIN SOON.
IT'D HAVE TO BE BEFORE THURSDAY, BECAUSE I'M GOING AWAY FOR A MEDITATION RETREAT IN THE CATSKILLS, AND THEN AREN'T YOU GOING TO CALIFORNIA?

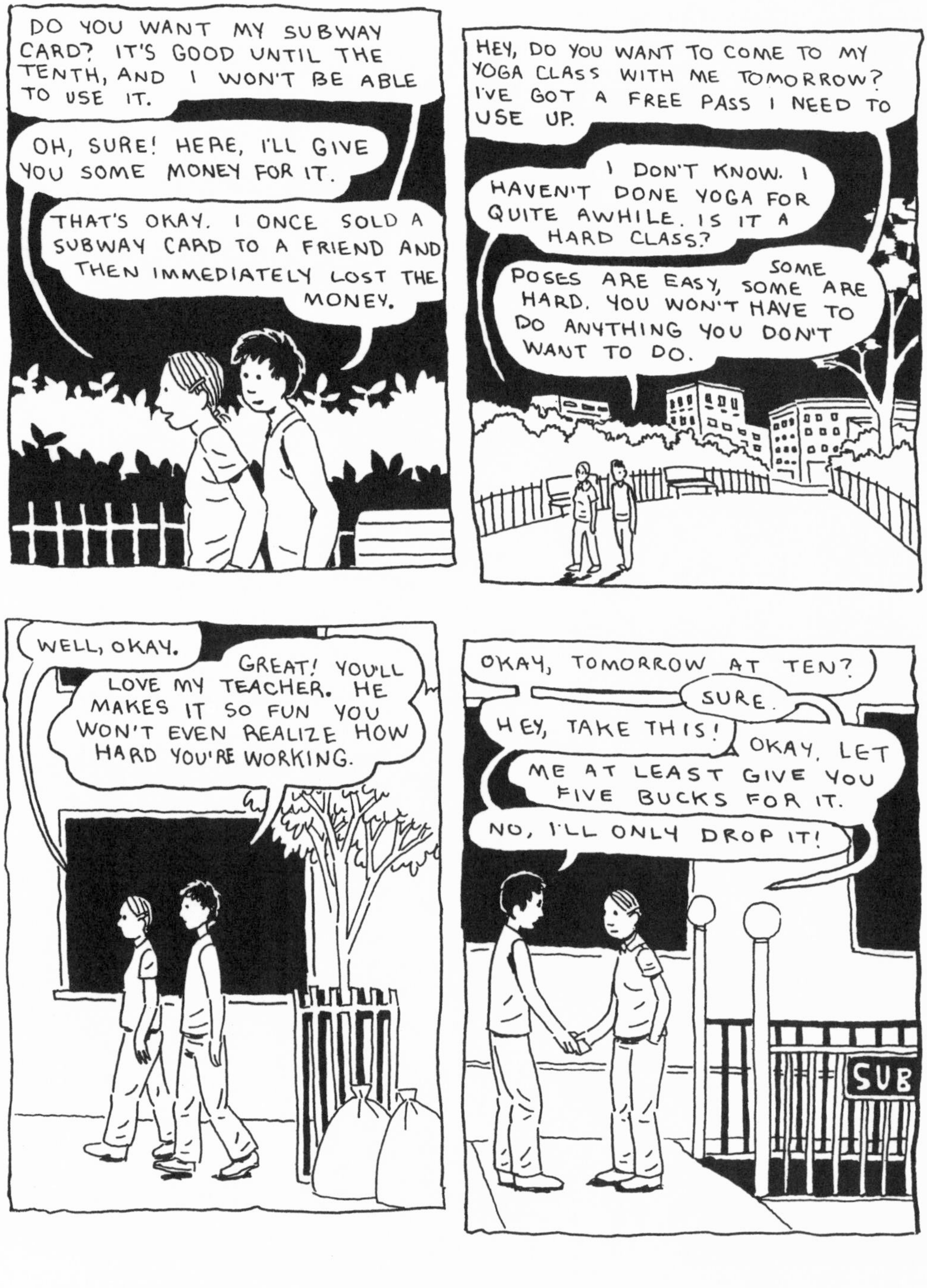
DO YOU WANT MY SUBWAY CARD? IT'S GOOD UNTIL THE TENTH, AND I WON'T BE ABLE TO USE IT.
OH, SURE! HERE, I'LL GIVE YOU SOME MONEY FOR IT.
THAT'S OKAY. I ONCE SOLD A SUBWAY CARD TO A FRIEND AND THEN IMMEDIATELY LOST THE MONEY.
HEY, DO YOU WANT TO COME TO MY YOGA CLASS WITH ME TOMORROW? I'VE GOT A FREE PASS I NEED TO USE UP.
I DON'T KNOW. I HAVEN'T DONE YOGA FOR QUITE AWHILE. IS IT A HARD CLASS?
SOME POSES ARE EASY, SOME ARE HARD. YOU WON'T HAVE TO DO ANYTHING YOU DON'T WANT TO DO.
WELL, OKAY.
GREAT! YOU'LL LOVE MY TEACHER. HE MAKES IT SO FUN YOU WON'T EVEN REALIZE HOW HARD YOU'RE WORKING.
OKAY, TOMORROW AT TEN?
SURE.
HEY, TAKE THIS!
OKAY, LET ME AT LEAST GIVE YOU FIVE BUCKS FOR IT.
NO, I'LL ONLY DROP IT!
SUB

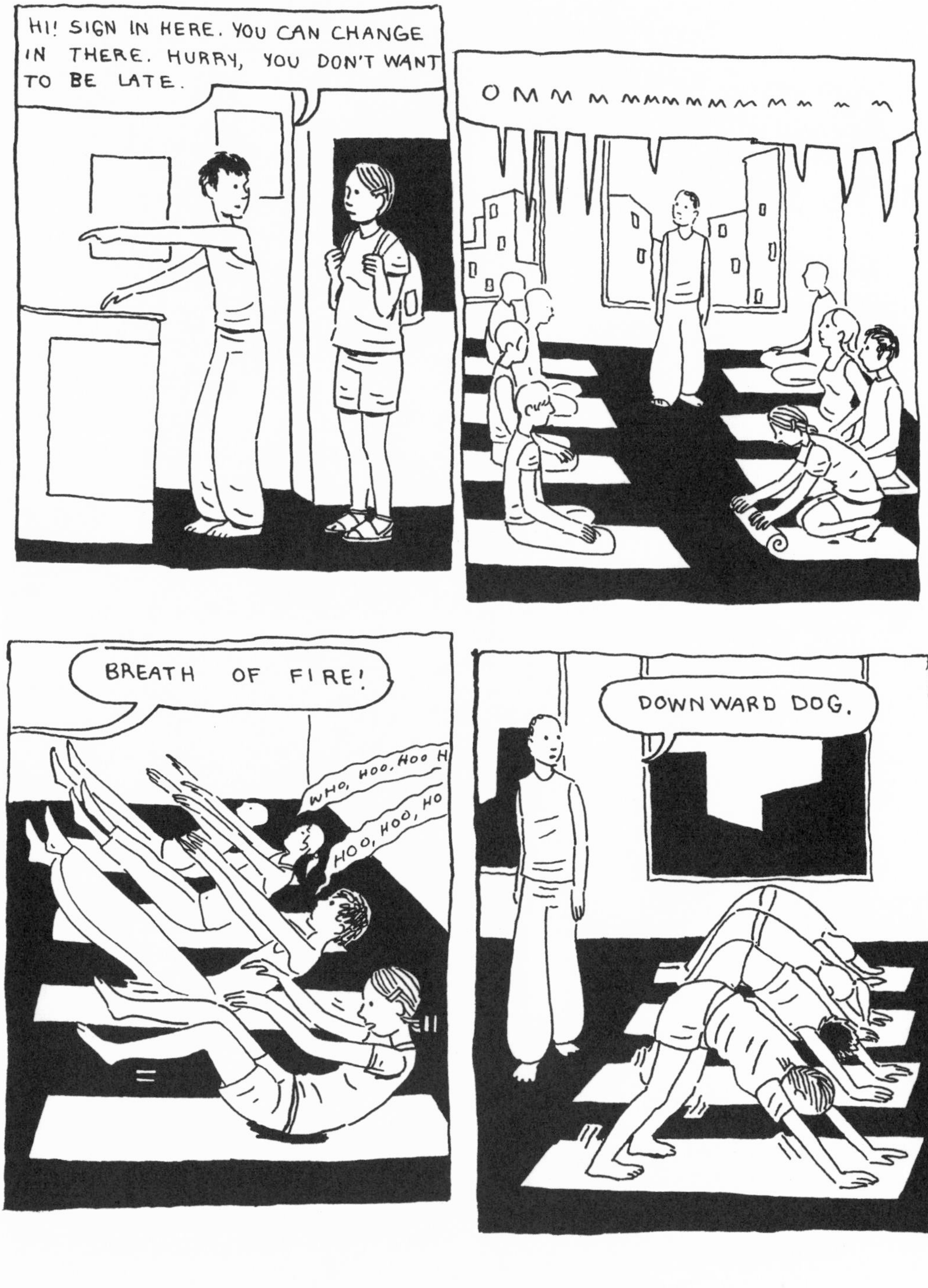
HI! SIGN IN HERE. YOU CAN CHANGE IN THERE. HURRY, YOU DON'T WANT TO BE LATE.
OMMMMMMMMMMMMMMM
BREATH OF FIRE!
WHO, HOO, HOO H
HOO, HOO, HO
DOWNWARD DOG.

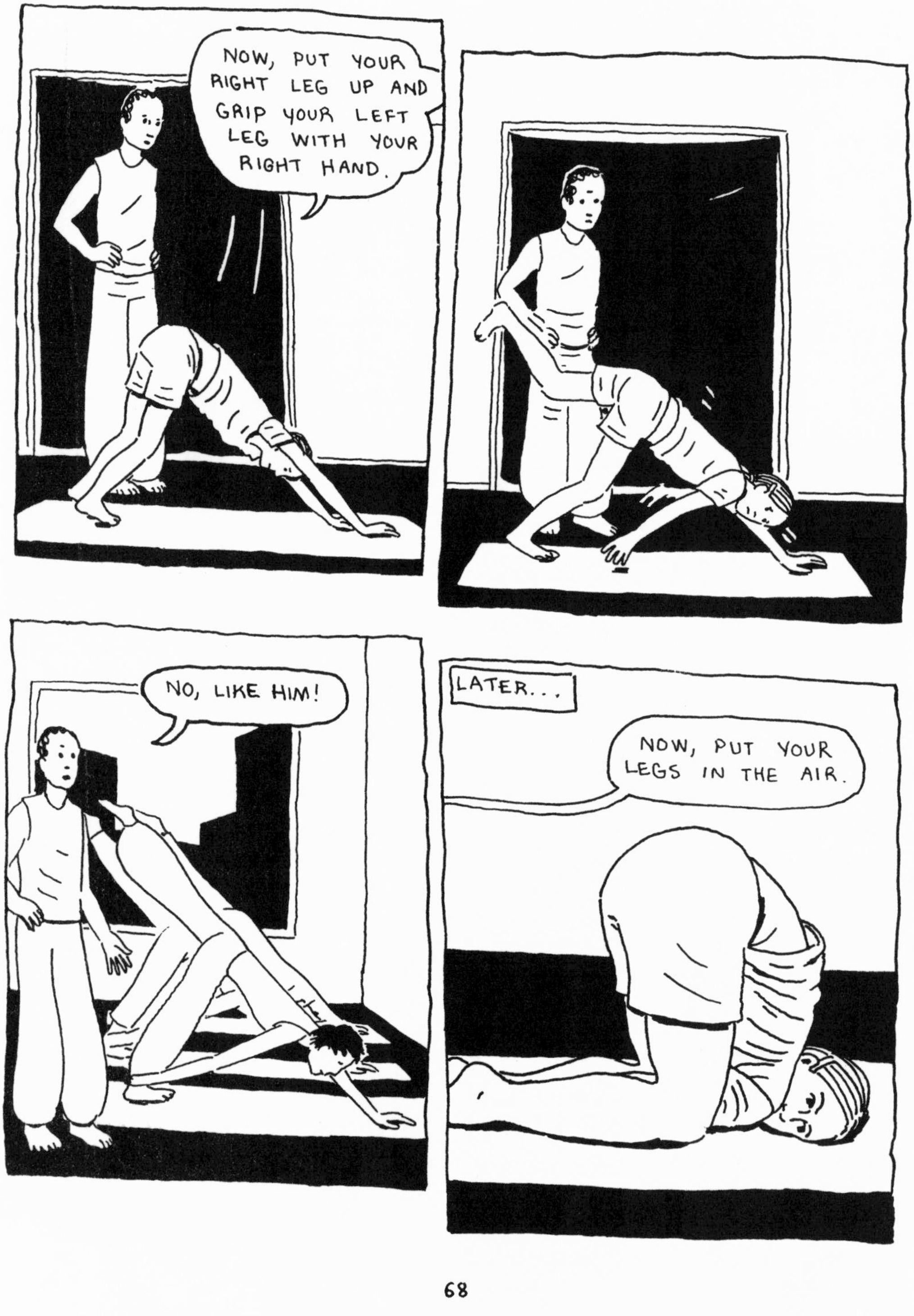
NOW, PUT YOUR RIGHT LEG UP AND GRIP YOUR LEFT LEG WITH YOUR RIGHT HAND.
NO, LIKE HIM!
LATER...
NOW, PUT YOUR LEGS IN THE AIR.

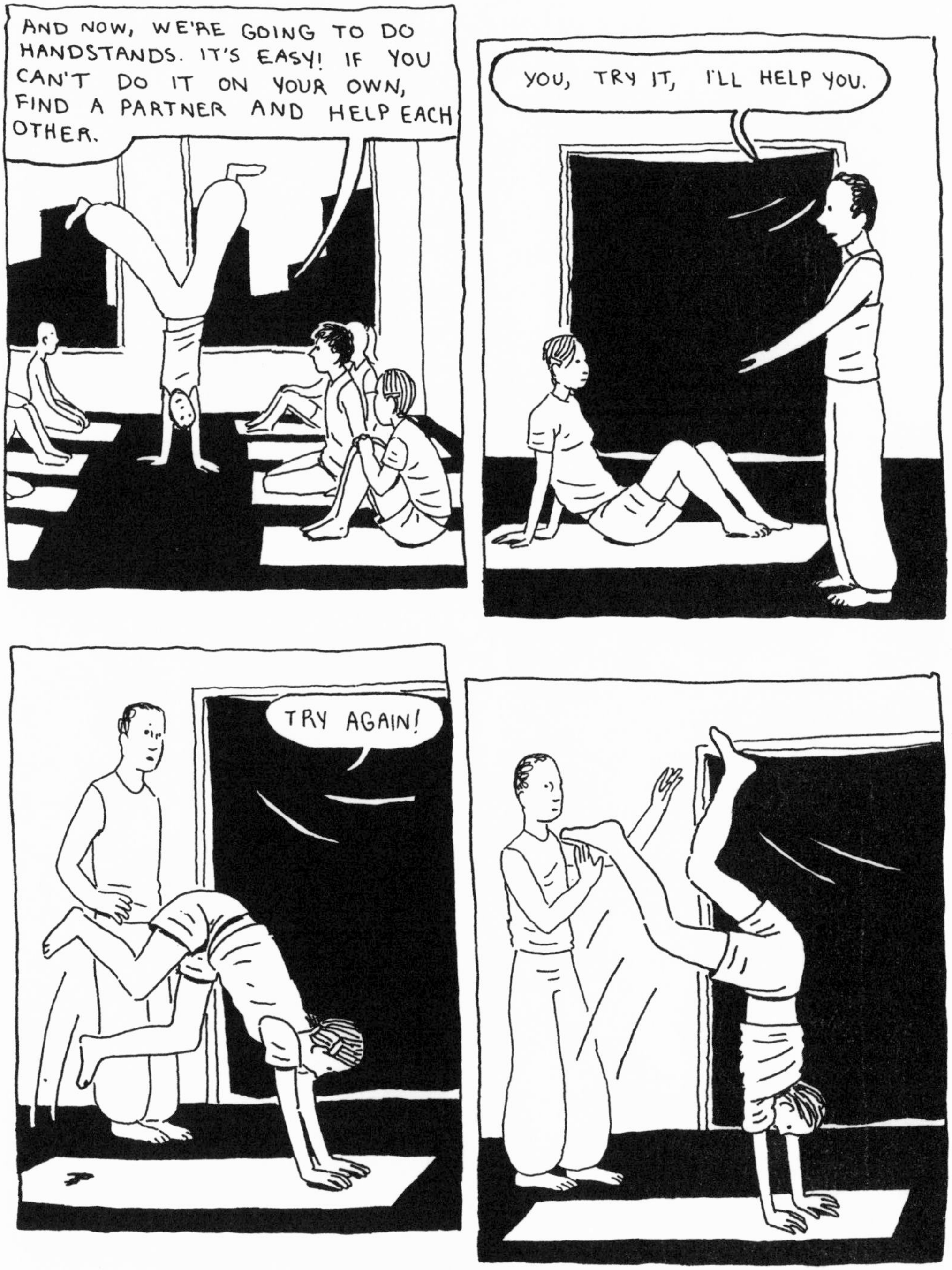
AND NOW, WE'RE GOING TO DO HANDSTANDS. IT'S EASY! IF YOU CAN'T DO IT ON YOUR OWN, FIND A PARTNER AND HELP EACH OTHER.
YOU, TRY IT, I'LL HELP YOU.
TRY AGAIN!

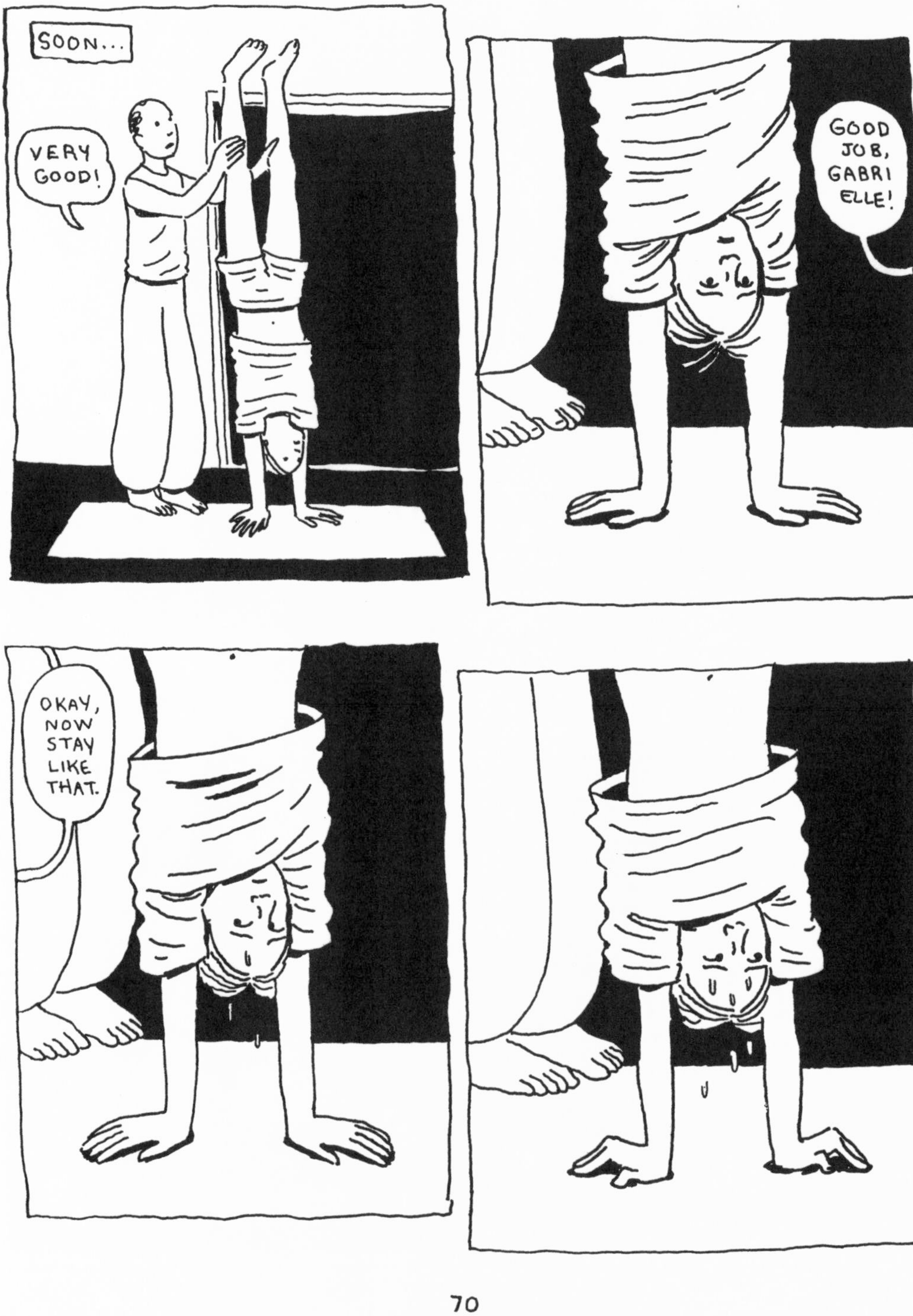
SOON...
VERY GOOD!
GOOD JOB, GABRIELLE!
OKAY, NOW STAY LIKE THAT.

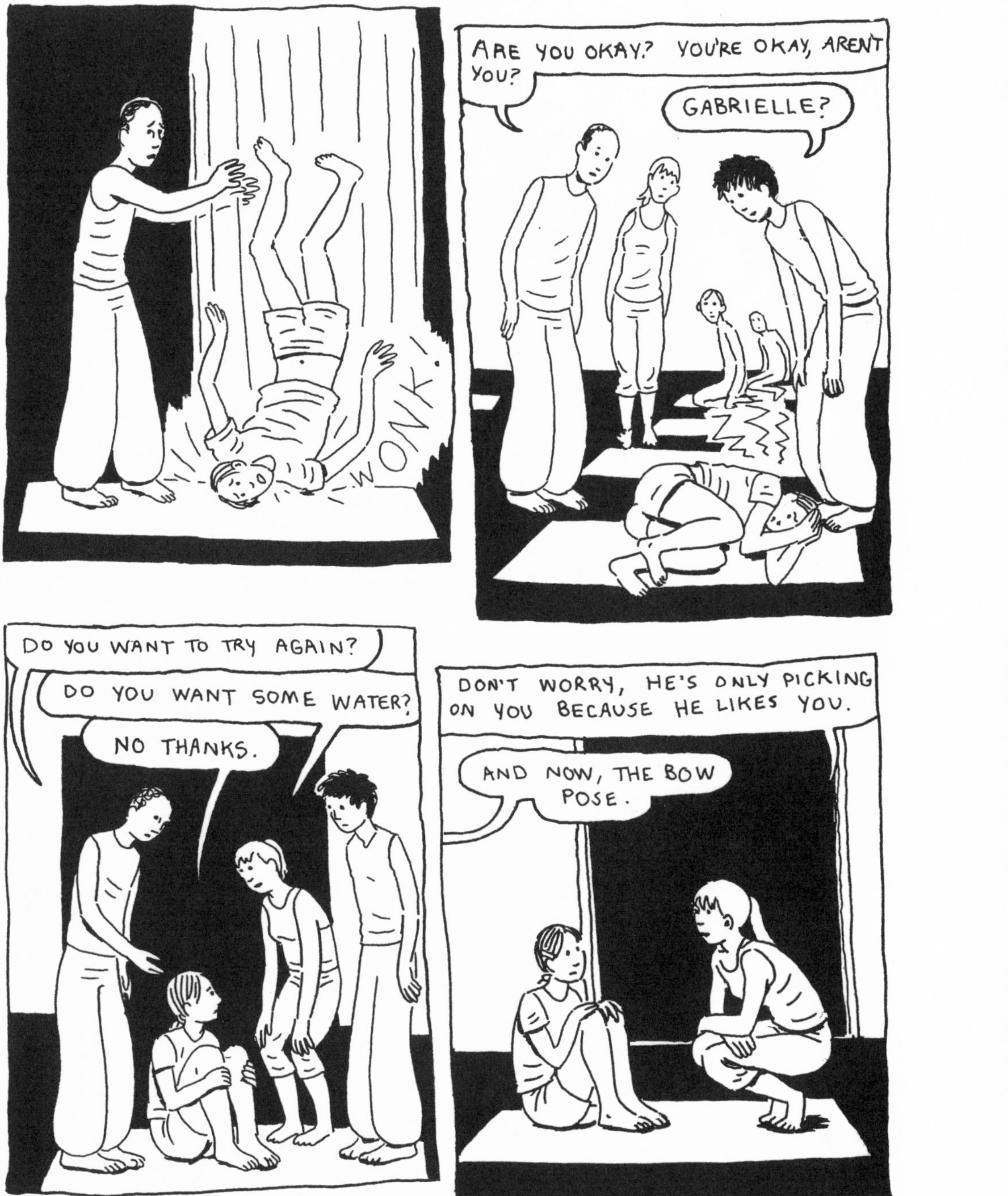
WONK!
ARE YOU OKAY? YOU'RE OKAY, AREN'T YOU?
GABRIELLE?
DO YOU WANT TO TRY AGAIN?
DO YOU WANT SOME WATER?
NO THANKS.
DON'T WORRY, HE'S ONLY PICKING ON YOU BECAUSE HE LIKES YOU.
AND NOW, THE BOW POSE.

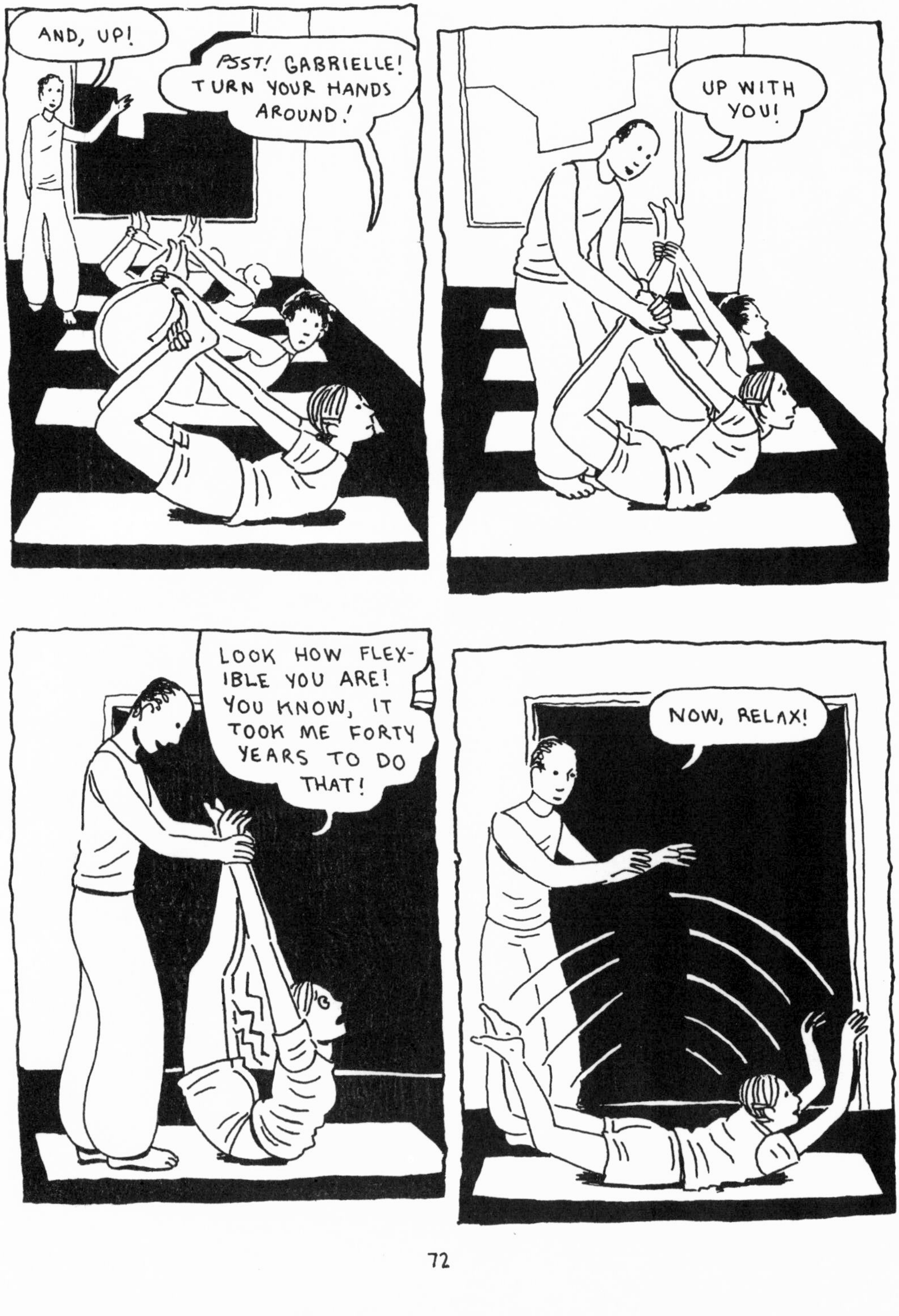
AND, UP!
PSST! GABRIELLE! TURN YOUR HANDS AROUND!
UP WITH YOU!
LOOK HOW FLEX-IBLE YOU ARE! YOU KNOW, IT TOOK ME FORTY YEARS TO DO THAT!
NOW, RELAX!

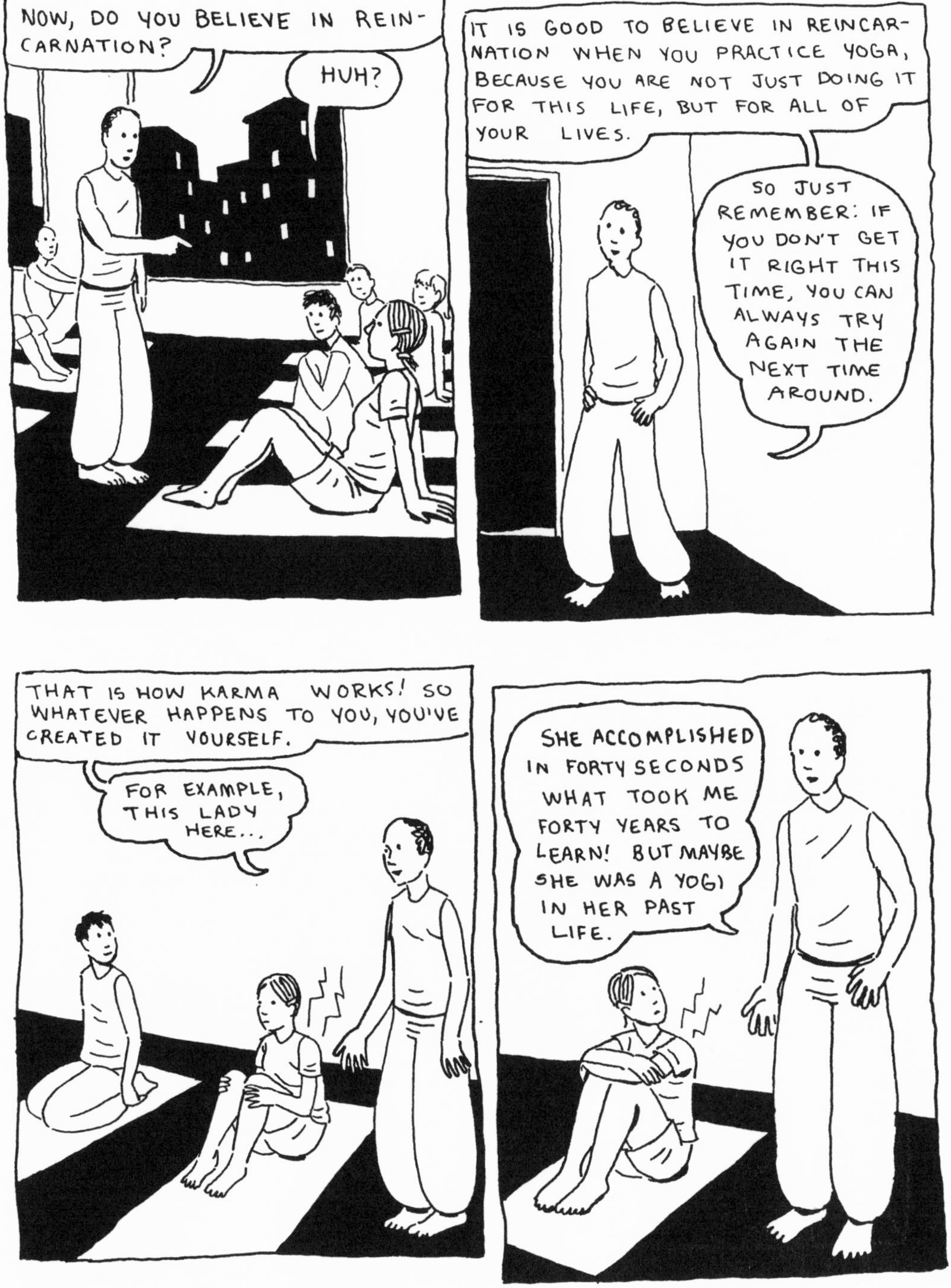
NOW, DO YOU BELIEVE IN REINCARNATION?
HUH?
IT IS GOOD TO BELIEVE IN REINCARNATION WHEN YOU PRACTICE YOGA, BECAUSE YOU ARE NOT JUST DOING IT FOR THIS LIFE, BUT FOR ALL OF YOUR LIVES.
SO JUST REMEMBER: IF YOU DON'T GET IT RIGHT THIS TIME, YOU CAN ALWAYS TRY AGAIN THE NEXT TIME AROUND.
THAT IS HOW KARMA WORKS! SO WHATEVER HAPPENS TO YOU, YOU'VE CREATED IT YOURSELF.
FOR EXAMPLE, THIS LADY HERE...
SHE ACCOMPLISHED IN FORTY SECONDS WHAT TOOK ME FORTY YEARS TO LEARN! BUT MAYBE SHE WAS A YOGI IN HER PAST LIFE.

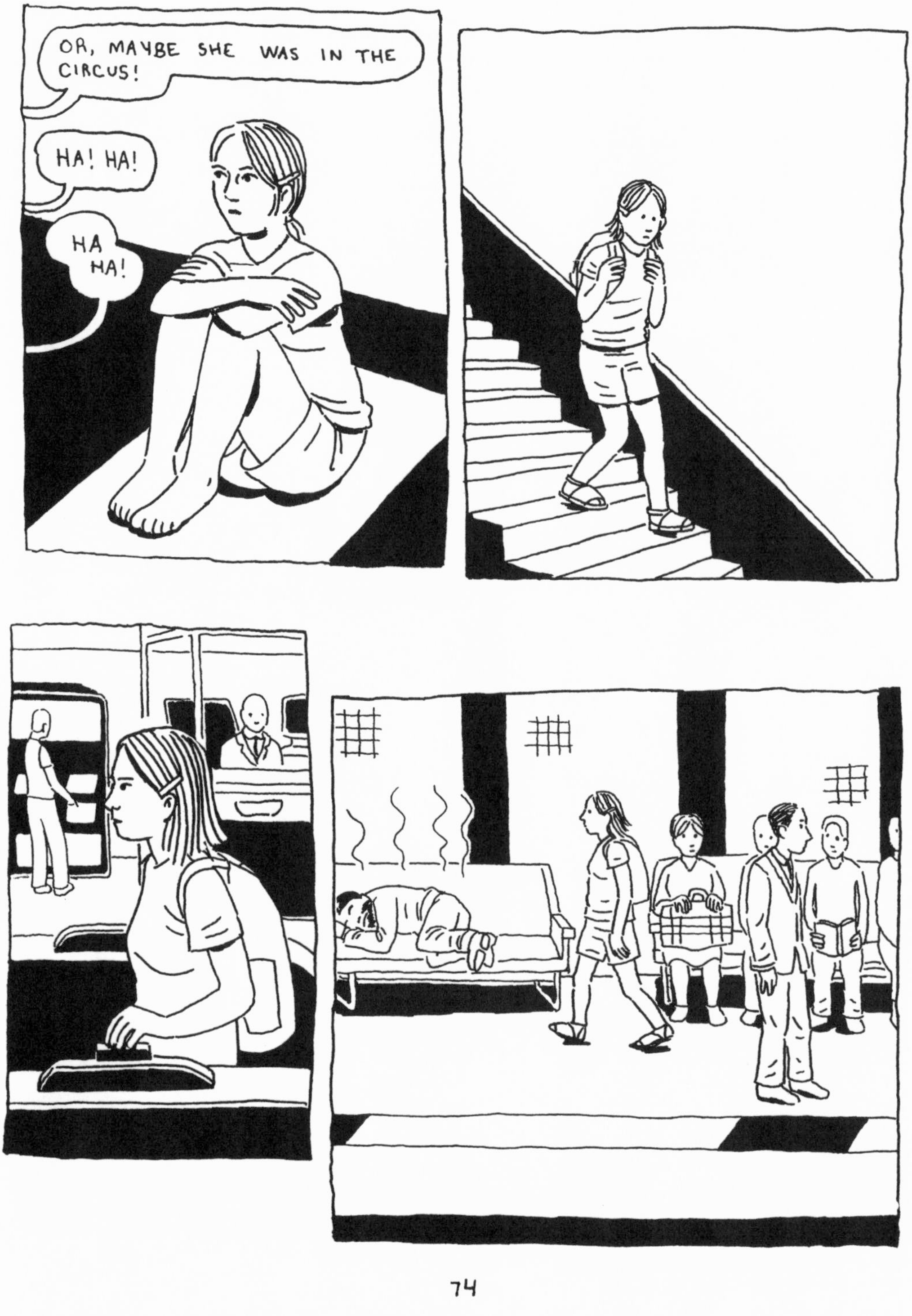
OR, MAYBE SHE WAS IN THE CIRCUS!
HA! HA!
HA HA!

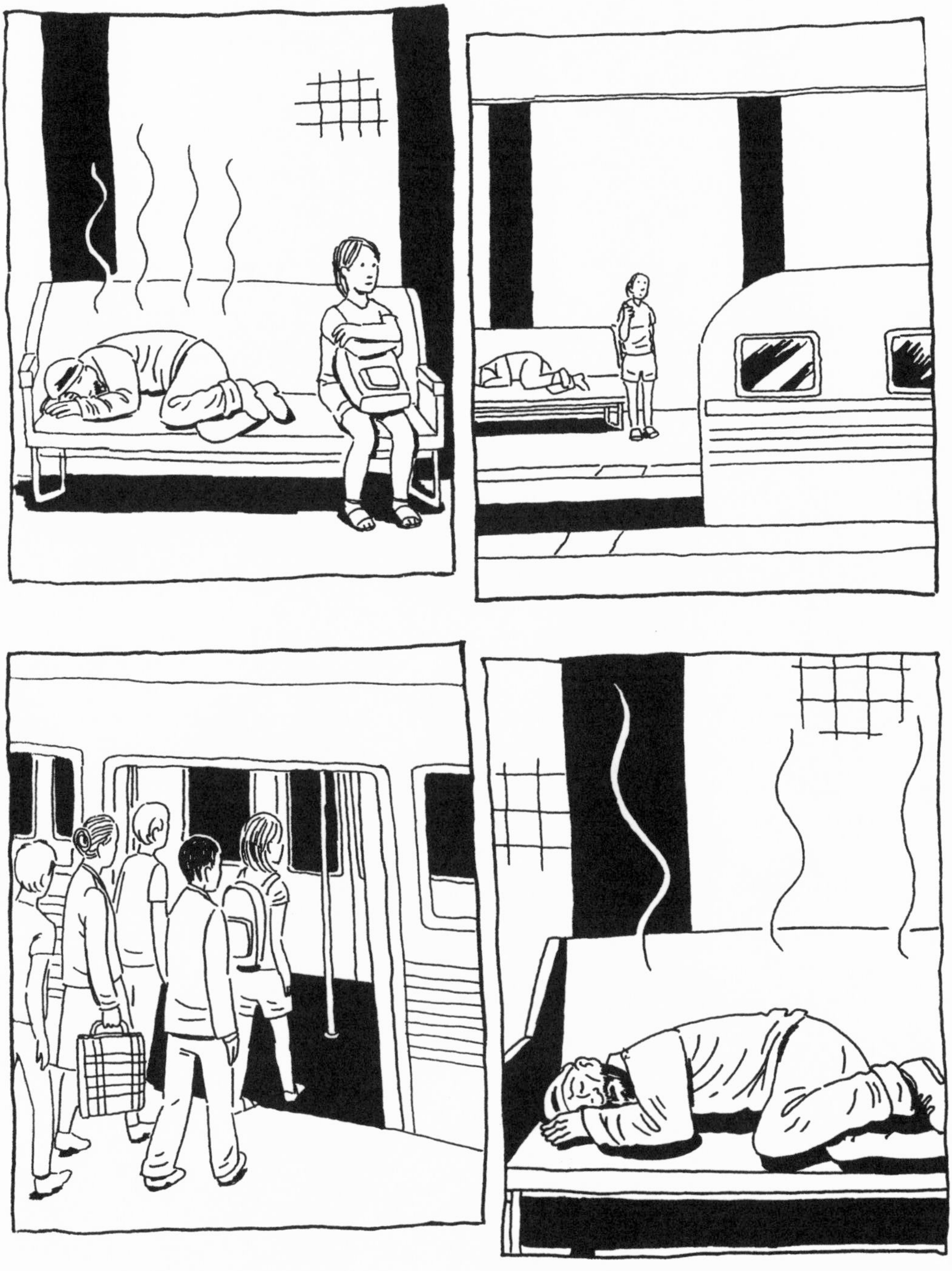

Lucky # 3 (May 2004)

A MATTER OF PERSPECTIVE

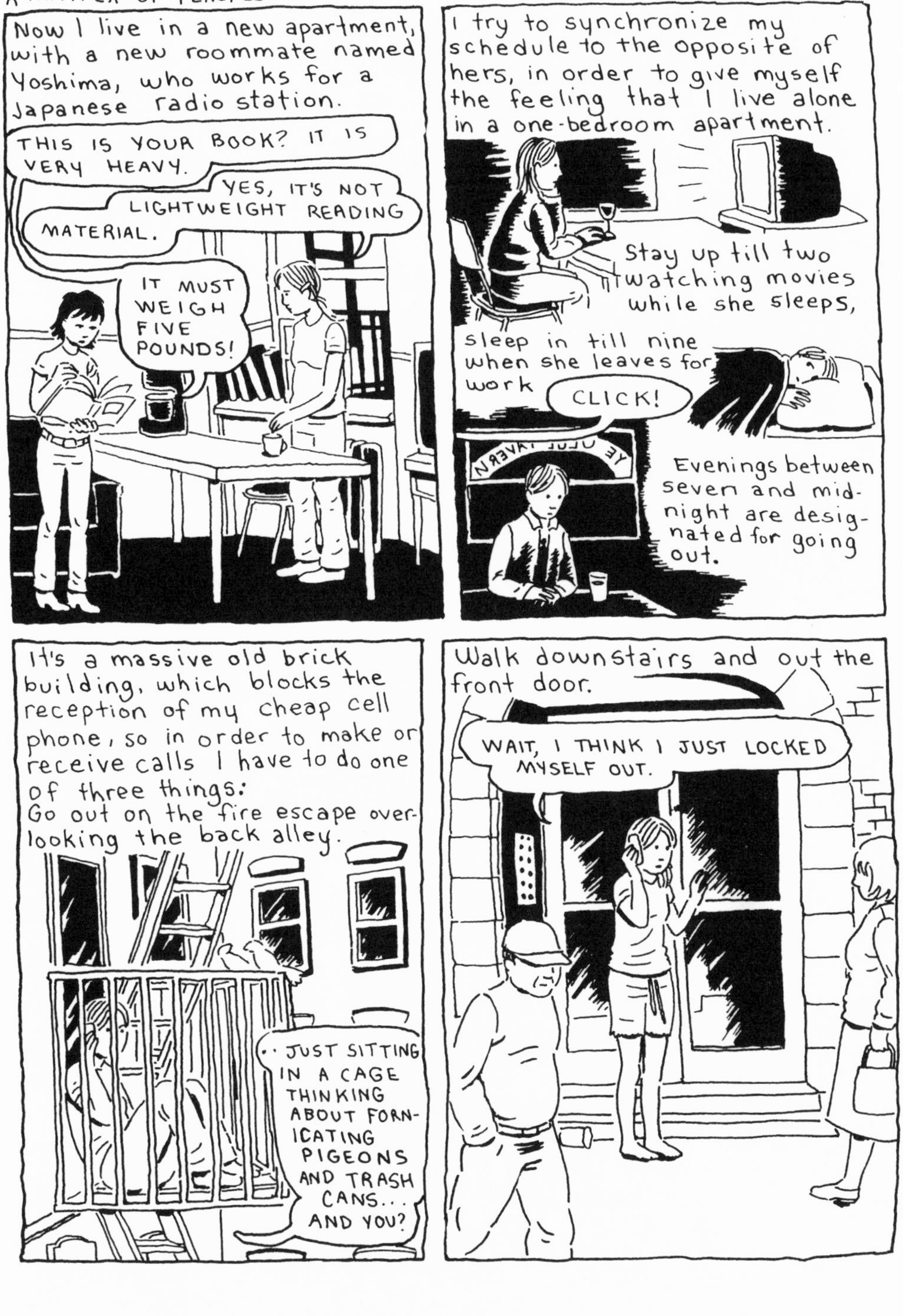
Now I live in a new apartment, with a new roommate named Yoshima, who works for a Japanese radio station.
THIS IS YOUR BOOK? IT IS VERY HEAVY.
YES, IT'S NOT LIGHTWEIGHT READING MATERIAL.
IT MUST WEIGH FIVE POUNDS!
I try to synchronize my schedule to the opposite of hers, in order to give myself the feeling that I live alone in a one-bedroom apartment.
Stay up till two watching movies while she sleeps,
sleep in till nine when she leaves for work
CLICK!
Evenings between seven and midnight are designated for going out.
It's a massive old brick building, which blocks the reception of my cheap cell phone, so in order to make or receive calls I have to do one of three things:
Go out on the fire escape overlooking the back alley.
..JUST SITTING IN A CAGE THINKING ABOUT FORNICATING PIGEONS AND TRASH CANS... AND YOU?
Walk downstairs and out the front door.
WAIT, I THINK I JUST LOCKED MYSELF OUT.

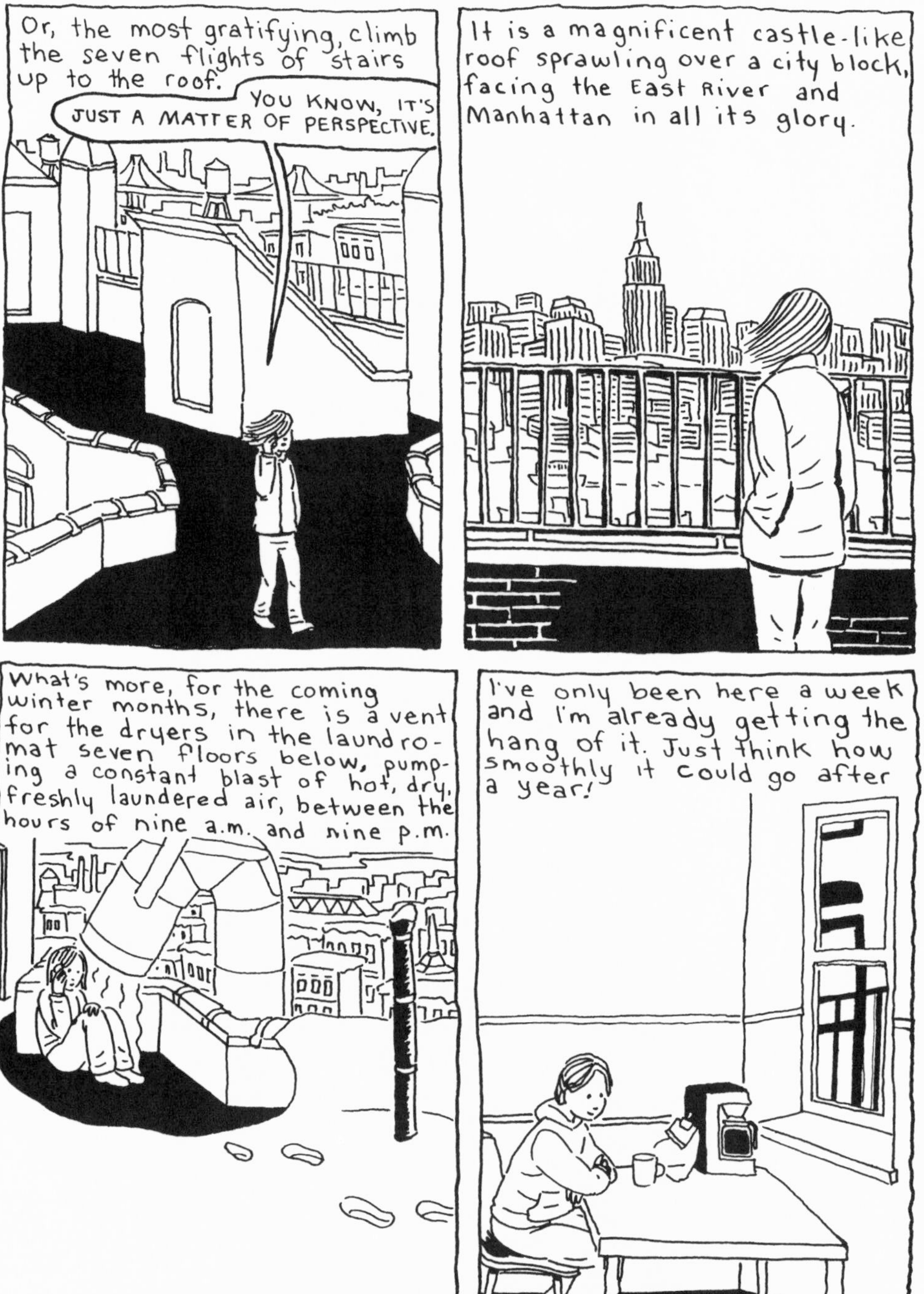

Or, the most gratifying, climb the seven flights of stairs up to the roof.
YOU KNOW, IT'S JUST A MATTER OF PERSPECTIVE.
It is a magnificent castle-like roof sprawling over a city block, facing the East River and Manhattan in all its glory.
What's more, for the coming winter months, there is a vent for the dryers in the laundromat seven floors below, pumping a constant blast of hot, dry, freshly laundered air, between the hours of nine a.m. and nine p.m.
I've only been here a week and I'm already getting the hang of it. Just think how smoothly it could go after a year!

# THE ARTIST'S ASSISTANT

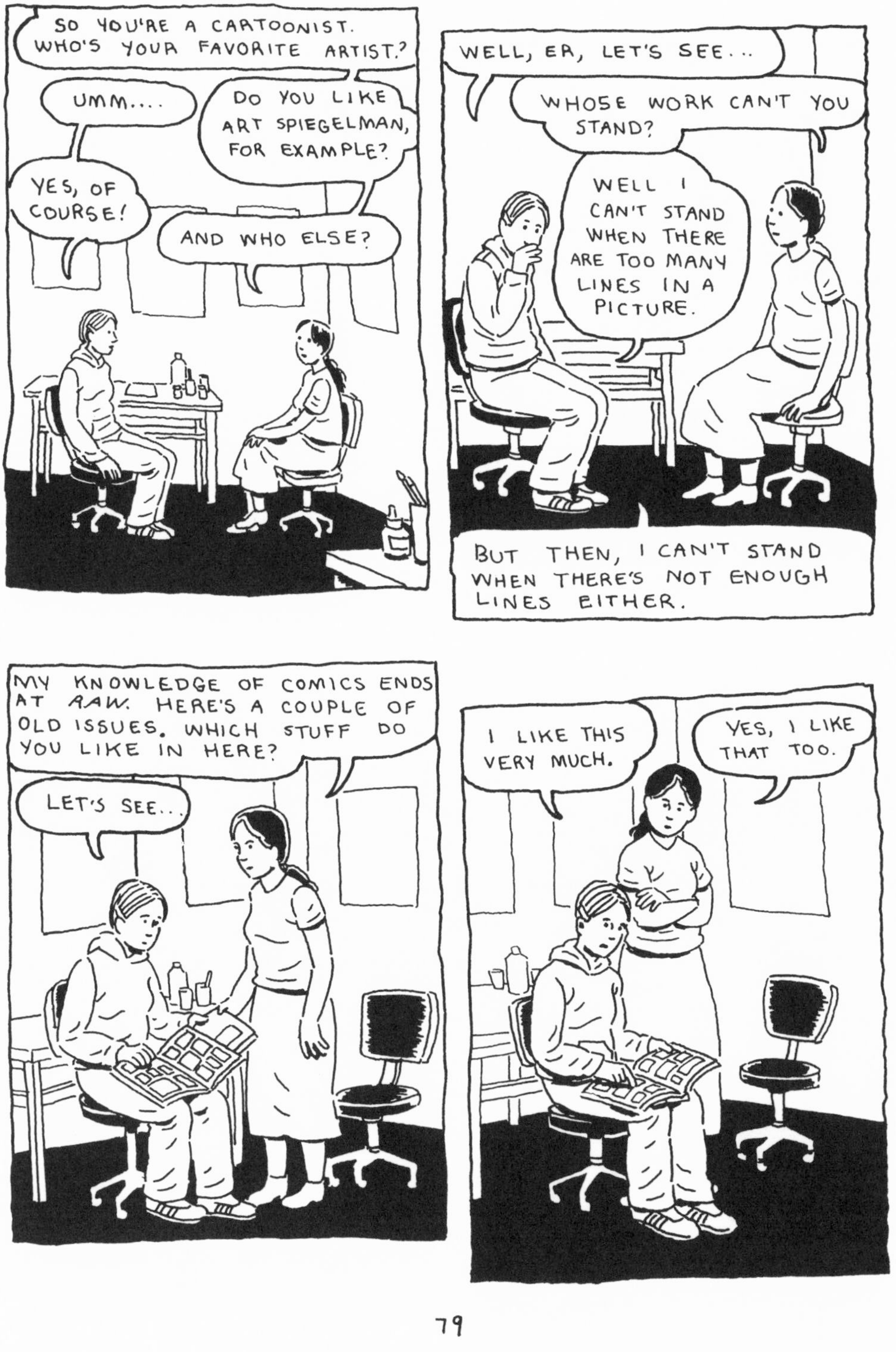
SO YOU'RE A CARTOONIST. WHO'S YOUR FAVORITE ARTIST?
UMM....
DO YOU LIKE ART SPIEGELMAN, FOR EXAMPLE?
YES, OF COURSE!
AND WHO ELSE?
WELL, ER, LET'S SEE...
WHOSE WORK CAN'T YOU STAND?
WELL I CAN'T STAND WHEN THERE ARE TOO MANY LINES IN A PICTURE.
BUT THEN, I CAN'T STAND WHEN THERE'S NOT ENOUGH LINES EITHER.
MY KNOWLEDGE OF COMICS ENDS AT RAW. HERE'S A COUPLE OF OLD ISSUES. WHICH STUFF DO YOU LIKE IN HERE?
LET'S SEE...
I LIKE THIS VERY MUCH.
YES, I LIKE THAT TOO.

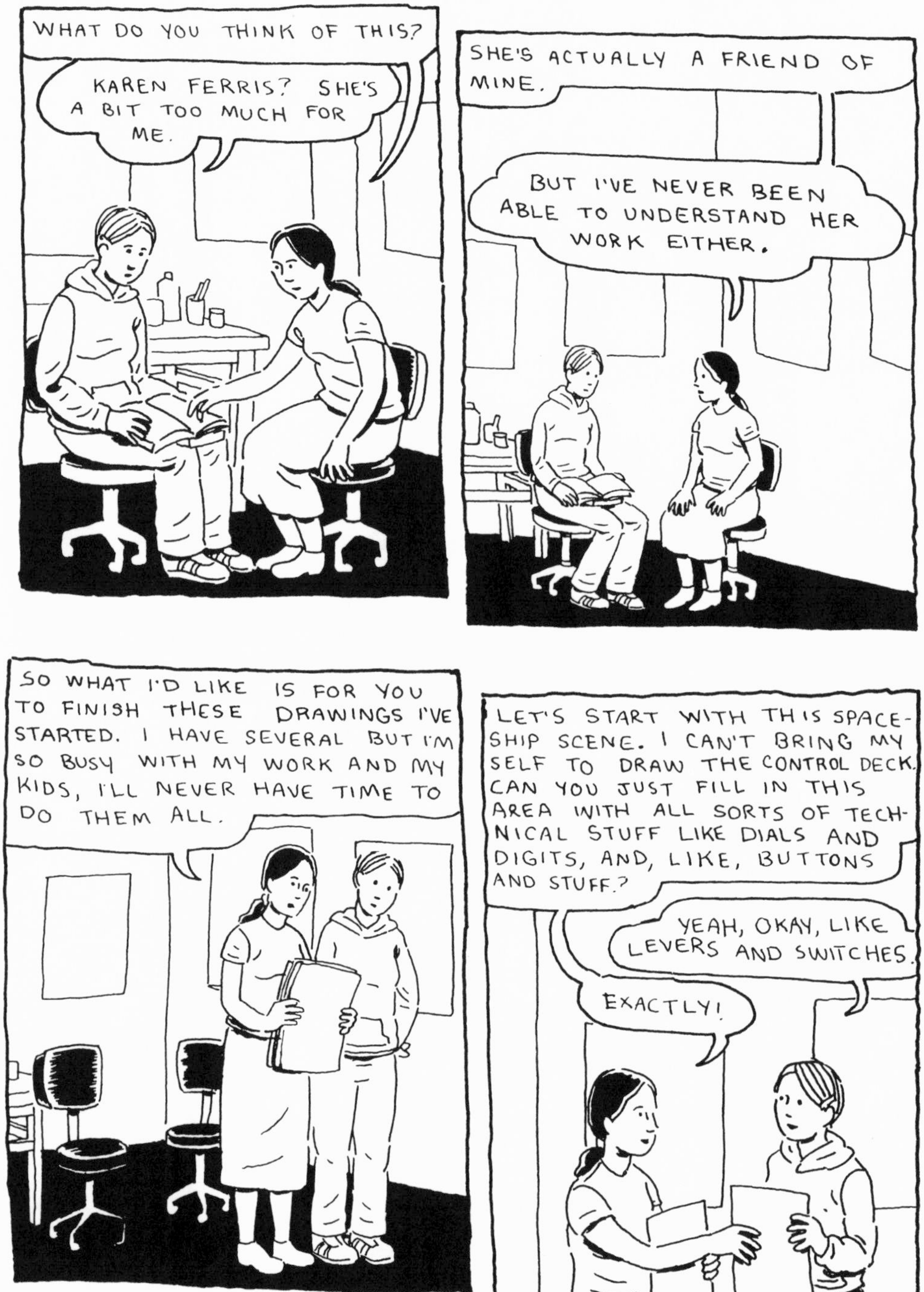
WHAT DO YOU THINK OF THIS?
KAREN FERRIS? SHE'S A BIT TOO MUCH FOR ME.
SHE'S ACTUALLY A FRIEND OF MINE.
BUT I'VE NEVER BEEN ABLE TO UNDERSTAND HER WORK EITHER.
SO WHAT I'D LIKE IS FOR YOU TO FINISH THESE DRAWINGS I'VE STARTED. I HAVE SEVERAL BUT I'M SO BUSY WITH MY WORK AND MY KIDS, I'LL NEVER HAVE TIME TO DO THEM ALL.
LET'S START WITH THIS SPACE-SHIP SCENE. I CAN'T BRING MY SELF TO DRAW THE CONTROL DECK. CAN YOU JUST FILL IN THIS AREA WITH ALL SORTS OF TECH-NICAL STUFF LIKE DIALS AND DIGITS, AND, LIKE, BUTTONS AND STUFF?
YEAH, OKAY, LIKE LEVERS AND SWITCHES.
EXACTLY!

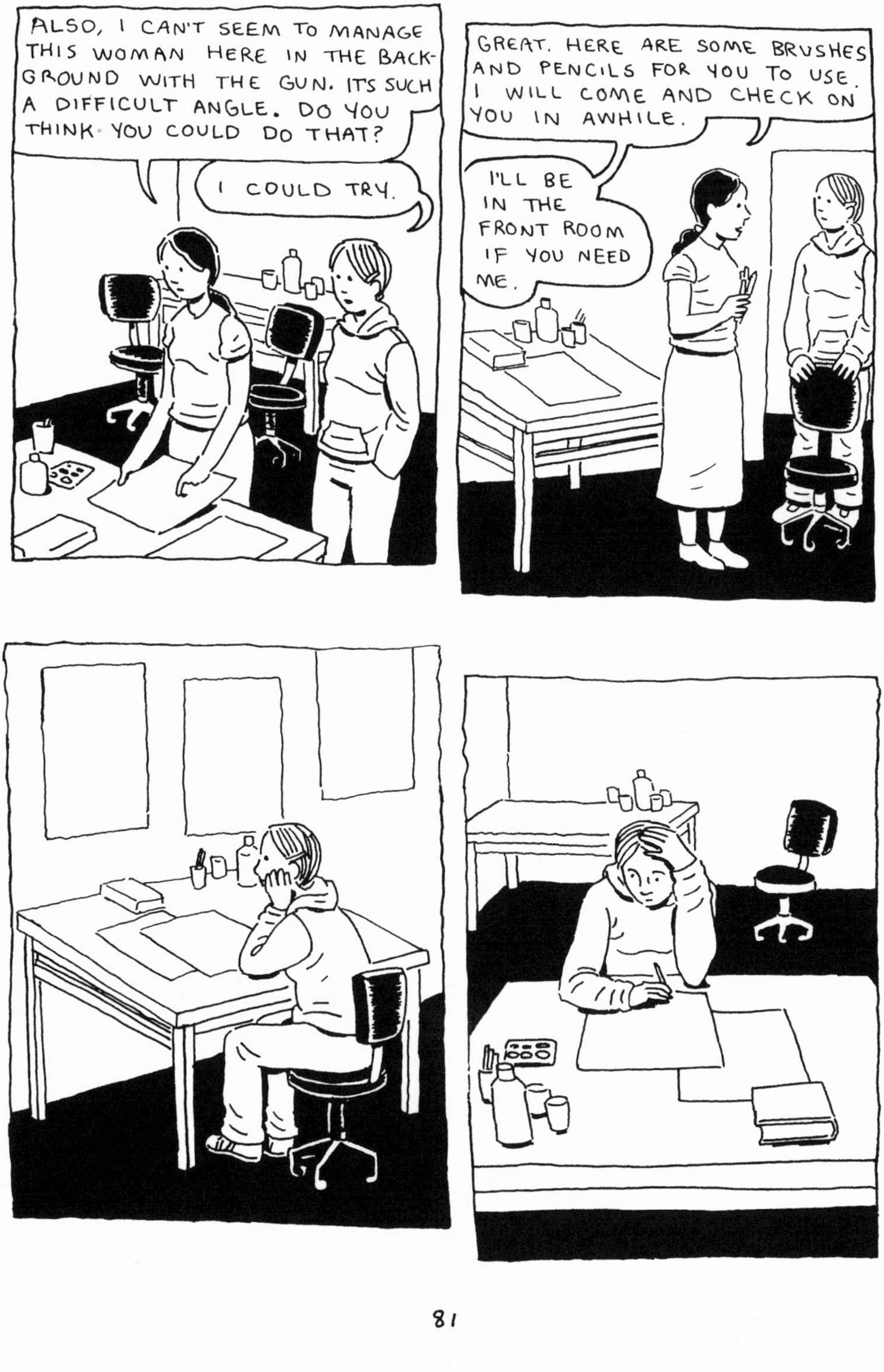
ALSO, I CAN'T SEEM TO MANAGE THIS WOMAN HERE IN THE BACKGROUND WITH THE GUN. IT'S SUCH A DIFFICULT ANGLE. DO YOU THINK YOU COULD DO THAT?
I COULD TRY.
GREAT. HERE ARE SOME BRUSHES AND PENCILS FOR YOU TO USE. I WILL COME AND CHECK ON YOU IN AWHILE.
I'LL BE IN THE FRONT ROOM IF YOU NEED ME.

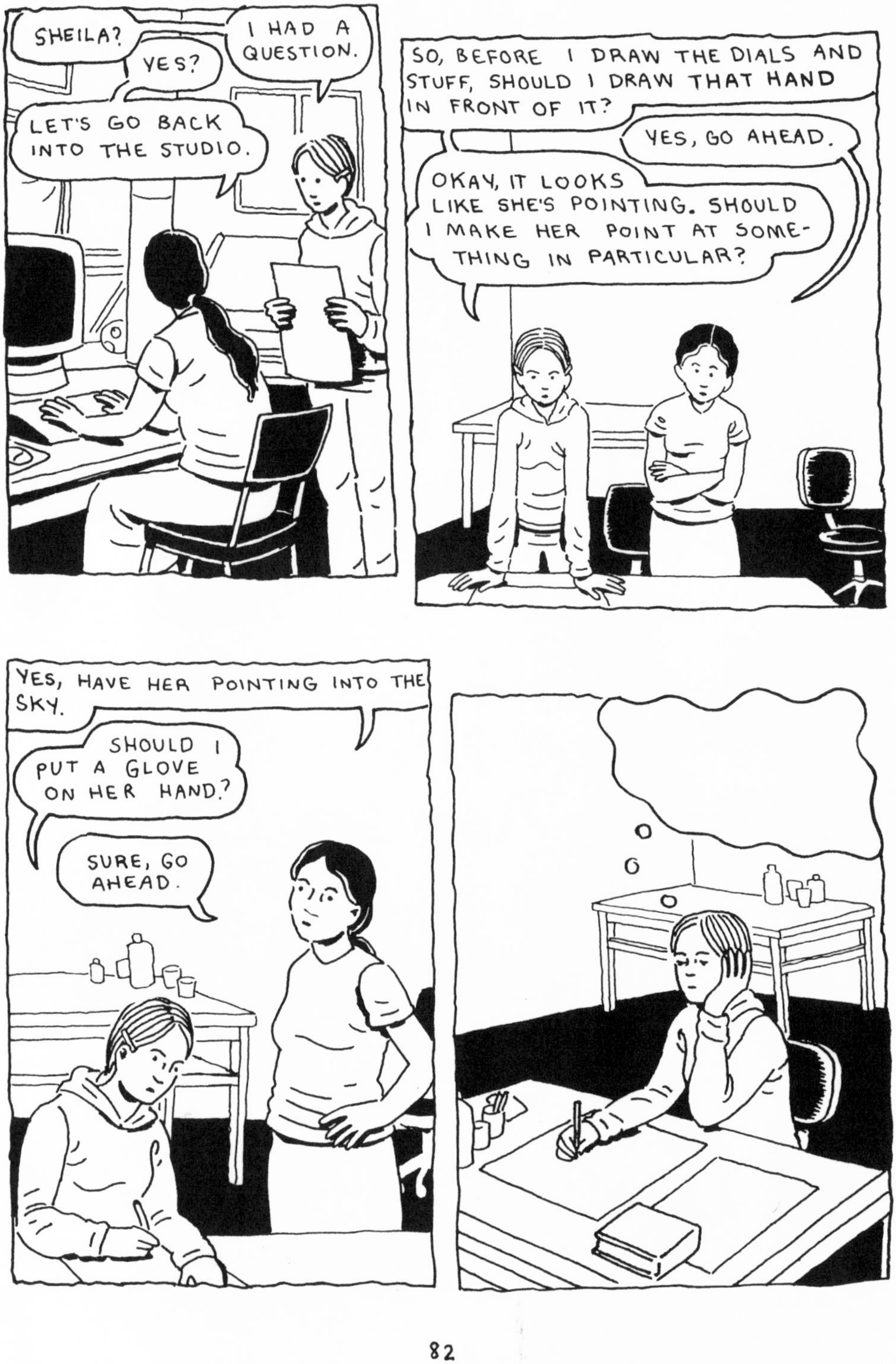
SHEILA?
YES?
I HAD A QUESTION.
LET'S GO BACK INTO THE STUDIO.
SO, BEFORE I DRAW THE DIALS AND STUFF, SHOULD I DRAW THAT HAND IN FRONT OF IT?
YES, GO AHEAD.
OKAY, IT LOOKS LIKE SHE'S POINTING. SHOULD I MAKE HER POINT AT SOMETHING IN PARTICULAR?
YES, HAVE HER POINTING INTO THE SKY.
SHOULD I PUT A GLOVE ON HER HAND?
SURE, GO AHEAD.

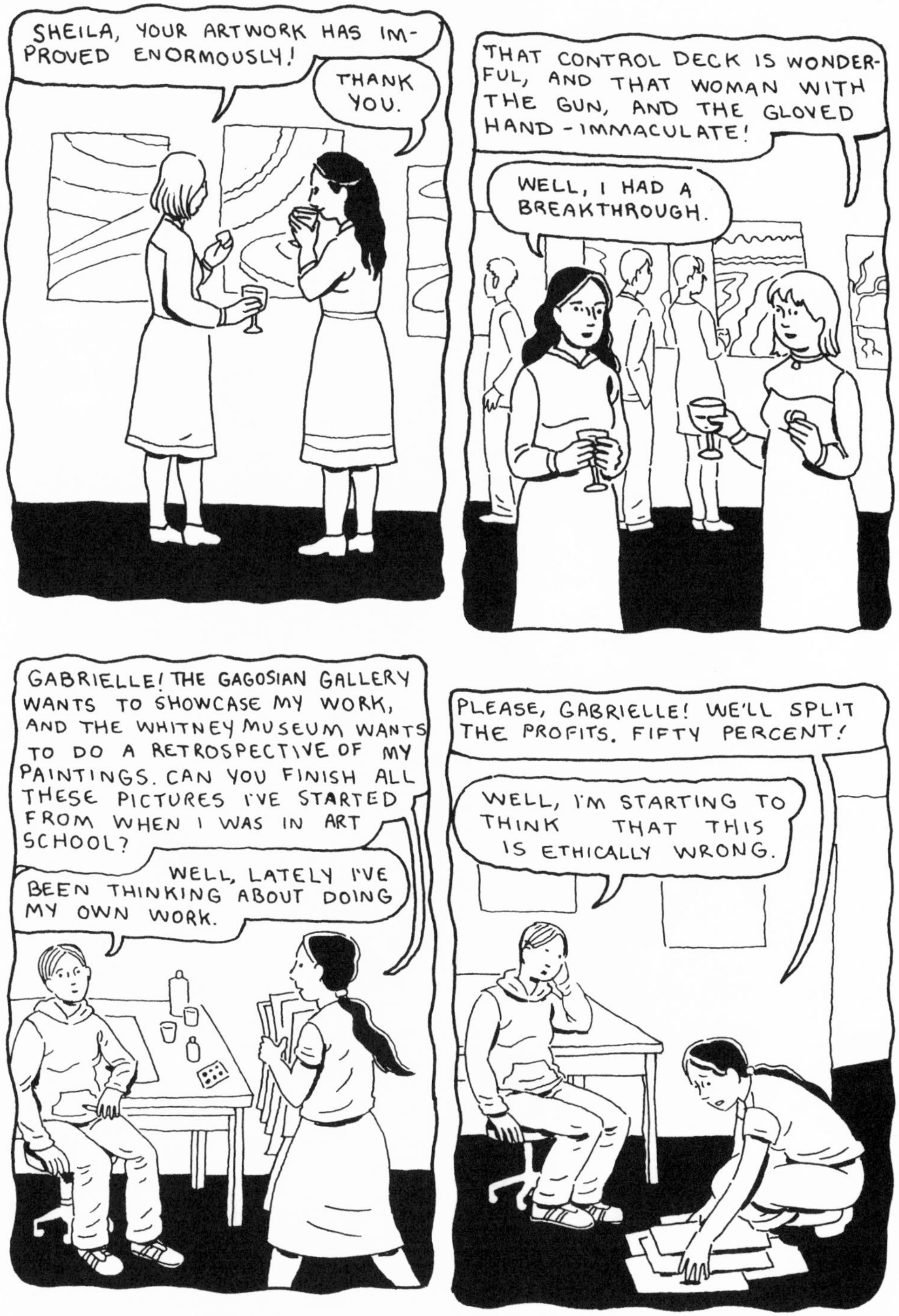
SHEILA, YOUR ARTWORK HAS IMPROVED ENORMOUSLY!
THANK YOU.
THAT CONTROL DECK IS WONDERFUL, AND THAT WOMAN WITH THE GUN, AND THE GLOVED HAND - IMMACULATE!
WELL, I HAD A BREAKTHROUGH.
GABRIELLE! THE GAGOSIAN GALLERY WANTS TO SHOWCASE MY WORK, AND THE WHITNEY MUSEUM WANTS TO DO A RETROSPECTIVE OF MY PAINTINGS. CAN YOU FINISH ALL THESE PICTURES I'VE STARTED FROM WHEN I WAS IN ART SCHOOL?
WELL, LATELY I'VE BEEN THINKING ABOUT DOING MY OWN WORK.
PLEASE, GABRIELLE! WE'LL SPLIT THE PROFITS. FIFTY PERCENT!
WELL, I'M STARTING TO THINK THAT THIS IS ETHICALLY WRONG.

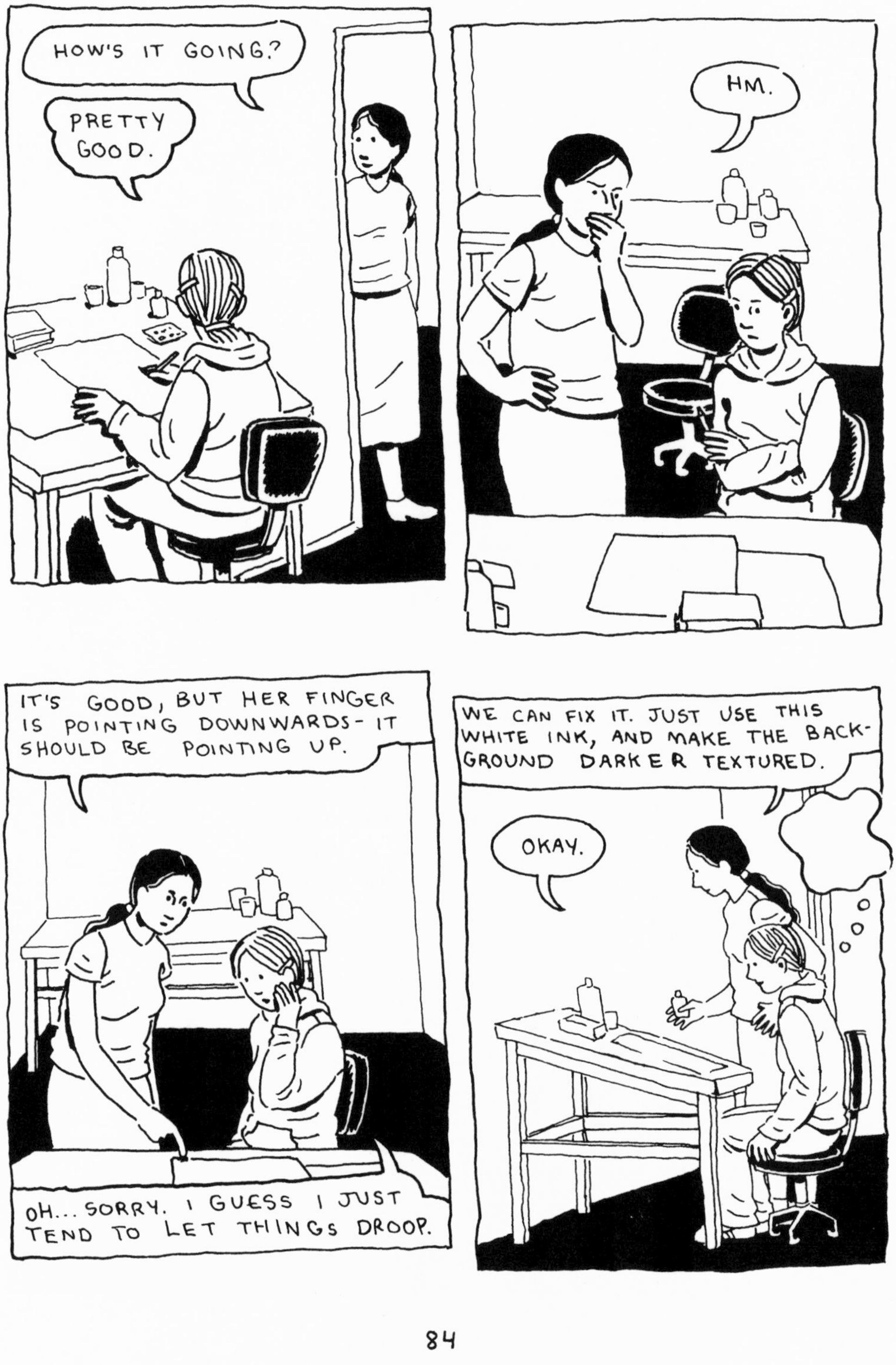
HOW'S IT GOING?
PRETTY GOOD.
HM.
IT'S GOOD, BUT HER FINGER IS POINTING DOWNWARDS- IT SHOULD BE POINTING UP.
OH... SORRY. I GUESS I JUST TEND TO LET THINGS DROOP.
WE CAN FIX IT. JUST USE THIS WHITE INK, AND MAKE THE BACK-GROUND DARKER TEXTURED.
OKAY.

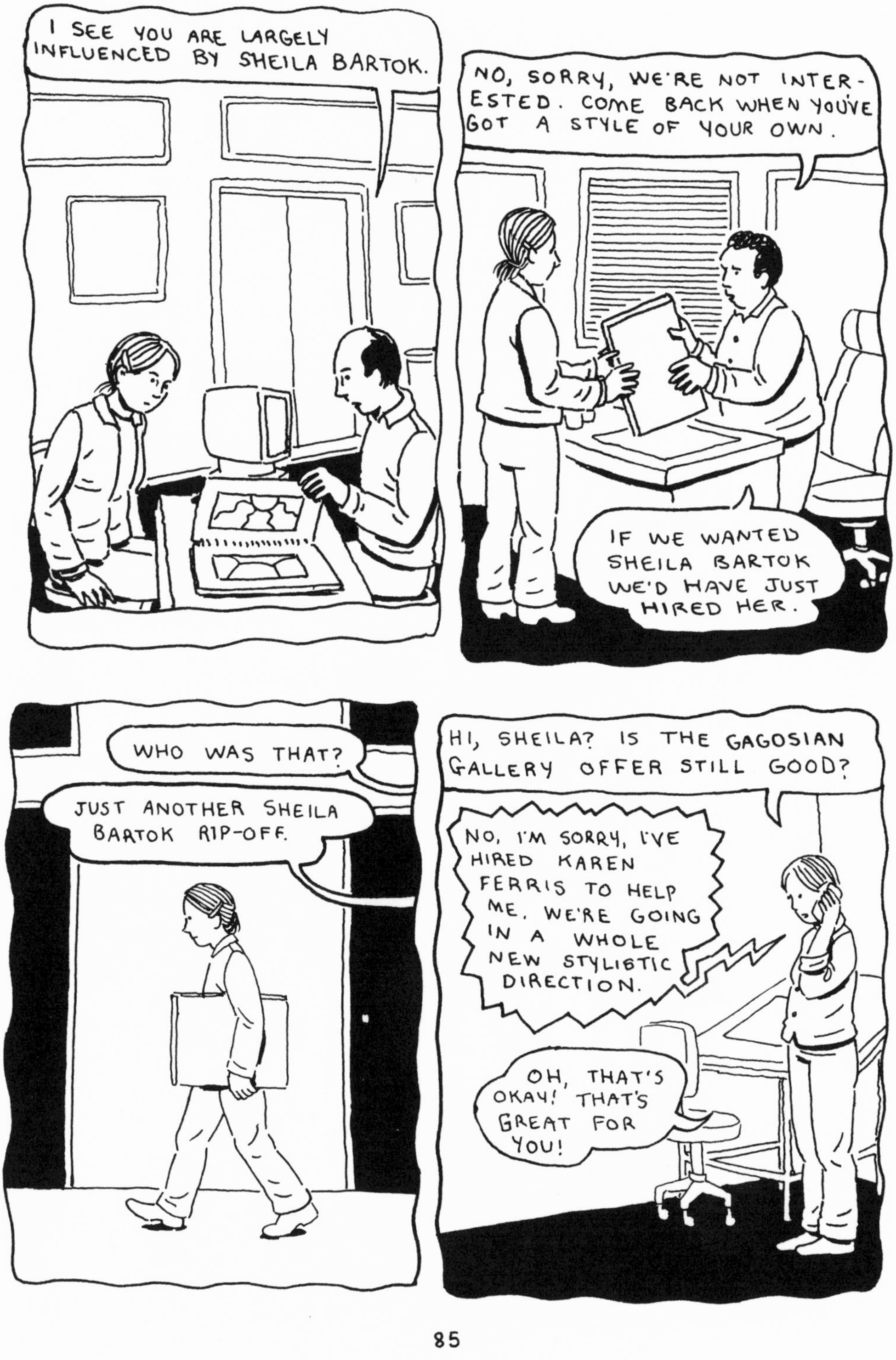
I SEE YOU ARE LARGELY INFLUENCED BY SHEILA BARTOK.
NO, SORRY, WE'RE NOT INTERESTED. COME BACK WHEN YOU'VE GOT A STYLE OF YOUR OWN.
IF WE WANTED SHEILA BARTOK WE'D HAVE JUST HIRED HER.
WHO WAS THAT?
JUST ANOTHER SHEILA BARTOK RIP-OFF.
HI, SHEILA? IS THE GAGOSIAN GALLERY OFFER STILL GOOD?
NO, I'M SORRY, I'VE HIRED KAREN FERRIS TO HELP ME. WE'RE GOING IN A WHOLE NEW STYLISTIC DIRECTION.
OH, THAT'S OKAY! THAT'S GREAT FOR YOU!

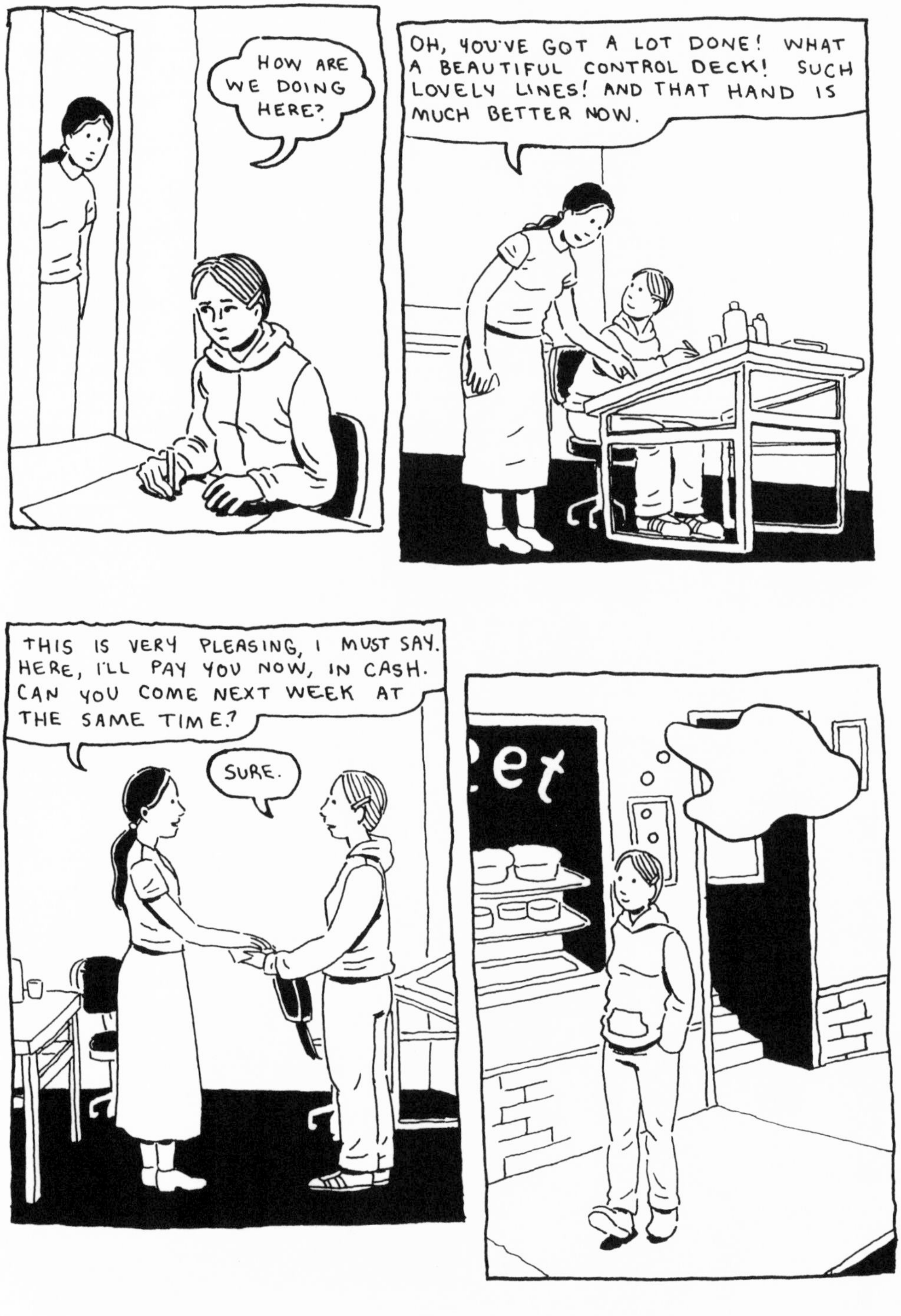
HOW ARE WE DOING HERE?
OH, YOU'VE GOT A LOT DONE! WHAT A BEAUTIFUL CONTROL DECK! SUCH LOVELY LINES! AND THAT HAND IS MUCH BETTER NOW.
THIS IS VERY PLEASING, I MUST SAY. HERE, I'LL PAY YOU NOW, IN CASH. CAN YOU COME NEXT WEEK AT THE SAME TIME?
SURE.

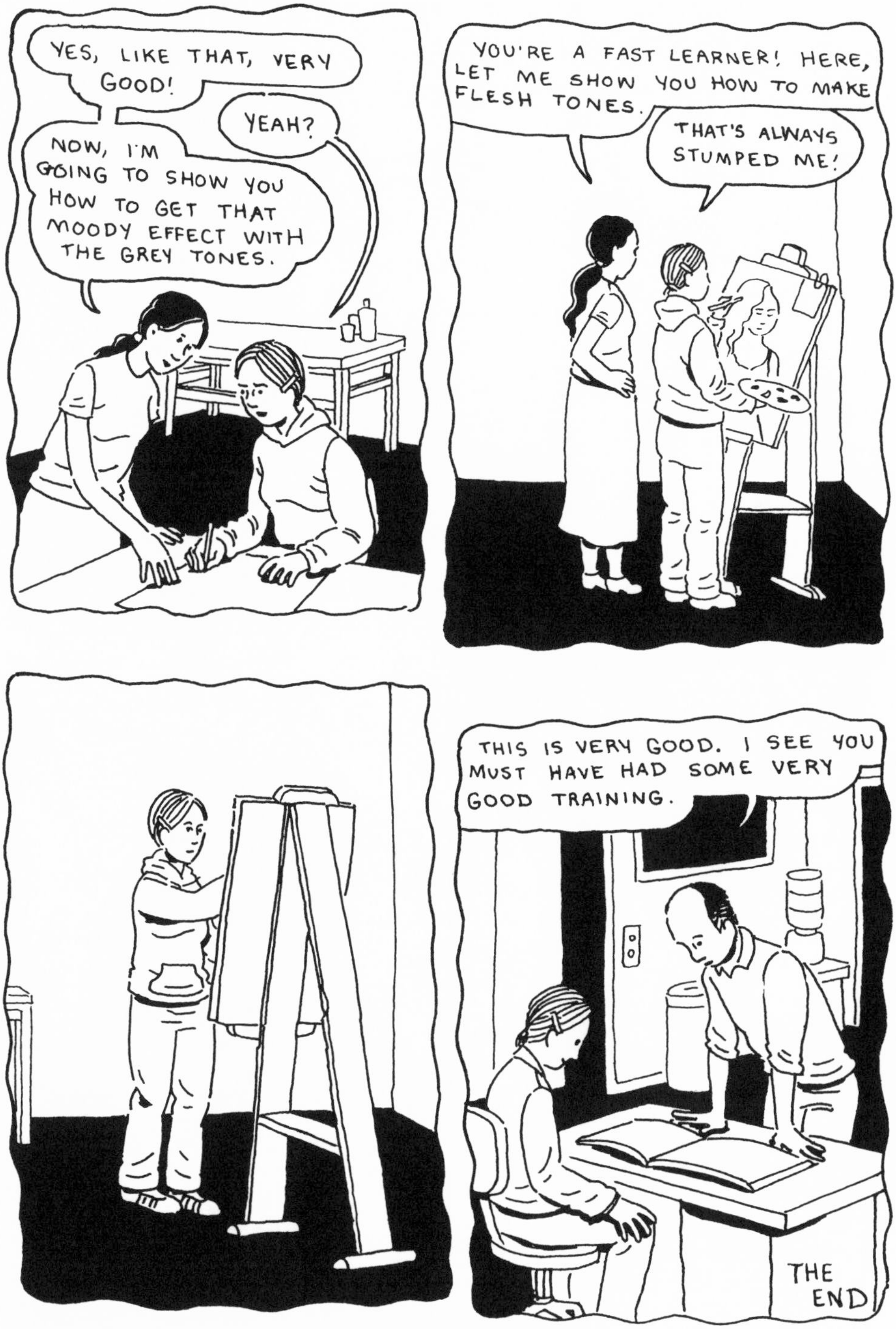
YES, LIKE THAT, VERY GOOD!
YEAH?
NOW, I'M GOING TO SHOW YOU HOW TO GET THAT MOODY EFFECT WITH THE GREY TONES.
YOU'RE A FAST LEARNER! HERE, LET ME SHOW YOU HOW TO MAKE FLESH TONES.
THAT'S ALWAYS STUMPED ME!
THIS IS VERY GOOD. I SEE YOU MUST HAVE HAD SOME VERY GOOD TRAINING.
THE END

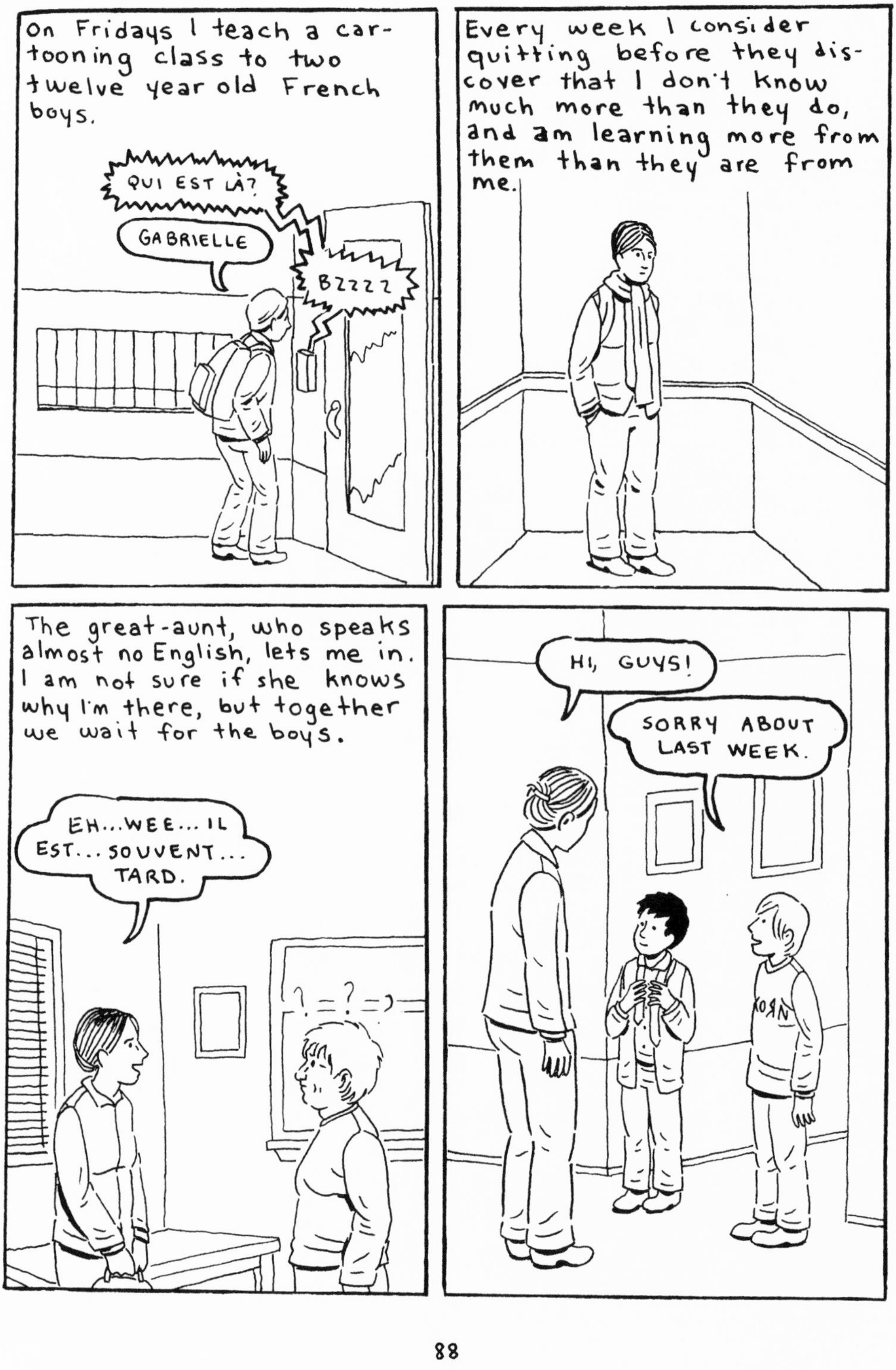

On Fridays I teach a cartooning class to two twelve year old French boys.
QUI EST LÀ?
GABRIELLE
BZZZZ
Every week I consider quitting before they discover that I don't know much more than they do, and am learning more from them than they are from me.
The great-aunt, who speaks almost no English, lets me in. I am not sure if she knows why I'm there, but together we wait for the boys.
EH...WEE...IL EST...SOUVENT...TARD.
? — ? — ?
HI, GUYS!
SORRY ABOUT LAST WEEK.
KORN

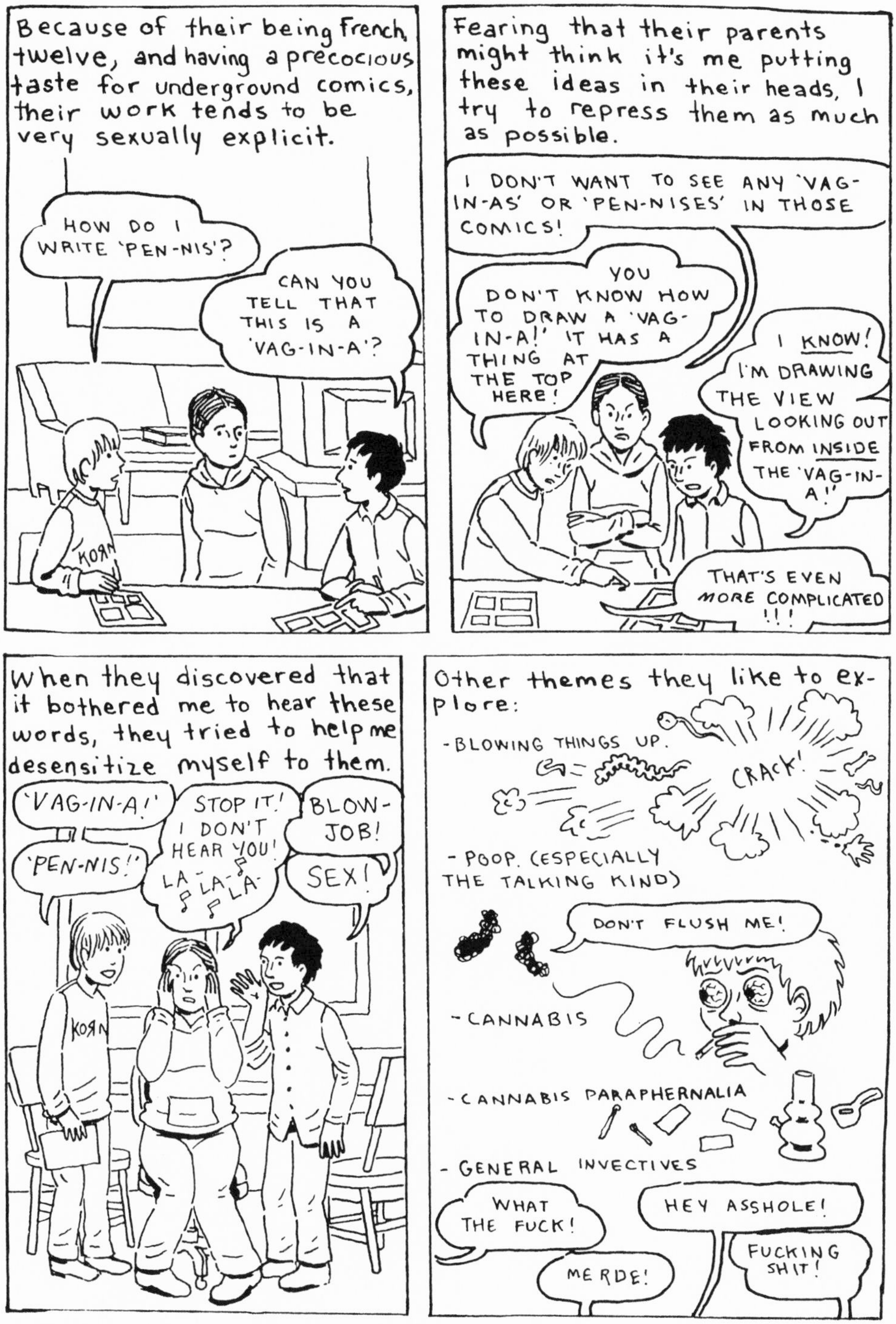
Because of their being French, twelve, and having a precocious taste for underground comics, their work tends to be very sexually explicit.
HOW DO I WRITE 'PEN-NIS'?
CAN YOU TELL THAT THIS IS A 'VAG-IN-A'?
KORN
Fearing that their parents might think it's me putting these ideas in their heads, I try to repress them as much as possible.
I DON'T WANT TO SEE ANY 'VAG-IN-AS' OR 'PEN-NISES' IN THOSE COMICS!
YOU DON'T KNOW HOW TO DRAW A 'VAG-IN-A!' IT HAS A THING AT THE TOP HERE!
I KNOW! I'M DRAWING THE VIEW LOOKING OUT FROM INSIDE THE 'VAG-IN-A!'
THAT'S EVEN MORE COMPLICATED!!!
When they discovered that it bothered me to hear these words, they tried to help me desensitize myself to them.
'VAG-IN-A!'
'PEN-NIS!'
STOP IT! I DON'T HEAR YOU! LA-LA-LA-
BLOW-JOB!
SEX!
KORN
Other themes they like to explore:
- BLOWING THINGS UP.
CRACK!
- POOP. (ESPECIALLY THE TALKING KIND)
DON'T FLUSH ME!
- CANNABIS
- CANNABIS PARAPHERNALIA
- GENERAL INVECTIVES
WHAT THE FUCK!
HEY ASSHOLE!
MERDE!
FUCKING SHIT!

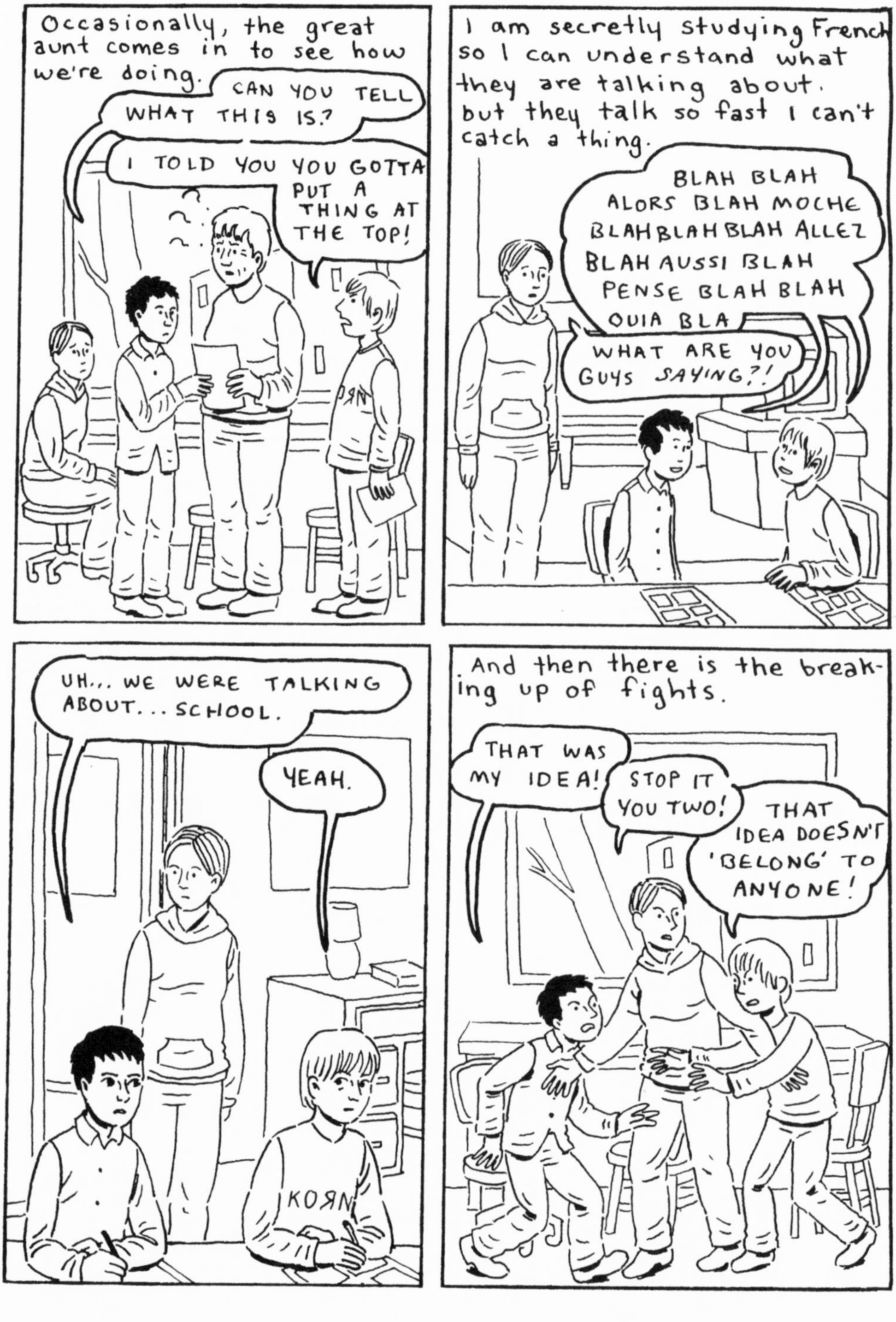
Occasionally, the great aunt comes in to see how we're doing.
CAN YOU TELL WHAT THIS IS?
I TOLD YOU YOU GOTTA PUT A THING AT THE TOP!
I am secretly studying French so I can understand what they are talking about. but they talk so fast I can't catch a thing.
BLAH BLAH ALORS BLAH MOCHE BLAHBLAHBLAH ALLEZ BLAH AUSSI BLAH PENSE BLAH BLAH OUIA BLA
WHAT ARE YOU GUYS SAYING?!
UH... WE WERE TALKING ABOUT... SCHOOL.
YEAH.
KORN
And then there is the breaking up of fights.
THAT WAS MY IDEA!
STOP IT YOU TWO!
THAT IDEA DOESN'T 'BELONG' TO ANYONE!

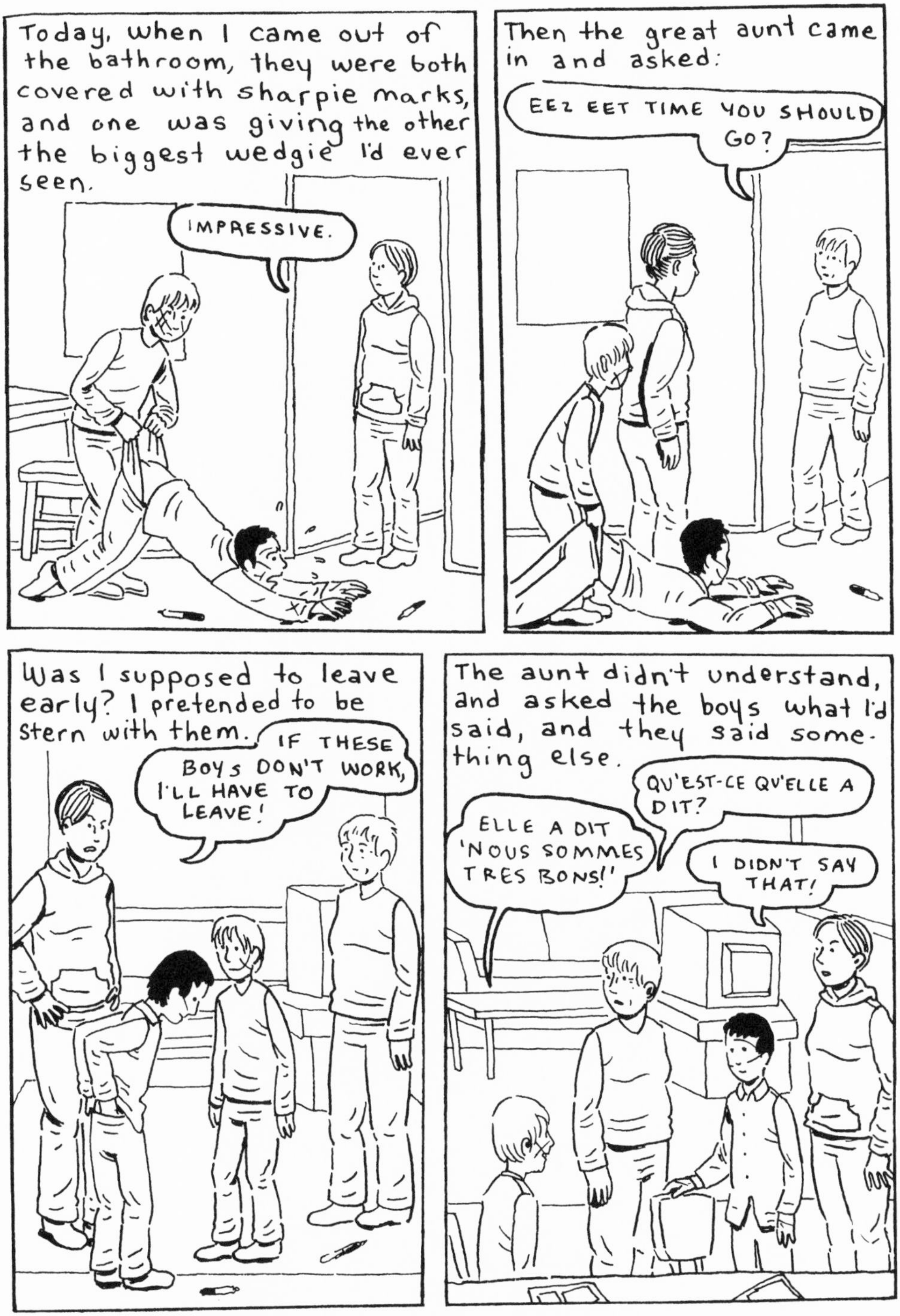
Today, when I came out of the bathroom, they were both covered with sharpie marks, and one was giving the other the biggest wedgie I'd ever seen.
IMPRESSIVE.
Then the great aunt came in and asked:
EEZ EET TIME YOU SHOULD GO?
Was I supposed to leave early? I pretended to be stern with them.
IF THESE BOYS DON'T WORK, I'LL HAVE TO LEAVE!
The aunt didn't understand, and asked the boys what I'd said, and they said something else.
QU'EST-CE QU'ELLE A DIT?
ELLE A DIT 'NOUS SOMMES TRES BONS!'
I DIDN'T SAY THAT!

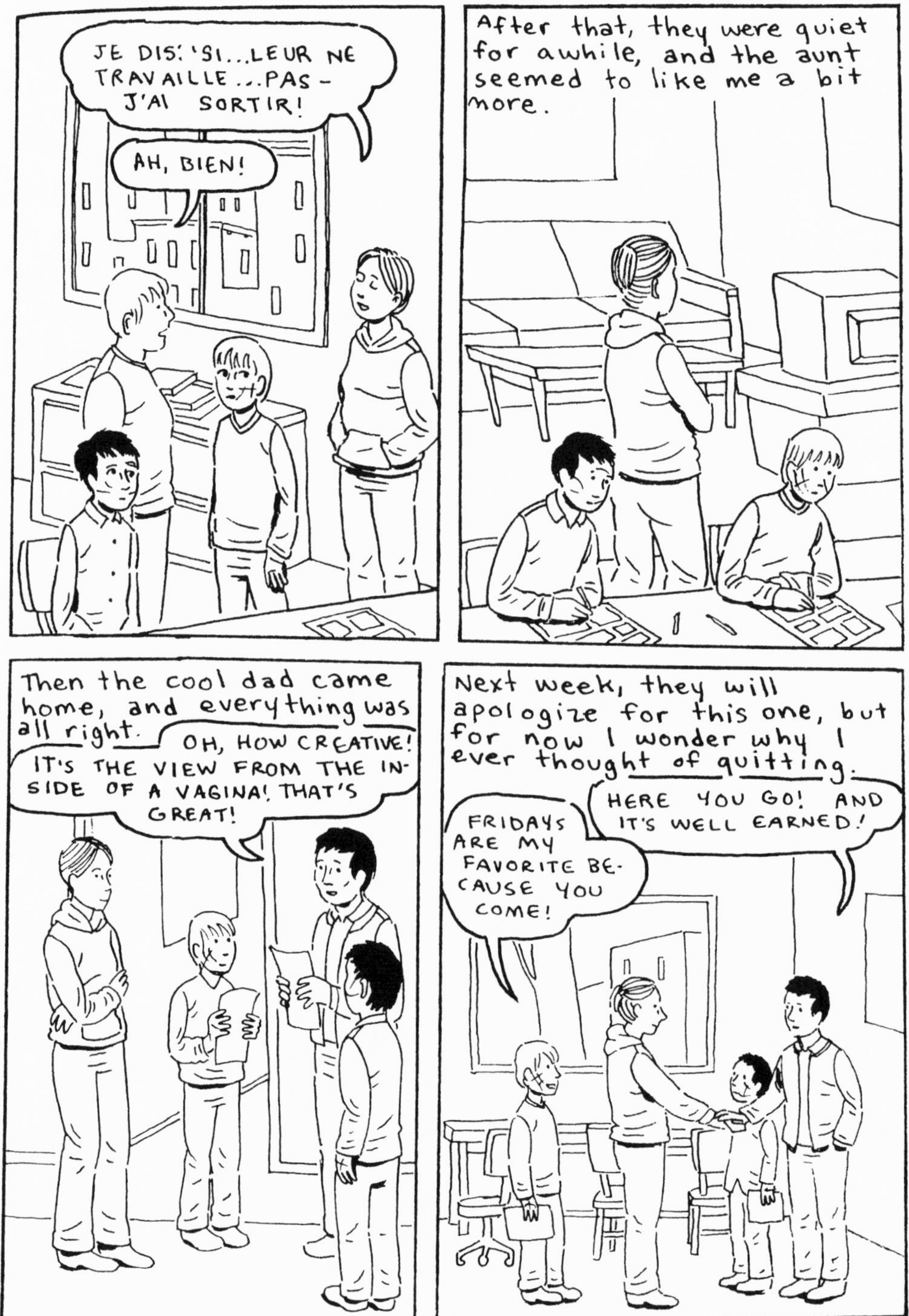
JE DIS: 'SI... LEUR NE TRAVAILLE... PAS - J'AI SORTIR!
AH, BIEN!
After that, they were quiet for awhile, and the aunt seemed to like me a bit more.
Then the cool dad came home, and everything was all right.
OH, HOW CREATIVE! IT'S THE VIEW FROM THE INSIDE OF A VAGINA! THAT'S GREAT!
Next week, they will apologize for this one, but for now I wonder why I ever thought of quitting.
HERE YOU GO! AND IT'S WELL EARNED!
FRIDAYS ARE MY FAVORITE BECAUSE YOU COME!

THE END

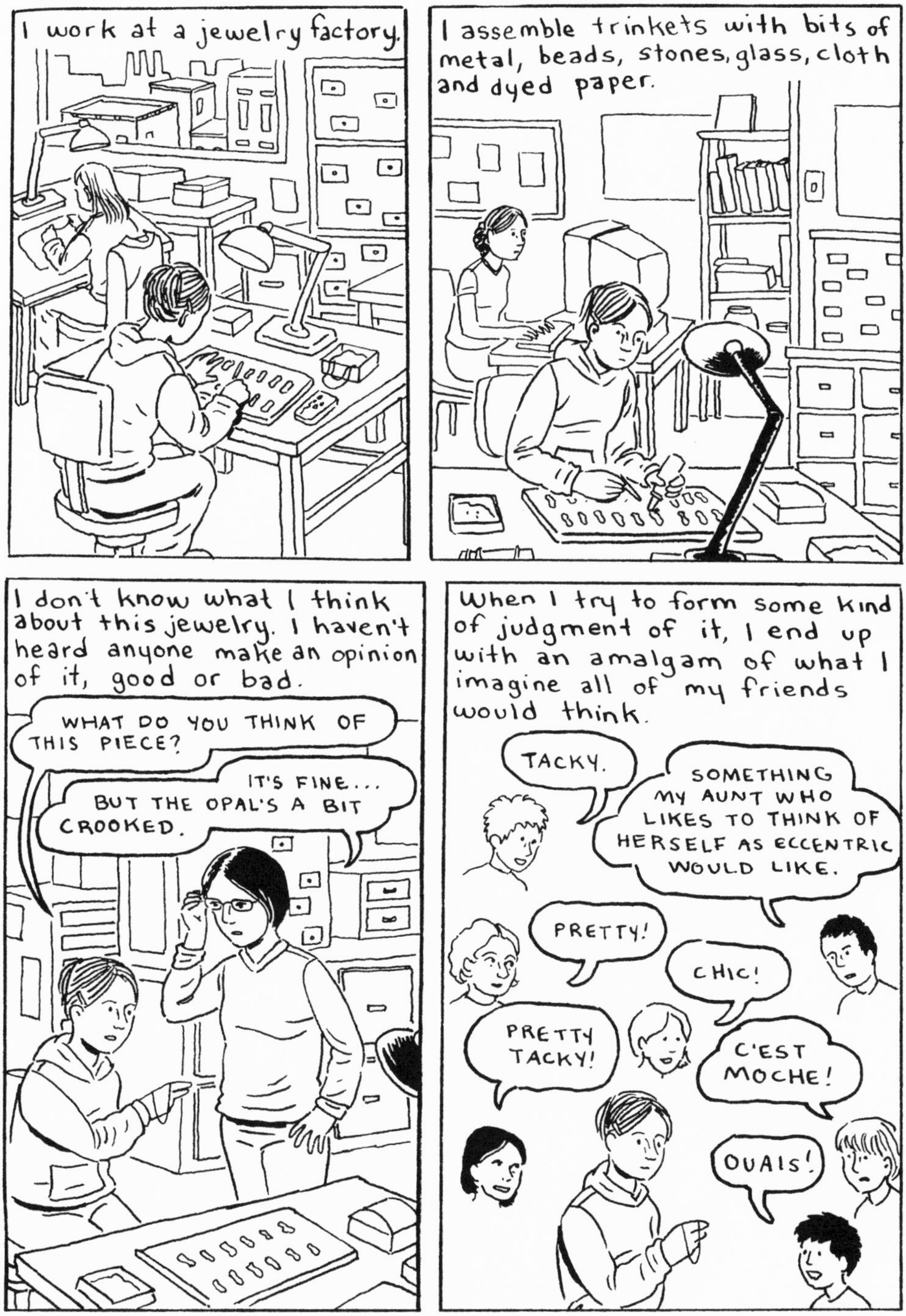
I work at a jewelry factory.
I assemble trinkets with bits of metal, beads, stones, glass, cloth and dyed paper.
I don't know what I think about this jewelry. I haven't heard anyone make an opinion of it, good or bad.
WHAT DO YOU THINK OF THIS PIECE?
IT'S FINE... BUT THE OPAL'S A BIT CROOKED.
When I try to form some kind of judgment of it, I end up with an amalgam of what I imagine all of my friends would think.
TACKY.
SOMETHING MY AUNT WHO LIKES TO THINK OF HERSELF AS ECCENTRIC WOULD LIKE.
PRETTY!
CHIC!
PRETTY TACKY!
C'EST MOCHE!
OUAIS!

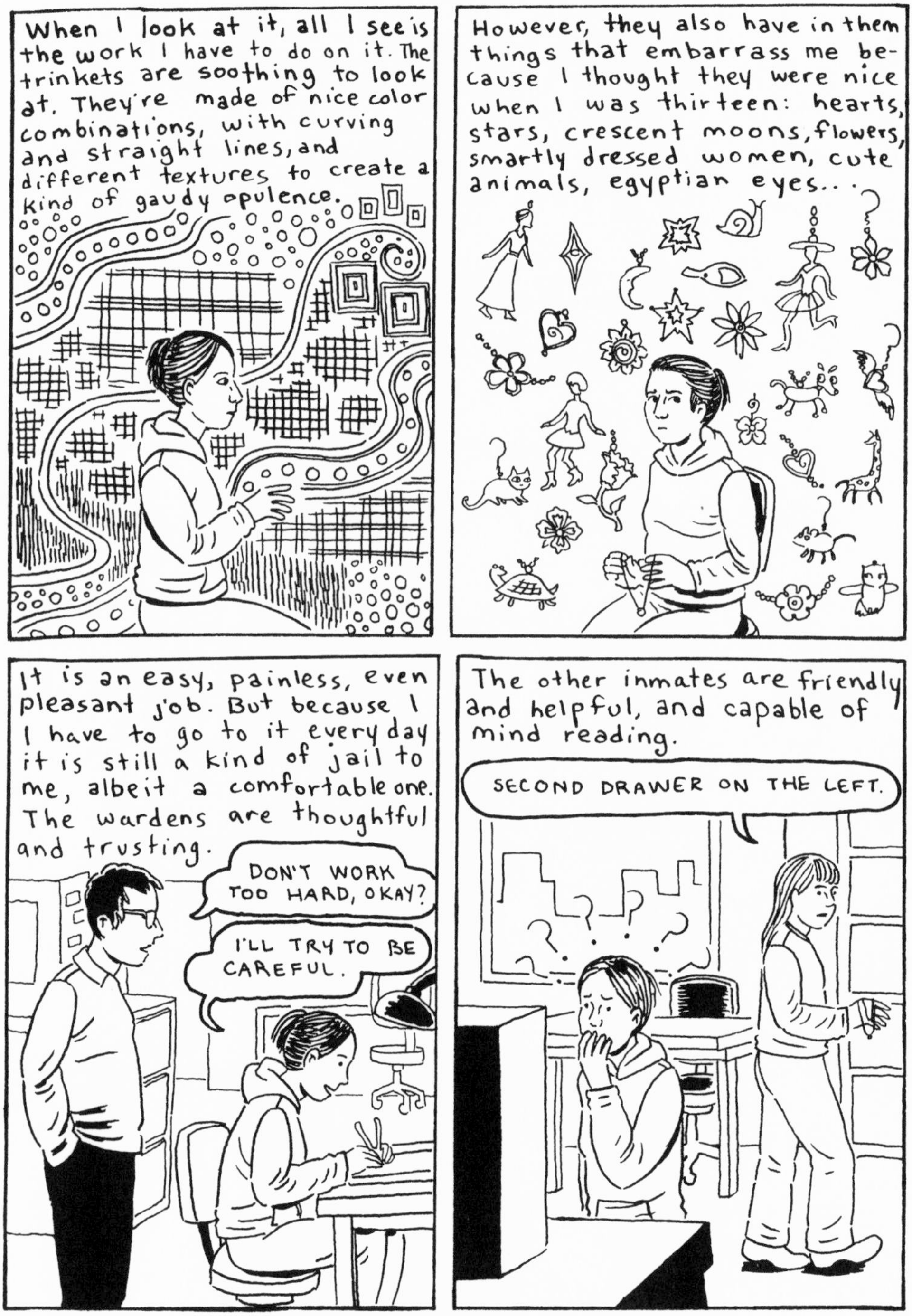
When I look at it, all I see is the work I have to do on it. The trinkets are soothing to look at. They're made of nice color combinations, with curving and straight lines, and different textures to create a kind of gaudy opulence.
However, they also have in them things that embarrass me because I thought they were nice when I was thirteen: hearts, stars, crescent moons, flowers, smartly dressed women, cute animals, egyptian eyes...
It is an easy, painless, even pleasant job. But because I I have to go to it every day it is still a kind of jail to me, albeit a comfortable one. The wardens are thoughtful and trusting.
DON'T WORK TOO HARD, OKAY?
I'LL TRY TO BE CAREFUL.
The other inmates are friendly and helpful, and capable of mind reading.
SECOND DRAWER ON THE LEFT.

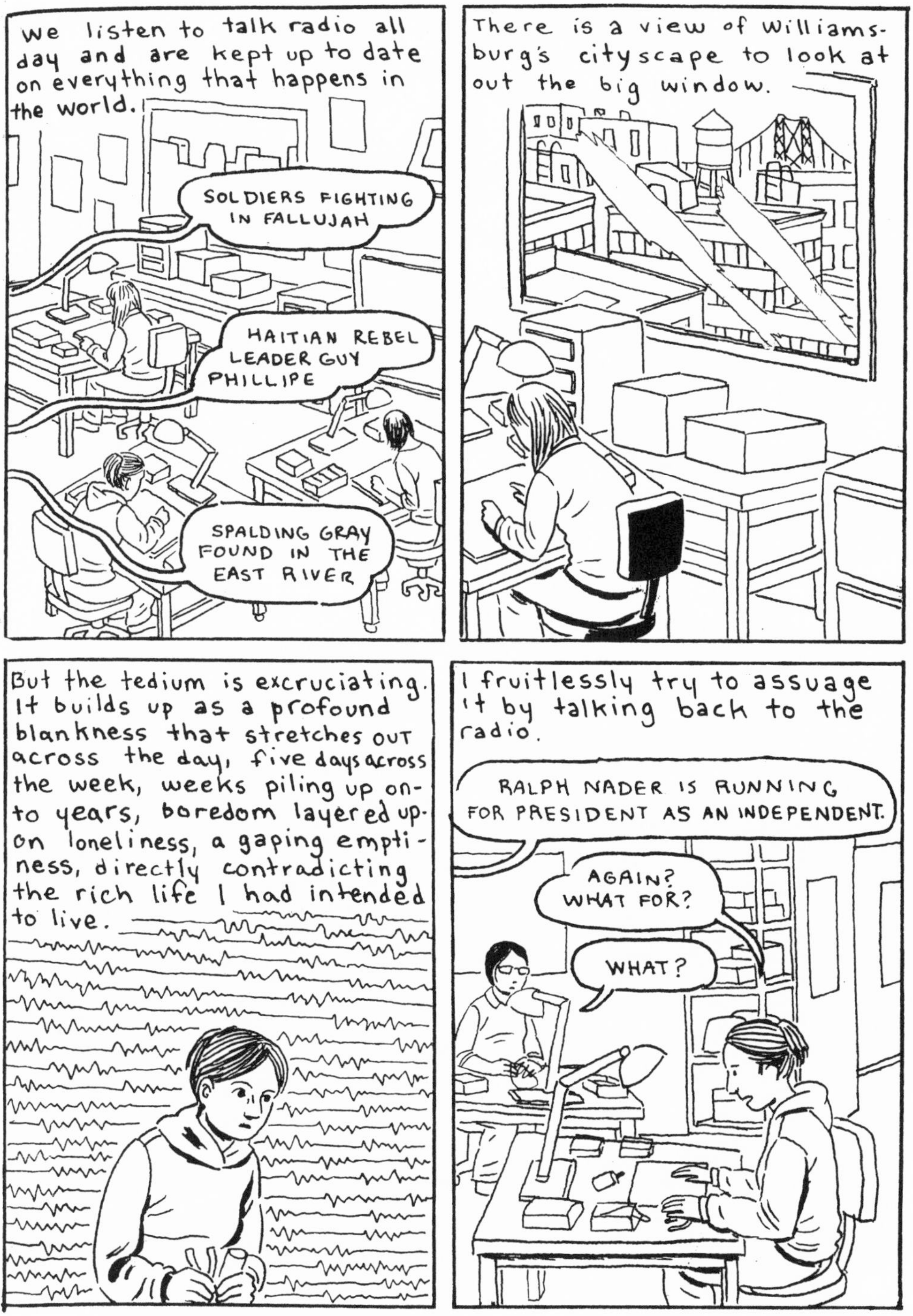
We listen to talk radio all day and are kept up to date on everything that happens in the world.
SOLDIERS FIGHTING IN FALLUJAH
HAITIAN REBEL LEADER GUY PHILLIPE
SPALDING GRAY FOUND IN THE EAST RIVER
There is a view of Williamsburg's cityscape to look at out the big window.
But the tedium is excruciating. It builds up as a profound blankness that stretches out across the day, five days across the week, weeks piling up onto years, boredom layered upon loneliness, a gaping emptiness, directly contradicting the rich life I had intended to live.
I fruitlessly try to assuage it by talking back to the radio.
RALPH NADER IS RUNNING FOR PRESIDENT AS AN INDEPENDENT.
AGAIN? WHAT FOR?
WHAT?

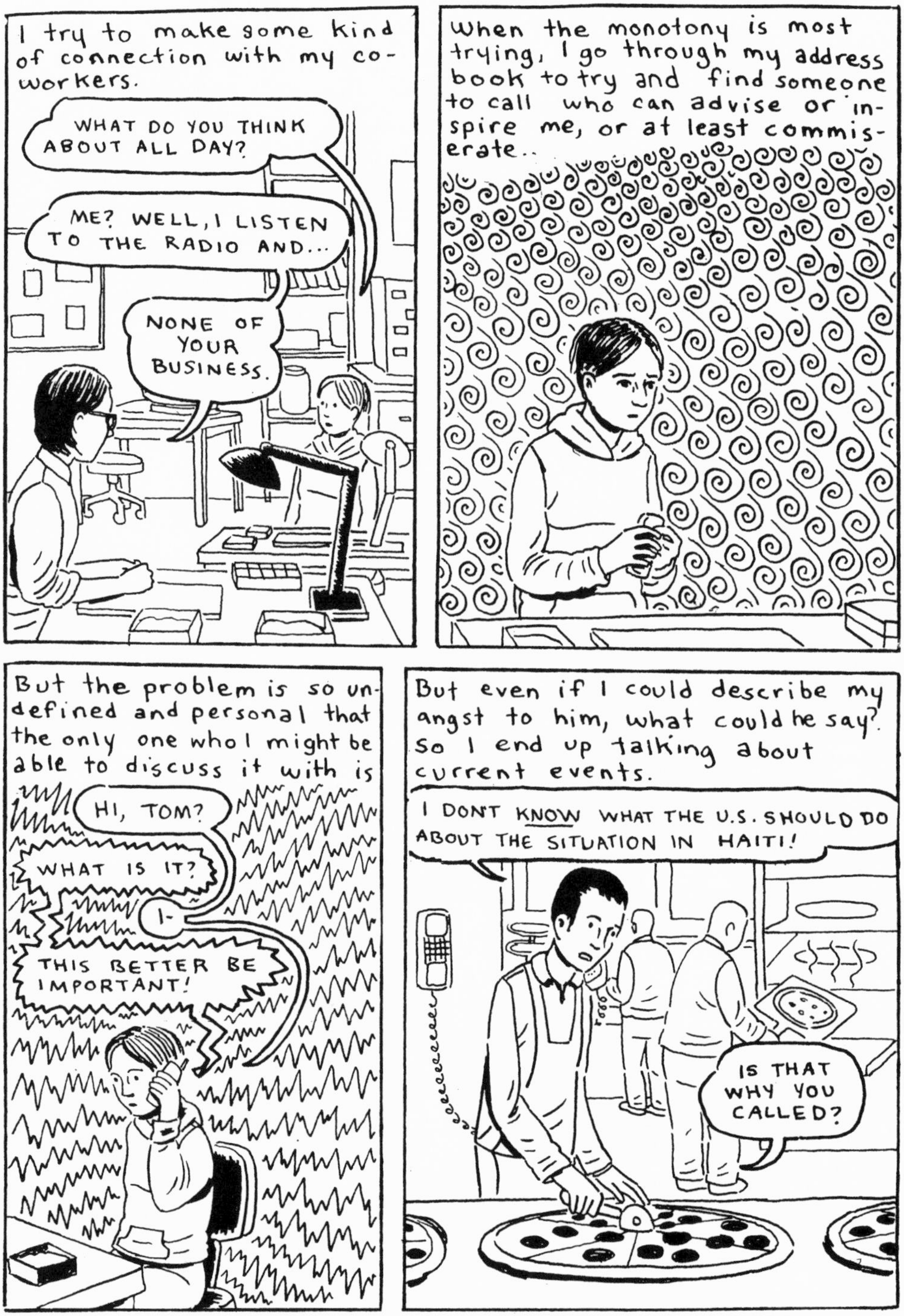
I try to make some kind of connection with my co-workers.
WHAT DO YOU THINK ABOUT ALL DAY?
ME? WELL, I LISTEN TO THE RADIO AND...
NONE OF YOUR BUSINESS.
When the monotony is most trying, I go through my address book to try and find someone to call who can advise or inspire me, or at least commiserate..
But the problem is so undefined and personal that the only one who I might be able to discuss it with is
HI, TOM?
WHAT IS IT?
I-
THIS BETTER BE IMPORTANT!
But even if I could describe my angst to him, what could he say? So I end up talking about current events.
I DON'T KNOW WHAT THE U.S. SHOULD DO ABOUT THE SITUATION IN HAITI!
IS THAT WHY YOU CALLED?

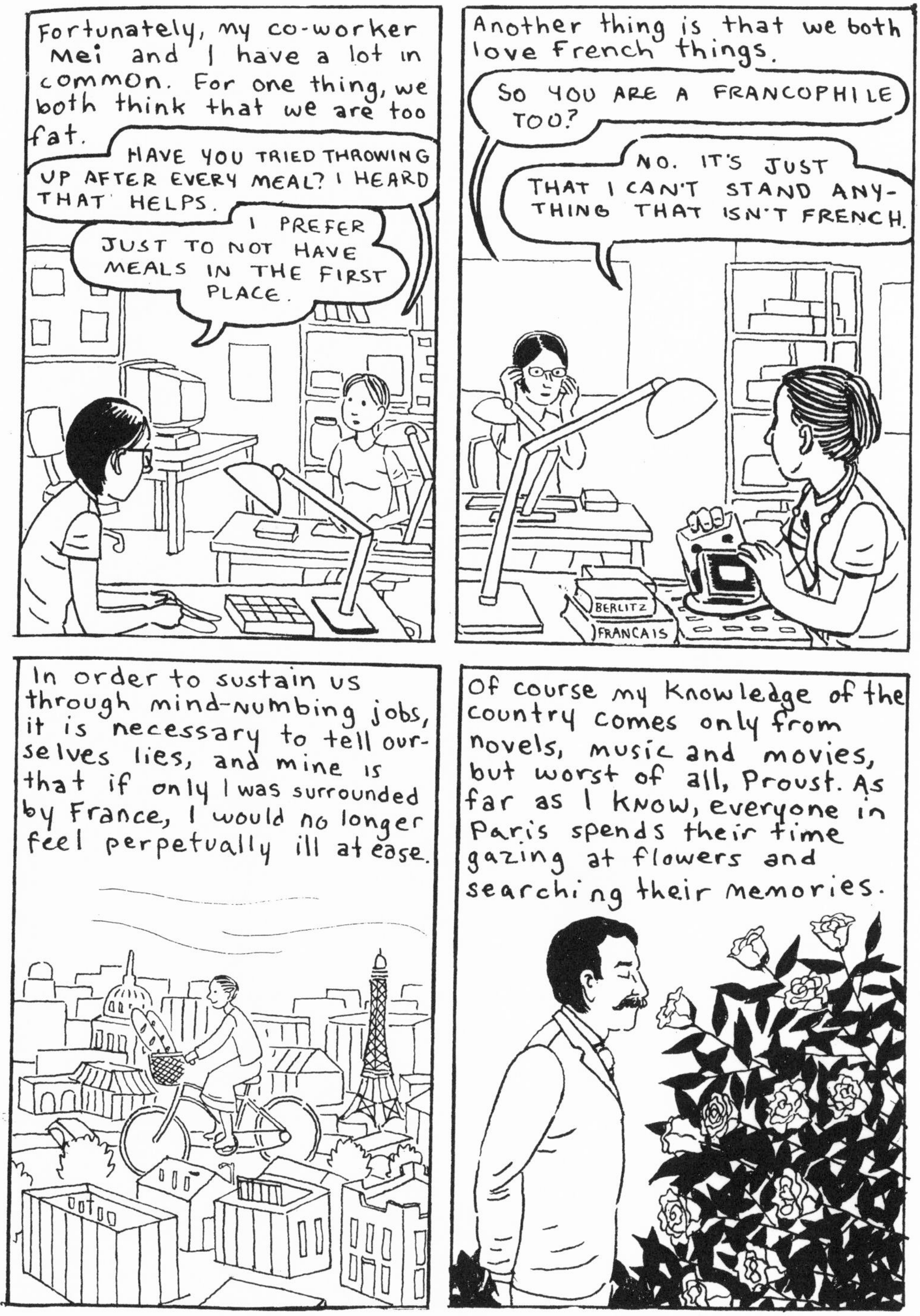
Fortunately, my co-worker Mei and I have a lot in common. For one thing, we both think that we are too fat.
HAVE YOU TRIED THROWING UP AFTER EVERY MEAL? I HEARD THAT HELPS.
I PREFER JUST TO NOT HAVE MEALS IN THE FIRST PLACE.
Another thing is that we both love French things.
SO YOU ARE A FRANCOPHILE TOO?
NO. IT'S JUST THAT I CAN'T STAND ANYTHING THAT ISN'T FRENCH.
BERLITZ
FRANCAIS
In order to sustain us through mind-numbing jobs, it is necessary to tell ourselves lies, and mine is that if only I was surrounded by France, I would no longer feel perpetually ill at ease.
Of course my knowledge of the country comes only from novels, music and movies, but worst of all, Proust. As far as I know, everyone in Paris spends their time gazing at flowers and searching their memories.

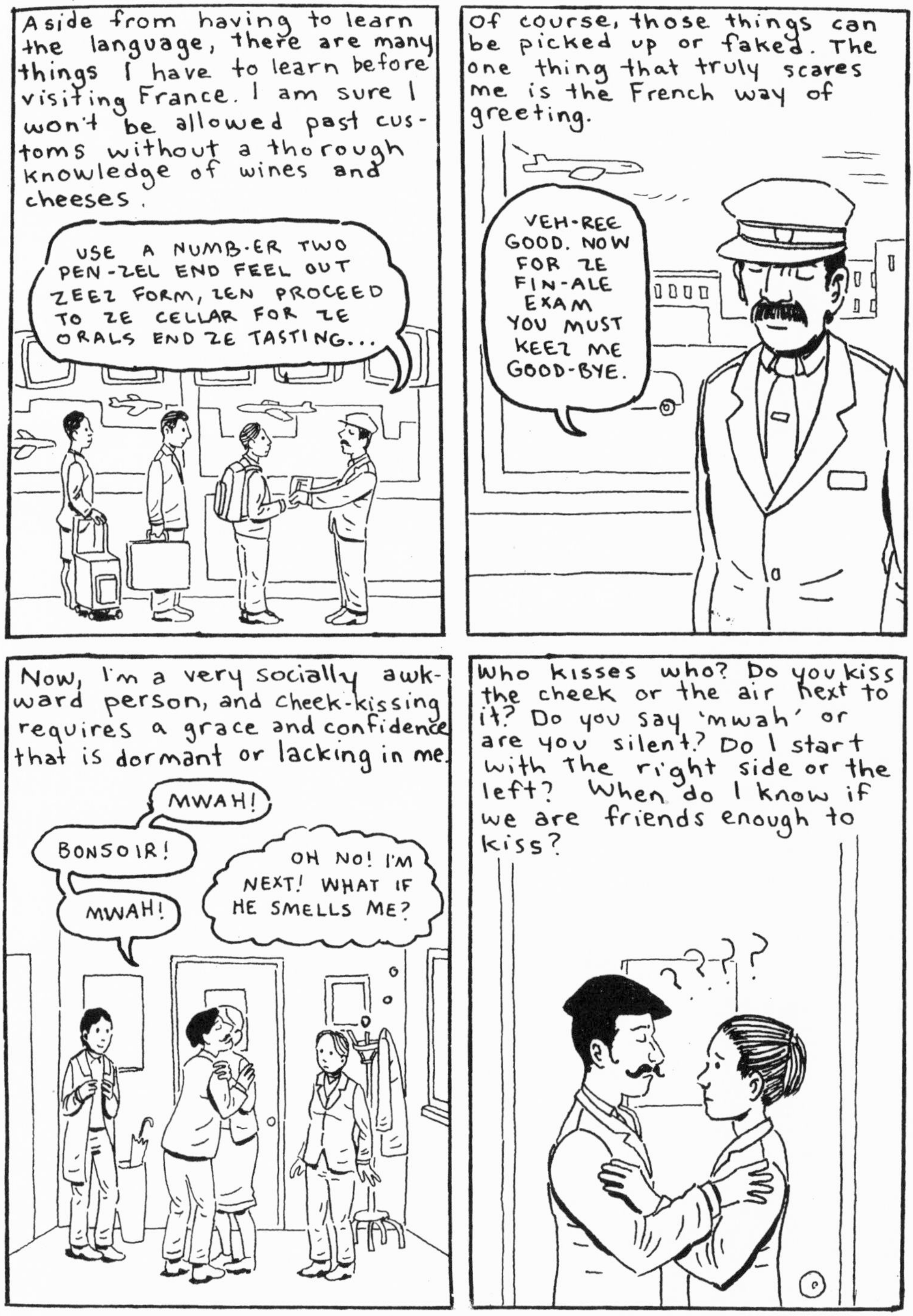
Aside from having to learn the language, there are many things I have to learn before visiting France. I am sure I won't be allowed past customs without a thorough knowledge of wines and cheeses.
USE A NUMB-ER TWO PEN-ZEL END FEEL OUT ZEEZ FORM, ZEN PROCEED TO ZE CELLAR FOR ZE ORALS END ZE TASTING...
Of course, those things can be picked up or faked. The one thing that truly scares me is the French way of greeting.
VEH-REE GOOD. NOW FOR ZE FIN-ALE EXAM YOU MUST KEEZ ME GOOD-BYE.
Now, I'm a very socially awkward person, and cheek-kissing requires a grace and confidence that is dormant or lacking in me.
MWAH!
BONSOIR!
MWAH!
OH NO! I'M NEXT! WHAT IF HE SMELLS ME?
Who kisses who? Do you kiss the cheek or the air next to it? Do you say 'mwah' or are you silent? Do I start with the right side or the left? When do I know if we are friends enough to kiss?
? ? ? ?

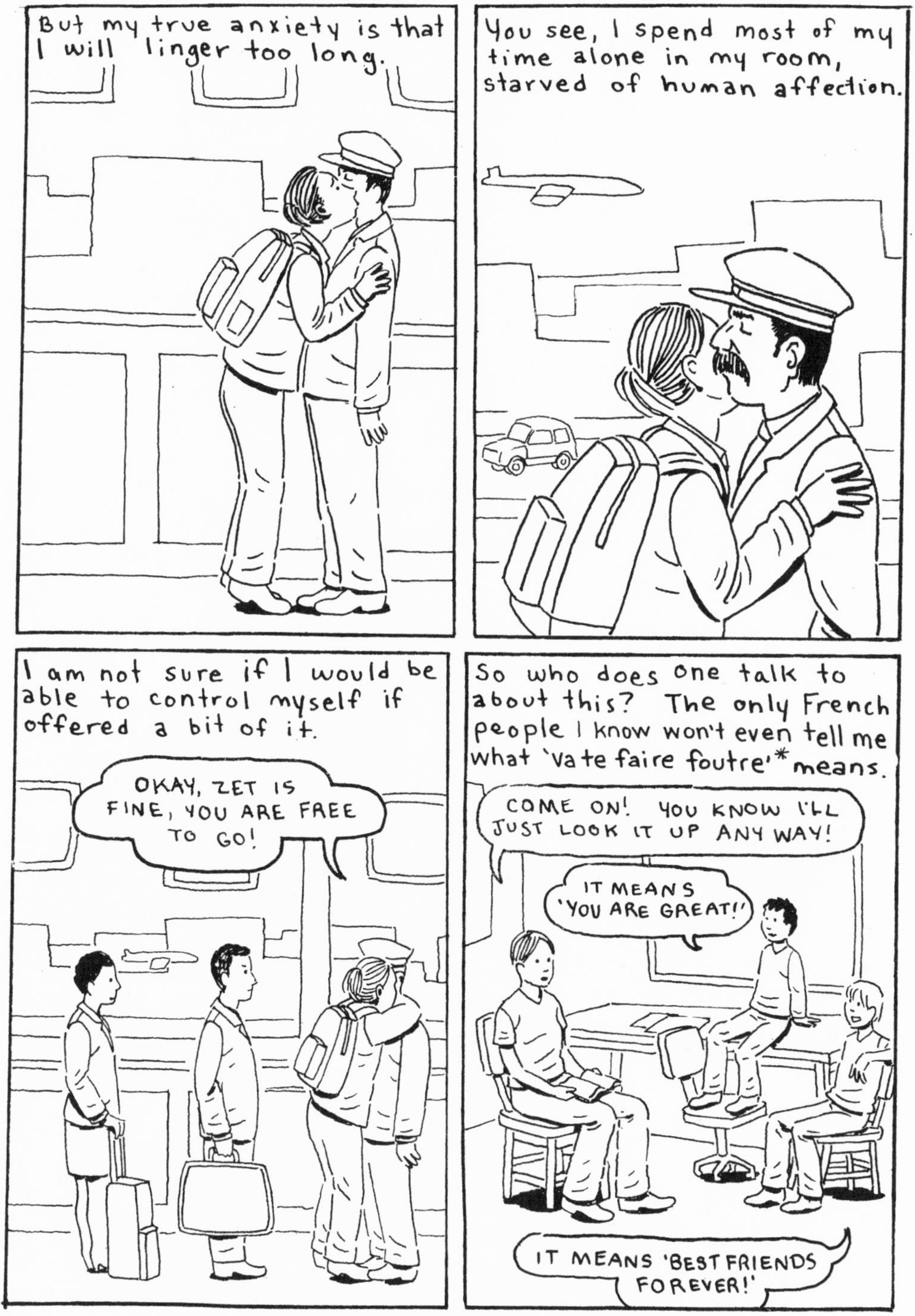
But my true anxiety is that I will linger too long.
You see, I spend most of my time alone in my room, starved of human affection.
I am not sure if I would be able to control myself if offered a bit of it.
OKAY, ZET IS FINE, YOU ARE FREE TO GO!
So who does one talk to about this? The only French people I know won't even tell me what 'va te faire foutre'* means.
COME ON! YOU KNOW I'LL JUST LOOK IT UP ANY WAY!
IT MEANS 'YOU ARE GREAT!'
IT MEANS 'BEST FRIENDS FOREVER!'

* IT MEANS, ROUGHLY, 'FUCK OFF'

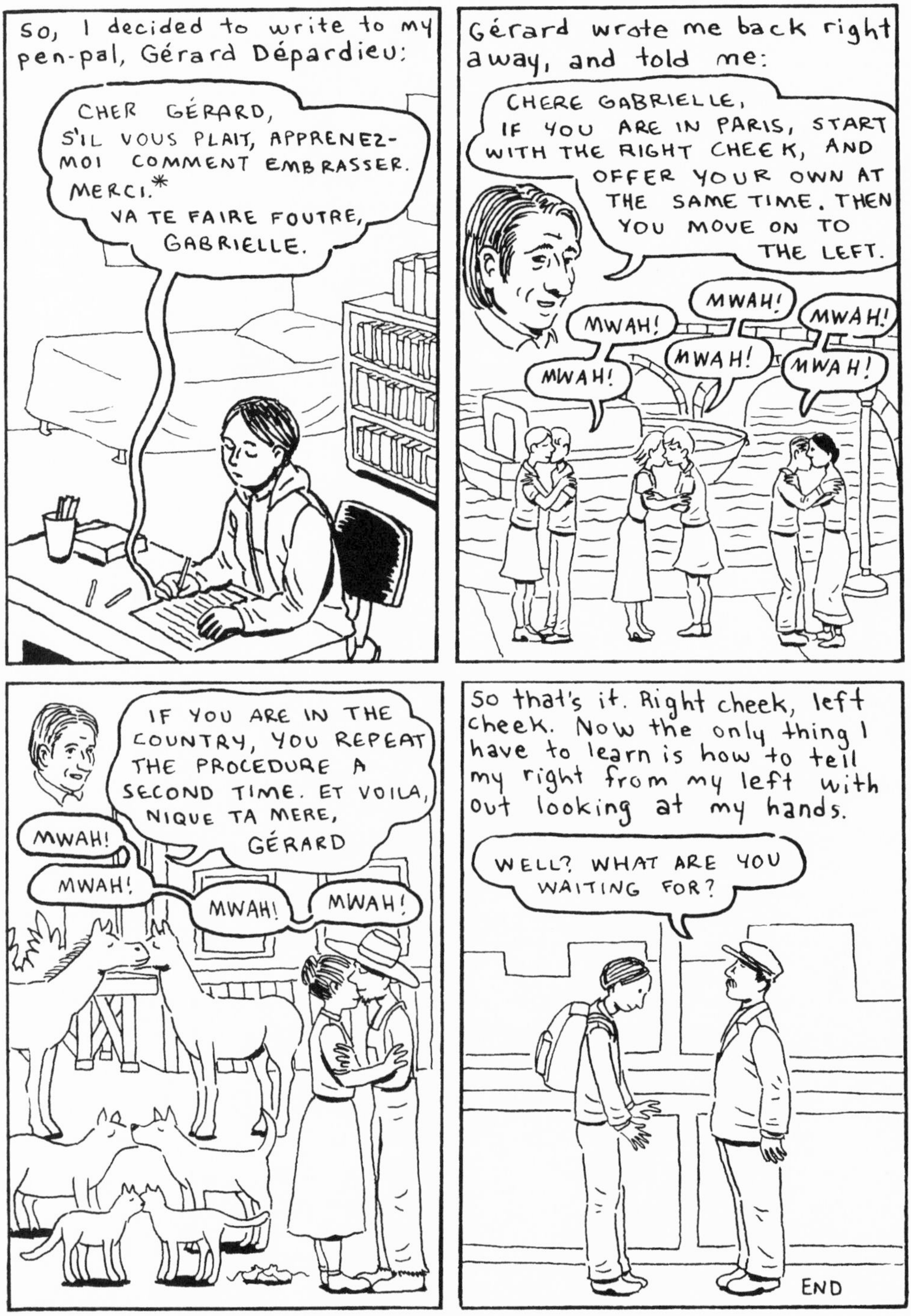
So, I decided to write to my pen-pal, Gérard Dépardieu:
CHER GÉRARD, S'IL VOUS PLAIT, APPRENEZ-MOI COMMENT EMBRASSER. MERCI.* VA TE FAIRE FOUTRE, GABRIELLE.
Gérard wrote me back right away, and told me:
CHERE GABRIELLE, IF YOU ARE IN PARIS, START WITH THE RIGHT CHEEK, AND OFFER YOUR OWN AT THE SAME TIME. THEN YOU MOVE ON TO THE LEFT.
MWAH!
MWAH!
MWAH!
MWAH!
MWAH!
MWAH!
IF YOU ARE IN THE COUNTRY, YOU REPEAT THE PROCEDURE A SECOND TIME. ET VOILA, NIQUE TA MERE, GÉRARD
MWAH!
MWAH!
MWAH!
MWAH!
So that's it. Right cheek, left cheek. Now the only thing I have to learn is how to tell my right from my left with out looking at my hands.
WELL? WHAT ARE YOU WAITING FOR?
END

* PLEASE TEACH ME HOW TO KISS.

Extra Stories

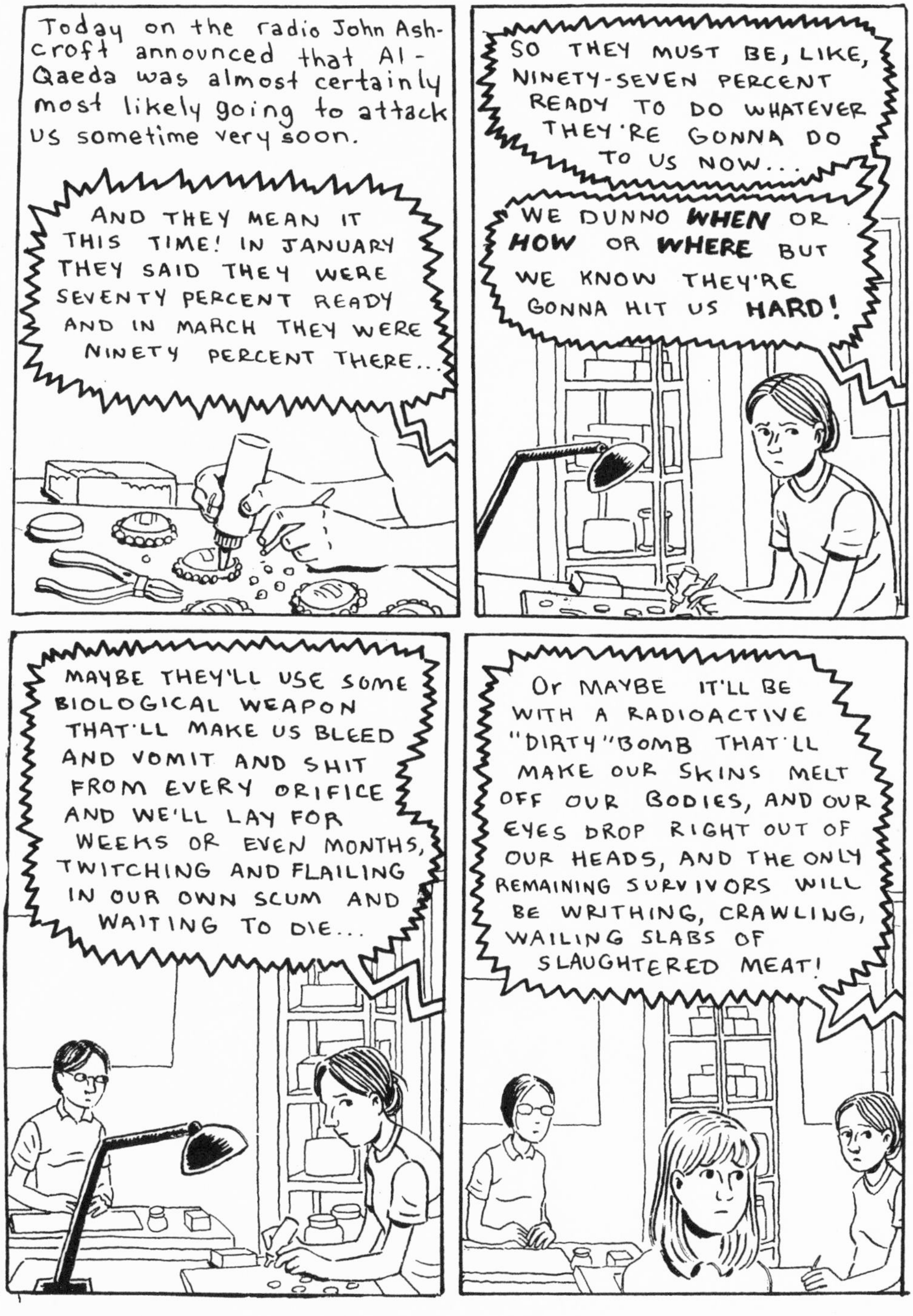
Today on the radio John Ashcroft announced that Al-Qaeda was almost certainly most likely going to attack us sometime very soon.
AND THEY MEAN IT THIS TIME! IN JANUARY THEY SAID THEY WERE SEVENTY PERCENT READY AND IN MARCH THEY WERE NINETY PERCENT THERE...
SO THEY MUST BE, LIKE, NINETY-SEVEN PERCENT READY TO DO WHATEVER THEY'RE GONNA DO TO US NOW...
WE DUNNO **WHEN** OR **HOW** OR **WHERE** BUT WE KNOW THEY'RE GONNA HIT US **HARD**!
MAYBE THEY'LL USE SOME BIOLOGICAL WEAPON THAT'LL MAKE US BLEED AND VOMIT AND SHIT FROM EVERY ORIFICE AND WE'LL LAY FOR WEEKS OR EVEN MONTHS, TWITCHING AND FLAILING IN OUR OWN SCUM AND WAITING TO DIE...
Or MAYBE IT'LL BE WITH A RADIOACTIVE "DIRTY" BOMB THAT'LL MAKE OUR SKINS MELT OFF OUR BODIES, AND OUR EYES DROP RIGHT OUT OF OUR HEADS, AND THE ONLY REMAINING SURVIVORS WILL BE WRITHING, CRAWLING, WAILING SLABS OF SLAUGHTERED MEAT!

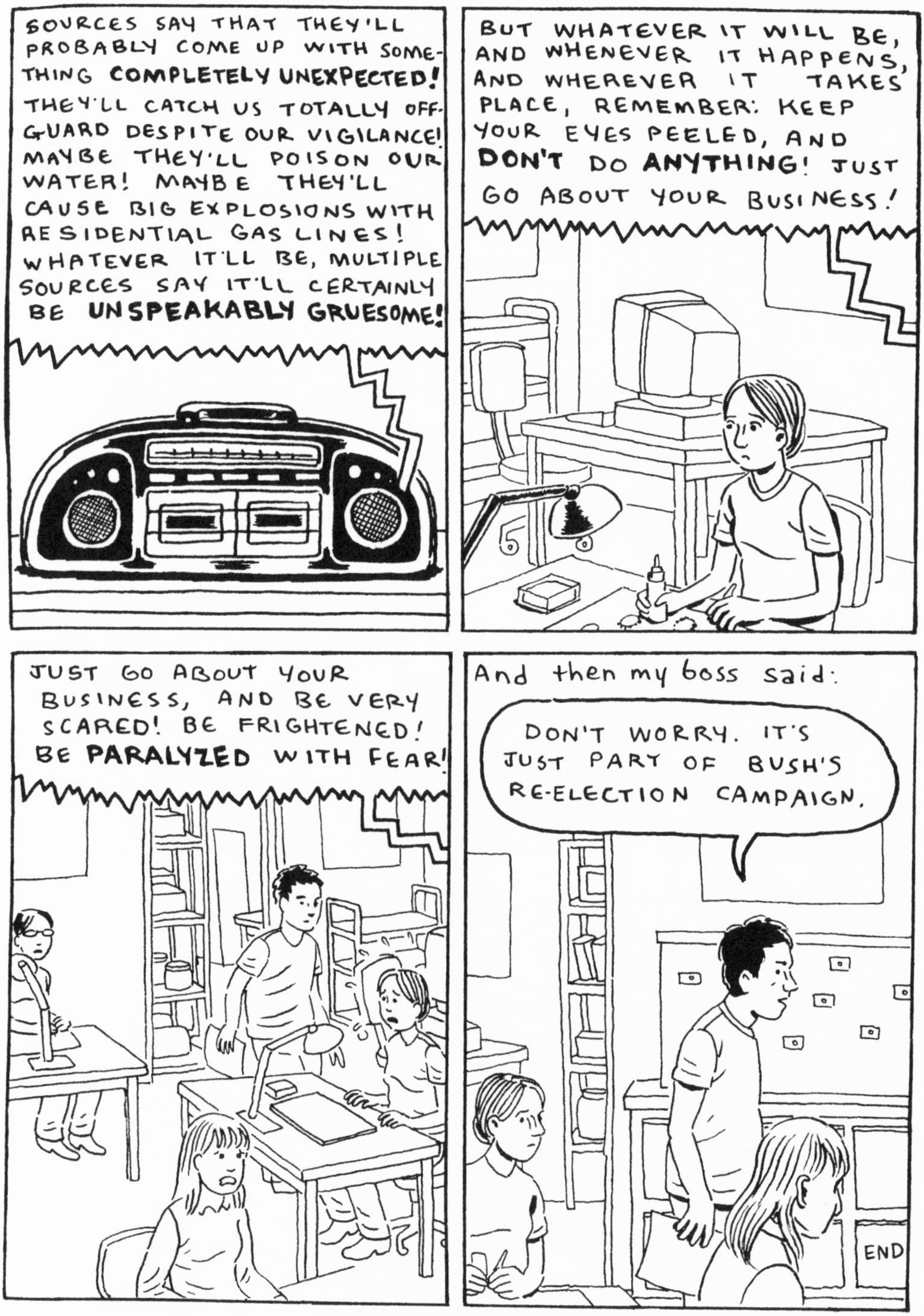
SOURCES SAY THAT THEY'LL PROBABLY COME UP WITH SOMETHING COMPLETELY UNEXPECTED! THEY'LL CATCH US TOTALLY OFF-GUARD DESPITE OUR VIGILANCE! MAYBE THEY'LL POISON OUR WATER! MAYBE THEY'LL CAUSE BIG EXPLOSIONS WITH RESIDENTIAL GAS LINES! WHATEVER IT'LL BE, MULTIPLE SOURCES SAY IT'LL CERTAINLY BE UNSPEAKABLY GRUESOME!
BUT WHATEVER IT WILL BE, AND WHENEVER IT HAPPENS, AND WHEREVER IT TAKES PLACE, REMEMBER: KEEP YOUR EYES PEELED, AND DON'T DO ANYTHING! JUST GO ABOUT YOUR BUSINESS!
JUST GO ABOUT YOUR BUSINESS, AND BE VERY SCARED! BE FRIGHTENED! BE PARALYZED WITH FEAR!
And then my boss said:
DON'T WORRY. IT'S JUST PART OF BUSH'S RE-ELECTION CAMPAIGN.
END

MOM

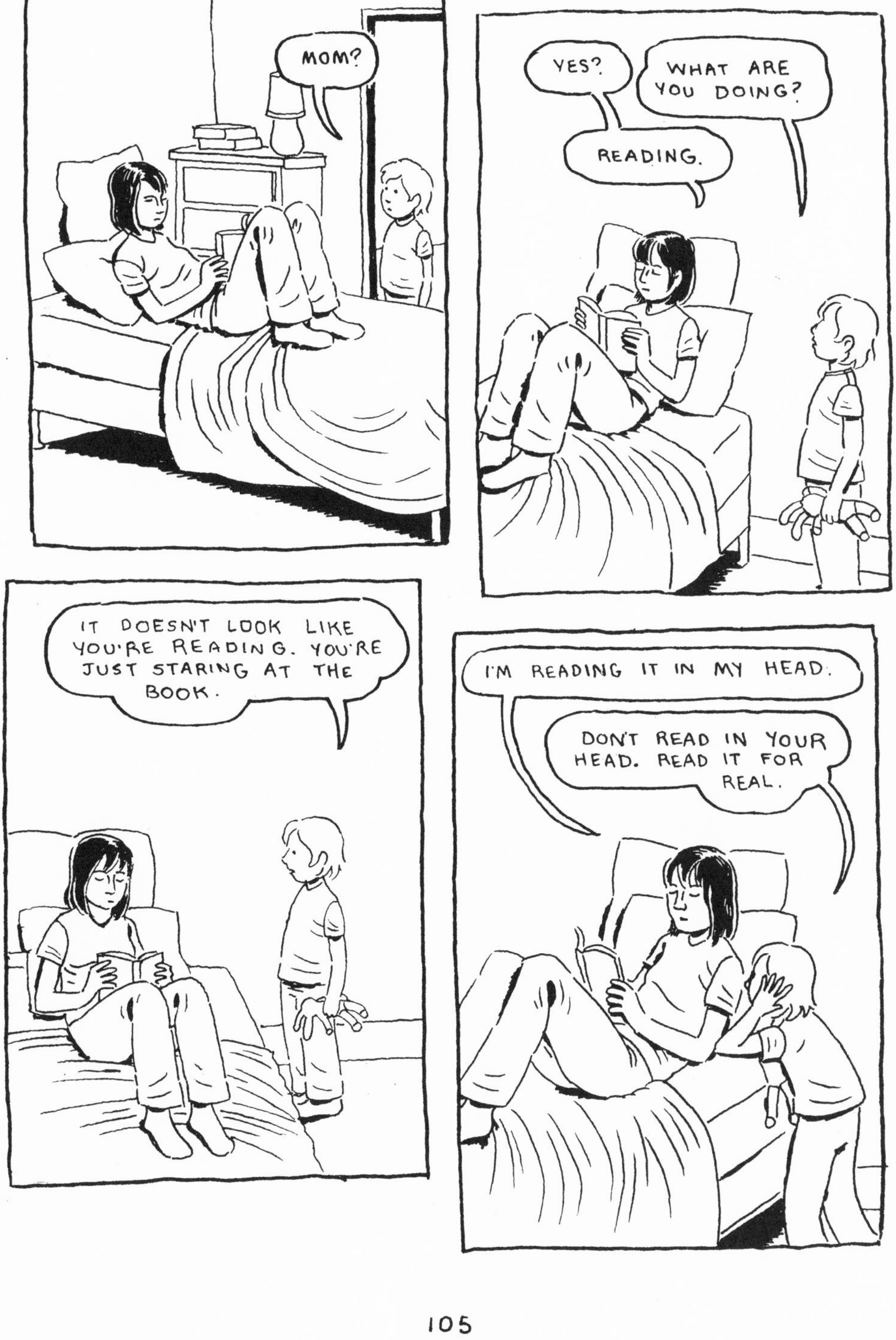

MOM?
YES?
WHAT ARE YOU DOING?
READING.
IT DOESN'T LOOK LIKE YOU'RE READING. YOU'RE JUST STARING AT THE BOOK.
I'M READING IT IN MY HEAD.
DON'T READ IN YOUR HEAD. READ IT FOR REAL.

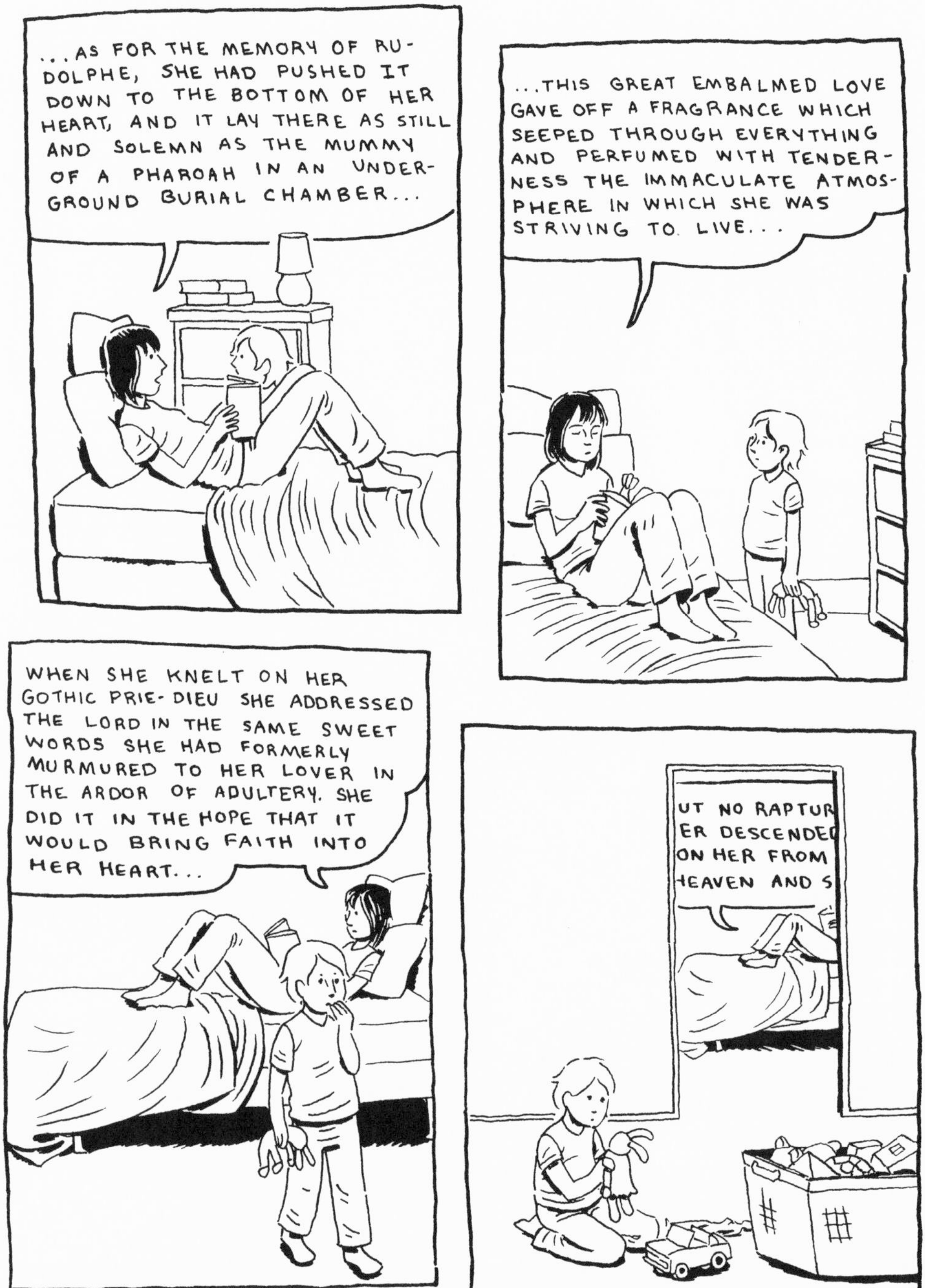
...AS FOR THE MEMORY OF RUDOLPHE, SHE HAD PUSHED IT DOWN TO THE BOTTOM OF HER HEART, AND IT LAY THERE AS STILL AND SOLEMN AS THE MUMMY OF A PHAROAH IN AN UNDERGROUND BURIAL CHAMBER...
...THIS GREAT EMBALMED LOVE GAVE OFF A FRAGRANCE WHICH SEEPED THROUGH EVERYTHING AND PERFUMED WITH TENDERNESS THE IMMACULATE ATMOSPHERE IN WHICH SHE WAS STRIVING TO LIVE...
WHEN SHE KNELT ON HER GOTHIC PRIE-DIEU SHE ADDRESSED THE LORD IN THE SAME SWEET WORDS SHE HAD FORMERLY MURMURED TO HER LOVER IN THE ARDOR OF ADULTERY. SHE DID IT IN THE HOPE THAT IT WOULD BRING FAITH INTO HER HEART...
UT NO RAPTUR ER DESCENDE ON HER FROM HEAVEN AND S

THE END

FAUX PAS AT THE BANK

# SADIE'S STORY BY SADIE AND GABRIELLE

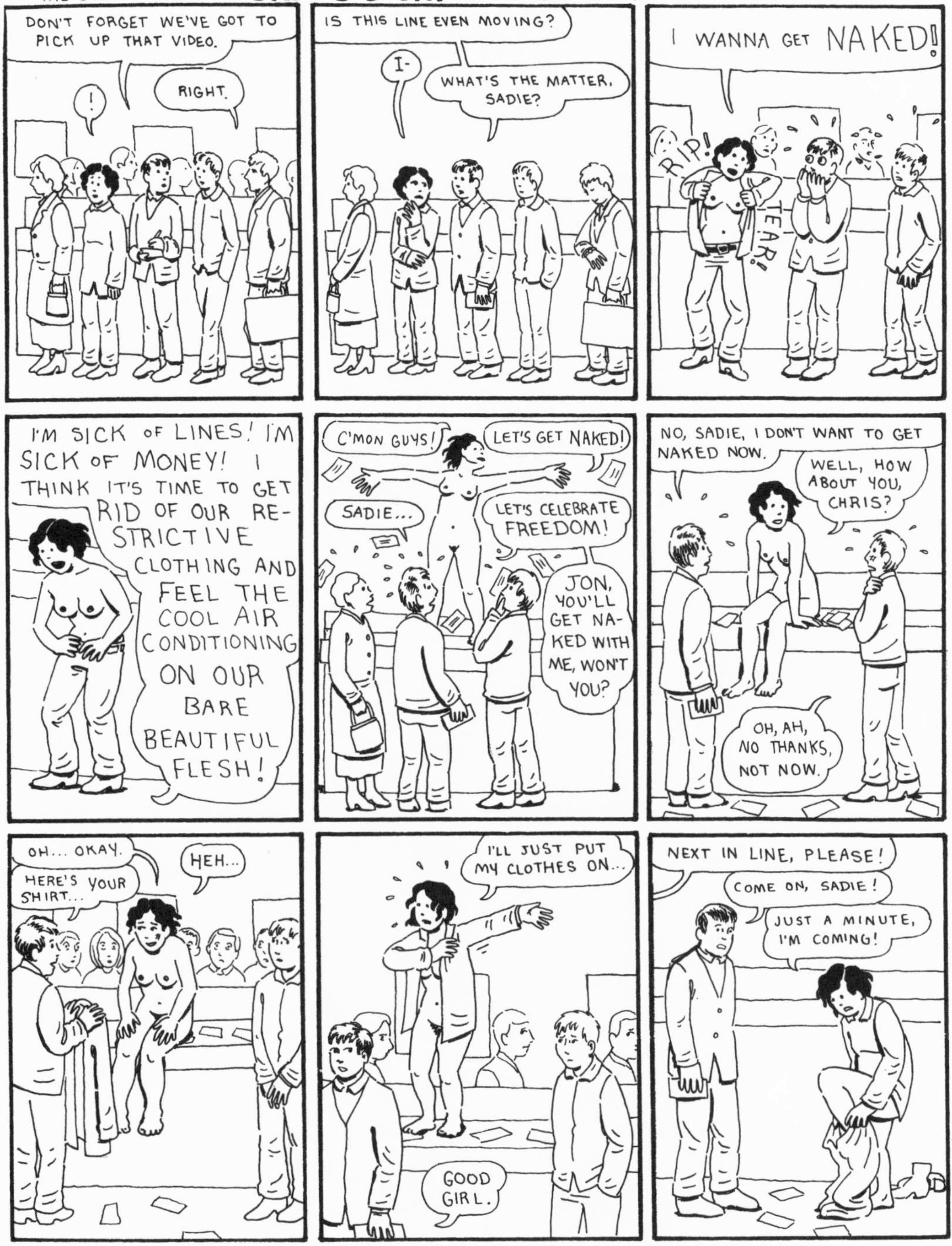
DON'T FORGET WE'VE GOT TO PICK UP THAT VIDEO.
!
RIGHT.
IS THIS LINE EVEN MOVING?
I-
WHAT'S THE MATTER, SADIE?
I WANNA GET NAKED!
RIP!
TEAR!
I'M SICK OF LINES! I'M SICK OF MONEY! I THINK IT'S TIME TO GET RID OF OUR RESTRICTIVE CLOTHING AND FEEL THE COOL AIR CONDITIONING ON OUR BARE BEAUTIFUL FLESH!
C'MON GUYS!
LET'S GET NAKED!
SADIE...
LET'S CELEBRATE FREEDOM!
JON, YOU'LL GET NAKED WITH ME, WON'T YOU?
NO, SADIE, I DON'T WANT TO GET NAKED NOW.
WELL, HOW ABOUT YOU, CHRIS?
OH, AH, NO THANKS, NOT NOW.
OH... OKAY.
HERE'S YOUR SHIRT...
HEH...
I'LL JUST PUT MY CLOTHES ON...
GOOD GIRL.
NEXT IN LINE, PLEASE!
COME ON, SADIE!
JUST A MINUTE, I'M COMING!

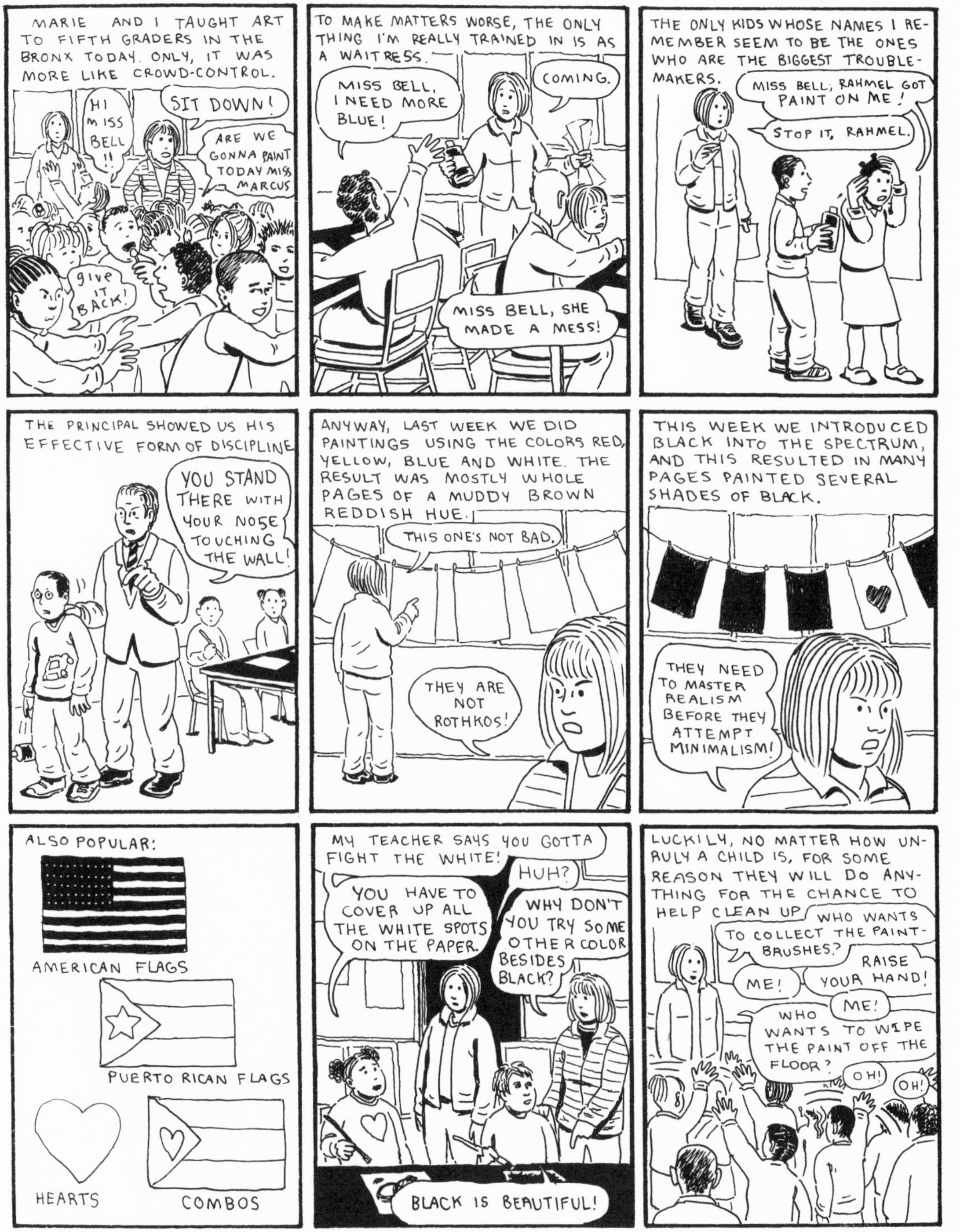
MARIE AND I TAUGHT ART TO FIFTH GRADERS IN THE BRONX TODAY. ONLY, IT WAS MORE LIKE CROWD-CONTROL.
HI MISS BELL!!
SIT DOWN!
ARE WE GONNA PAINT TODAY MISS MARCUS
GIVE IT BACK!
TO MAKE MATTERS WORSE, THE ONLY THING I'M REALLY TRAINED IN IS AS A WAITRESS.
MISS BELL, I NEED MORE BLUE!
COMING.
MISS BELL, SHE MADE A MESS!
THE ONLY KIDS WHOSE NAMES I REMEMBER SEEM TO BE THE ONES WHO ARE THE BIGGEST TROUBLE-MAKERS.
MISS BELL; RAHMEL GOT PAINT ON ME!
STOP IT, RAHMEL.
THE PRINCIPAL SHOWED US HIS EFFECTIVE FORM OF DISCIPLINE
YOU STAND THERE WITH YOUR NOSE TOUCHING THE WALL!
ANYWAY, LAST WEEK WE DID PAINTINGS USING THE COLORS RED, YELLOW, BLUE AND WHITE. THE RESULT WAS MOSTLY WHOLE PAGES OF A MUDDY BROWN REDDISH HUE.
THIS ONE'S NOT BAD.
THEY ARE NOT ROTHKOS!
THIS WEEK WE INTRODUCED BLACK INTO THE SPECTRUM, AND THIS RESULTED IN MANY PAGES PAINTED SEVERAL SHADES OF BLACK.
THEY NEED TO MASTER REALISM BEFORE THEY ATTEMPT MINIMALISM!
ALSO POPULAR:
AMERICAN FLAGS
PUERTO RICAN FLAGS
HEARTS
COMBOS
MY TEACHER SAYS YOU GOTTA FIGHT THE WHITE!
HUH?
YOU HAVE TO COVER UP ALL THE WHITE SPOTS ON THE PAPER.
WHY DON'T YOU TRY SOME OTHER COLOR BESIDES BLACK?
BLACK IS BEAUTIFUL!
LUCKILY, NO MATTER HOW UNRULY A CHILD IS, FOR SOME REASON THEY WILL DO ANYTHING FOR THE CHANCE TO HELP CLEAN UP.
WHO WANTS TO COLLECT THE PAINT-BRUSHES?
RAISE YOUR HAND!
ME!
ME!
WHO WANTS TO WIPE THE PAINT OFF THE FLOOR?
OH!
OH!

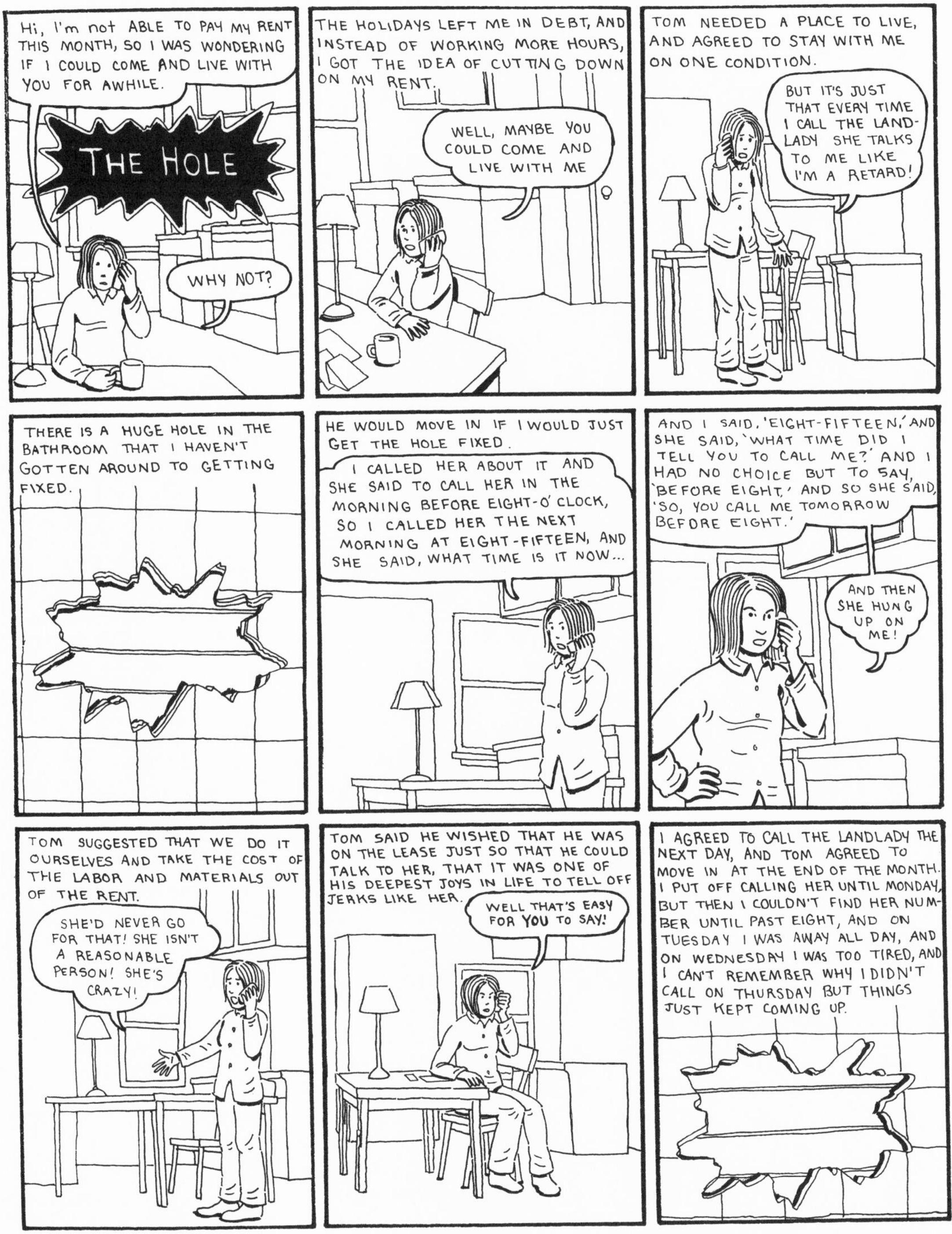
Hi, I'm not ABLE TO PAY MY RENT THIS MONTH, SO I WAS WONDERING IF I COULD COME AND LIVE WITH YOU FOR AWHILE.
THE HOLE
WHY NOT?
THE HOLIDAYS LEFT ME IN DEBT, AND INSTEAD OF WORKING MORE HOURS, I GOT THE IDEA OF CUTTING DOWN ON MY RENT.
WELL, MAYBE YOU COULD COME AND LIVE WITH ME
TOM NEEDED A PLACE TO LIVE, AND AGREED TO STAY WITH ME ON ONE CONDITION.
BUT IT'S JUST THAT EVERY TIME I CALL THE LAND-LADY SHE TALKS TO ME LIKE I'M A RETARD!
THERE IS A HUGE HOLE IN THE BATHROOM THAT I HAVEN'T GOTTEN AROUND TO GETTING FIXED.
HE WOULD MOVE IN IF I WOULD JUST GET THE HOLE FIXED.
I CALLED HER ABOUT IT AND SHE SAID TO CALL HER IN THE MORNING BEFORE EIGHT-O' CLOCK, SO I CALLED HER THE NEXT MORNING AT EIGHT-FIFTEEN, AND SHE SAID, WHAT TIME IS IT NOW...
AND I SAID, 'EIGHT-FIFTEEN,' AND SHE SAID, 'WHAT TIME DID I TELL YOU TO CALL ME?' AND I HAD NO CHOICE BUT TO SAY, 'BEFORE EIGHT,' AND SO SHE SAID, 'SO, YOU CALL ME TOMORROW BEFORE EIGHT.'
AND THEN SHE HUNG UP ON ME!
TOM SUGGESTED THAT WE DO IT OURSELVES AND TAKE THE COST OF THE LABOR AND MATERIALS OUT OF THE RENT.
SHE'D NEVER GO FOR THAT! SHE ISN'T A REASONABLE PERSON! SHE'S CRAZY!
TOM SAID HE WISHED THAT HE WAS ON THE LEASE JUST SO THAT HE COULD TALK TO HER, THAT IT WAS ONE OF HIS DEEPEST JOYS IN LIFE TO TELL OFF JERKS LIKE HER.
WELL THAT'S EASY FOR YOU TO SAY!
I AGREED TO CALL THE LANDLADY THE NEXT DAY, AND TOM AGREED TO MOVE IN AT THE END OF THE MONTH. I PUT OFF CALLING HER UNTIL MONDAY, BUT THEN I COULDN'T FIND HER NUMBER UNTIL PAST EIGHT, AND ON TUESDAY I WAS AWAY ALL DAY, AND ON WEDNESDAY I WAS TOO TIRED, AND I CAN'T REMEMBER WHY I DIDN'T CALL ON THURSDAY BUT THINGS JUST KEPT COMING UP.

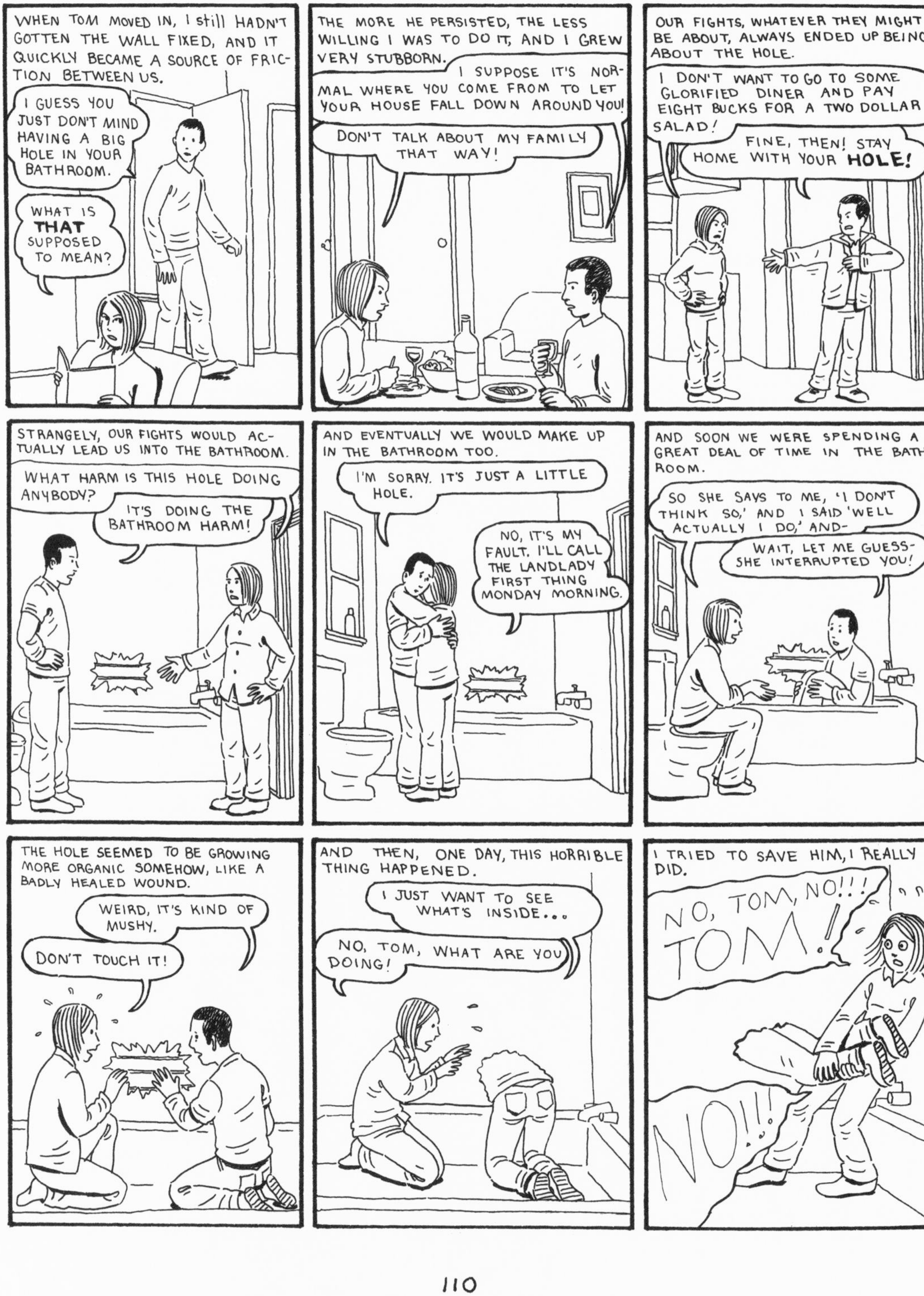
WHEN TOM MOVED IN, I still HADN'T GOTTEN THE WALL FIXED, AND IT QUICKLY BECAME A SOURCE OF FRICTION BETWEEN US.
I GUESS YOU JUST DON'T MIND HAVING A BIG HOLE IN YOUR BATHROOM.
WHAT IS **THAT** SUPPOSED TO MEAN?
THE MORE HE PERSISTED, THE LESS WILLING I WAS TO DO IT, AND I GREW VERY STUBBORN.
I SUPPOSE IT'S NORMAL WHERE YOU COME FROM TO LET YOUR HOUSE FALL DOWN AROUND YOU!
DON'T TALK ABOUT MY FAMILY THAT WAY!
OUR FIGHTS, WHATEVER THEY MIGHT BE ABOUT, ALWAYS ENDED UP BEING ABOUT THE HOLE.
I DON'T WANT TO GO TO SOME GLORIFIED DINER AND PAY EIGHT BUCKS FOR A TWO DOLLAR SALAD!
FINE, THEN! STAY HOME WITH YOUR **HOLE!**
STRANGELY, OUR FIGHTS WOULD ACTUALLY LEAD US INTO THE BATHROOM.
WHAT HARM IS THIS HOLE DOING ANYBODY?
IT'S DOING THE BATHROOM HARM!
AND EVENTUALLY WE WOULD MAKE UP IN THE BATHROOM TOO.
I'M SORRY. IT'S JUST A LITTLE HOLE.
NO, IT'S MY FAULT. I'LL CALL THE LANDLADY FIRST THING MONDAY MORNING.
AND SOON WE WERE SPENDING A GREAT DEAL OF TIME IN THE BATHROOM.
SO SHE SAYS TO ME, 'I DON'T THINK SO,' AND I SAID 'WELL ACTUALLY I DO,' AND-
WAIT, LET ME GUESS-SHE INTERRUPTED YOU!
THE HOLE SEEMED TO BE GROWING MORE ORGANIC SOMEHOW, LIKE A BADLY HEALED WOUND.
WEIRD, IT'S KIND OF MUSHY.
DON'T TOUCH IT!
AND THEN, ONE DAY, THIS HORRIBLE THING HAPPENED.
I JUST WANT TO SEE WHAT'S INSIDE...
NO, TOM, WHAT ARE YOU DOING!
I TRIED TO SAVE HIM, I REALLY DID.
NO, TOM, NO!!! TOM!
NO!!!

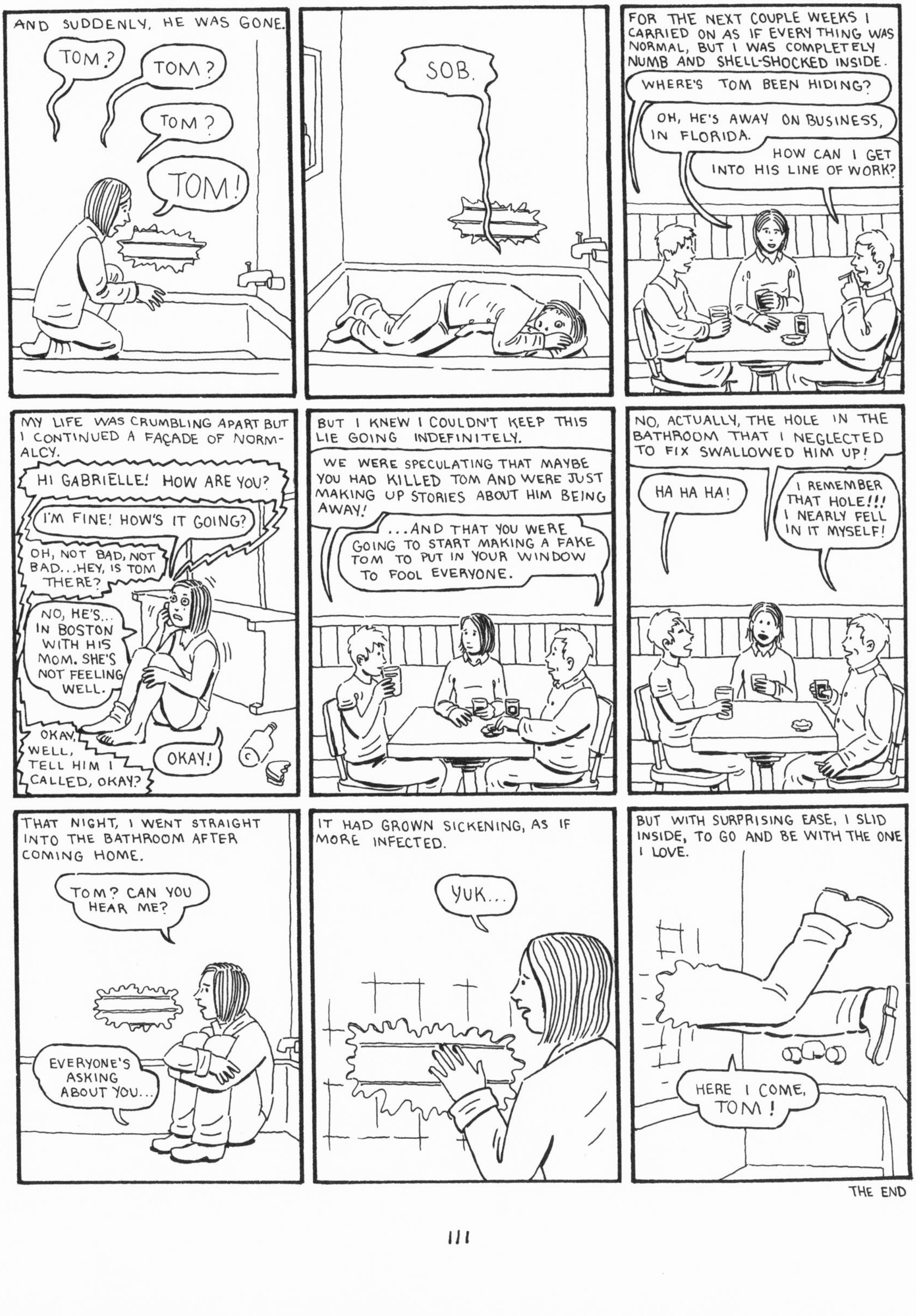
AND SUDDENLY, HE WAS GONE.
TOM?
TOM?
TOM?
TOM!
SOB.
FOR THE NEXT COUPLE WEEKS I CARRIED ON AS IF EVERYTHING WAS NORMAL, BUT I WAS COMPLETELY NUMB AND SHELL-SHOCKED INSIDE.
WHERE'S TOM BEEN HIDING?
OH, HE'S AWAY ON BUSINESS, IN FLORIDA.
HOW CAN I GET INTO HIS LINE OF WORK?
MY LIFE WAS CRUMBLING APART BUT I CONTINUED A FAÇADE OF NORMALCY.
HI GABRIELLE! HOW ARE YOU?
I'M FINE! HOW'S IT GOING?
OH, NOT BAD, NOT BAD...HEY, IS TOM THERE?
NO, HE'S... IN BOSTON WITH HIS MOM. SHE'S NOT FEELING WELL.
OKAY, WELL, TELL HIM I CALLED, OKAY?
OKAY!
BUT I KNEW I COULDN'T KEEP THIS LIE GOING INDEFINITELY.
WE WERE SPECULATING THAT MAYBE YOU HAD KILLED TOM AND WERE JUST MAKING UP STORIES ABOUT HIM BEING AWAY!
...AND THAT YOU WERE GOING TO START MAKING A FAKE TOM TO PUT IN YOUR WINDOW TO FOOL EVERYONE.
NO, ACTUALLY, THE HOLE IN THE BATHROOM THAT I NEGLECTED TO FIX SWALLOWED HIM UP!
HA HA HA!
I REMEMBER THAT HOLE!!! I NEARLY FELL IN IT MYSELF!
THAT NIGHT, I WENT STRAIGHT INTO THE BATHROOM AFTER COMING HOME.
TOM? CAN YOU HEAR ME?
EVERYONE'S ASKING ABOUT YOU...
IT HAD GROWN SICKENING, AS IF MORE INFECTED.
YUK...
BUT WITH SURPRISING EASE, I SLID INSIDE, TO GO AND BE WITH THE ONE I LOVE.
HERE I COME, TOM!

THE END

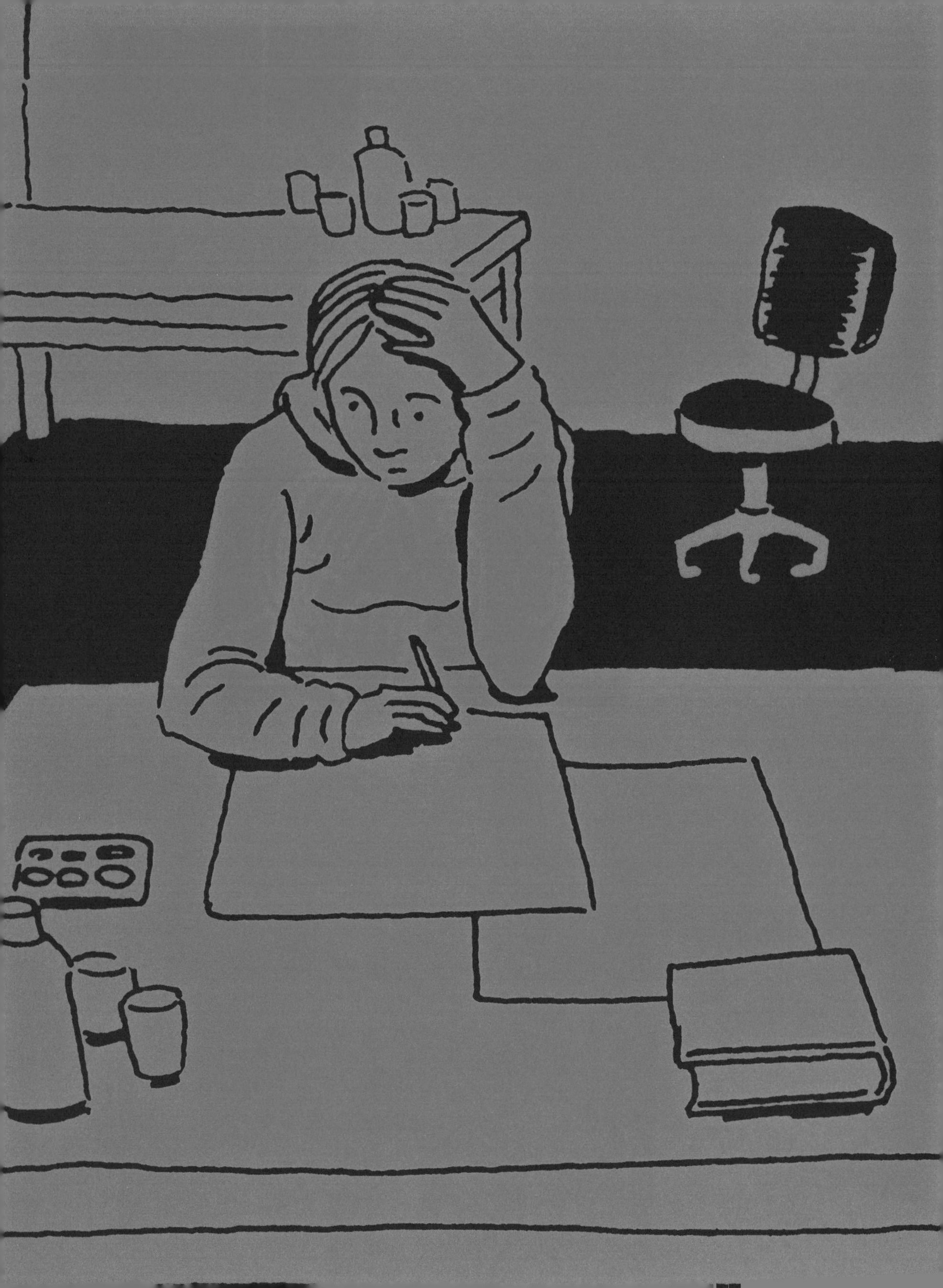

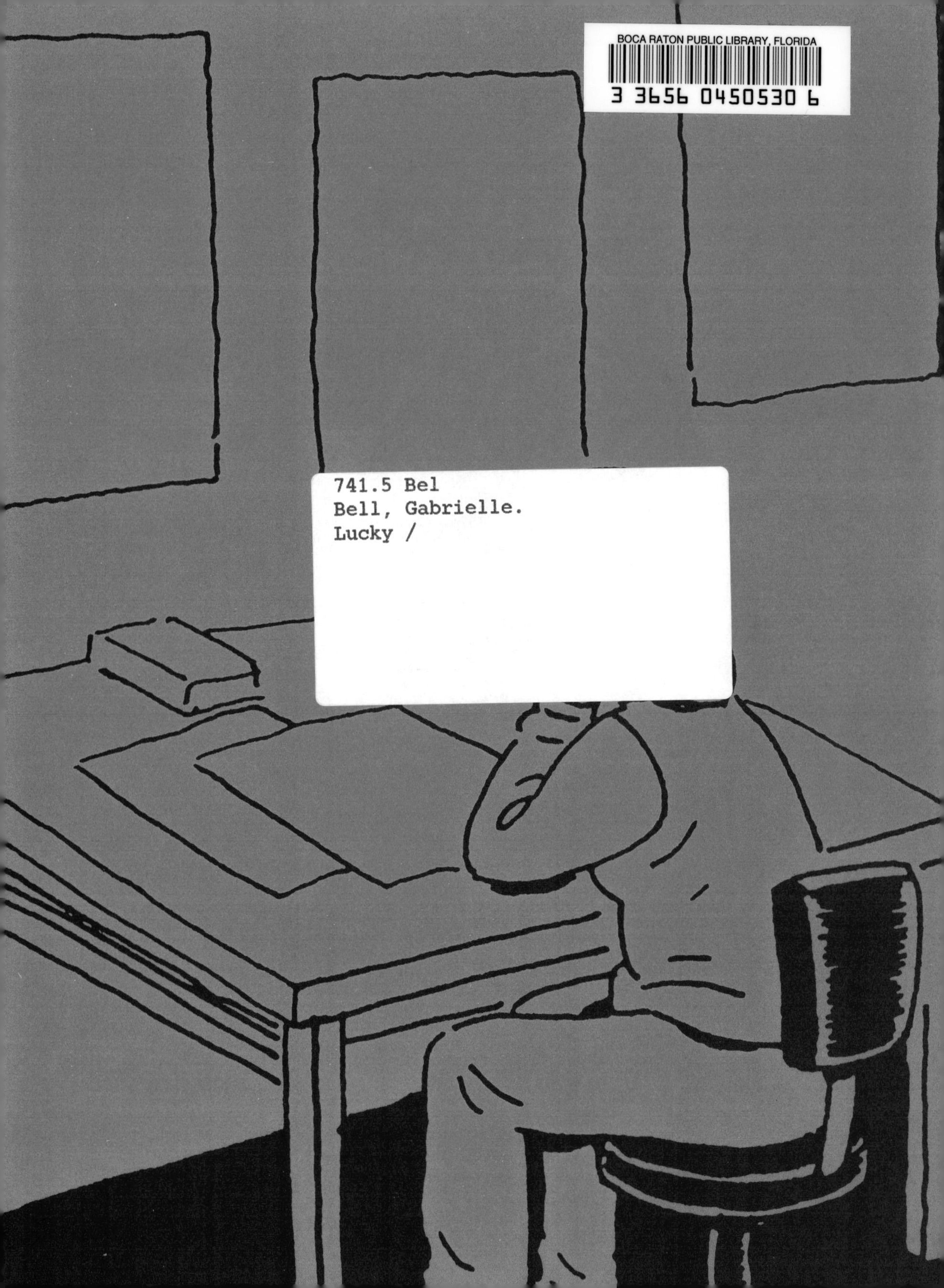